Microsoft QuickBASIC for Scientists

Microsoft QuickBASIC for Scientists: A Guide to Writing Better Programs

JAMES W. COOPER
IBM T. J. Watson Research Center
Yorktown Heights, New York

WILEY

A WILEY-INTERSCIENCE PUBLICATION

JOHN WILEY & SONS

New York / Chichester / Brisbane / Toronto / Singapore

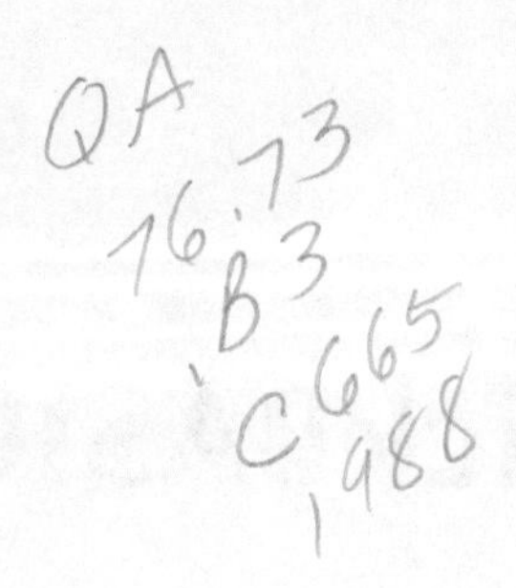

Library of Congress Cataloging-in-Publication Data:

Cooper, James William, 1943–
Microsoft QuickBASIC for Scientists: A Guide to Writing Better Programs/James W. Cooper.
p. cm.
"A Wiley-Interscience publication."
Bibliography: p.
Includes index.
ISBN 0-471-61301-0
1. BASIC (Computer program language). 2. Microsoft QuickBASIC (Computer program) I. Title.
QA76.73.B3C665 1988
005.13′3--dc19 88-10140
CIP

Printed in the United States of America

10 9 8 7 6 5 4 3 2 1

Preface

Soon after I began using QuickBASIC, I realized that it was not just a good implementation of a BASIC compiler. In fact, QuickBASIC is nearly a new language which overcomes every objection that has ever been raised to the original BASIC language dialect as implemented on the PC. QuickBASIC does not require line numbers, has subprograms which allow the passing of arguments, allows both global and local variables, allows separate compilation of routines and the linking of libraries, can make use of the math coprocessor, eliminates the 64K limit to program code, and is orders of magnitude faster than the original BASIC interpreter.

Most important perhaps is the fact that QuickBASIC is a *structured* language with looping constructs which make it a powerful language for serious programming work. Gone is the need to ever use the GOTO statement, the ON . . . GOSUB statement, or even the GOSUB statement itself.

Since QuickBASIC is in effect a new language, it seemed to me that a textbook ought to be prepared describing how to program in this language—how to write structured programs in a modern fashion without reference to the preconceptions of the original BASIC language. This is the purpose of this book.

My only difficulty along the way has been that Microsoft has continued to improve QuickBASIC even as I was writing, leapfrogging my chapters as I wrote them. This text describes what I believe is a settled version of the language and its features. I have found working in this language to be a delightful surprise and hope that each reader will feel the same way.

I particularly want to thank Dr. Jack Fowble of the Ohio State University College of Pharmacy and Professor Joseph Noggle of the University of Delaware chemistry department for their meticulous reading of my manuscript and for their helpful comments. I also wish to thank the Wilton Y Wahoo Swim Team for the loan of their IBM Proprinter II. I also want to thank my children, Vaughn and Nicole, for their advice on the manuscript and my wife, Vicki, for her endless patience with my solitary pursuit.

JAMES W. COOPER
WILTON, CONNECTICUT
AUGUST, 1988

Contents

Trademark Notices

QuickBASIC is a trademark of Microsoft Corporation.

Personal Computer AT is a registered trademark of the IBM Corporation.

PC/XT, PS/2, and Personal System/2 are trademarks of the IBM Corporation.

Microsoft and MS-DOS are registered trademarks of Microsoft Corporation.

Microsoft QuickBASIC for Scientists

1 Introduction to QuickBASIC

The Microsoft QuickBASIC 4.0 Compiler has revolutionized programming in BASIC. With this language you can write programs using a sophisticated text editor and run them at high speed, since QuickBASIC actually compiles the programs and runs them right there in memory.

Furthermore, QuickBASIC is not like old versions of BASIC on the IBM PC and compatibles. It is structured, doesn't require line numbers, allows subroutines with arguments, and allows you to use all of the memory in your PC instead of restricting you to 64K bytes. This is such a departure from the "old" way of writing and debugging BASIC programs that it merits a book of its own, describing how to program in this new, faster, structured BASIC.

WHY IS A COMPILER BETTER?

The BASIC and BASICA (or GWBASIC) programs that came with your PC are BASIC *interpreters*. This means that the actual program text is scanned by the BASIC program *each time* it is executed and then interpreted and executed. Thus, if you write some calculation loop which is executed many times, an interpreter must reinterpret the program statements each time it executes the loop. This is rather slow and inefficient. The advantage is that you can make rapid changes in the text and have them executed at once.

A *compiler,* on the other hand, first converts all of the BASIC program's text into machine instructions, and then executes those. The compilation step is usually slow and cumbersome but the execution much faster. QuickBASIC has merged these two approaches by having the compiler operate on the text in memory just as the interpreter did and store the compiled machine instructions in memory as well. The program thus compiles quite rapidly and executes much more rapidly (up to 10 times faster) than the same interpreted program.

WHAT DO I NEED TO RUN QUICKBASIC?

An IBM PC or PS/2 or compatible system with at least 512K of memory and one or more diskette drives is required. A hard disk drive is particularly useful since QuickBASIC is a large program filling much of a single diskette. Since hard disk drives have become so inexpensive, we will assume that you have one.

COPYING THE PROGRAMS

QuickBASIC is provided on three diskettes, which you should copy onto backup diskettes. If you have a hard disk drive, you should put all of the files in some subdirectory such as \BIN or \UTILS which is accessible from any subdirectory. To do this, create the subdirectory UTILS

```
md utils
```

and then change to it:

```
cd\utils
```

and copy all of both diskettes into this subdirectory:

```
copy a:*.* c:
```

Then you should use the PATH command to tell DOS to always look in this subdirectory for any files you try to run:

```
path c:\utils;
```

You can include this PATH command in your AUTOEXEC.BAT file, and it will be executed every time you start your computer.

If you aren't familiar with the PATH command and subdirectories, they are discussed in the chapter on DOS commands in this book as well as in the DOS manual that came with your computer.

The most important of the files you copy will be the file QB.EXE, the QuickBASIC program itself. Once you have copied it onto your hard disk as above, you can start it and run it by just typing "qb" from any subdirectory.

STARTING QUICKBASIC

To start QuickBASIC, just type

```
qb
```

and wait while the program is loaded. A list of commands appears across the top of the screen:

```
File  Edit  View  Search  Run  Debug  Calls          F1 = Help
```

which you can select by holding down the *Alt* key and typing an F, E, V, S, R or C. We'll see how to use these commands in the following chapters.

TYPING IN A SIMPLE PROGRAM

You can type in any BASIC program on the screen, and have QuickBASIC execute it for you. Let's type in a simple program to add two numbers together, and run it using QuickBASIC.

```
'Program to add two numbers together
  a = 5.6
  b = 7.7
  c = a + b
  PRINT "The sum of "; a; " and "; b; " is "; c
END
```

This simple program assigns the value 5.6 to the variable A, and 7.7 to the variable named B. It adds them and prints out their sum.

Note how simple the layout of the program is. QuickBASIC does not require line numbers, and since they have no real purpose we are not using them here. The first line is a comment, and begins with an apostrophe (').

To type this program in, just type the first line followed by pressing the Enter or Return ↵ key, and then type in a blank line by pressing the Enter key again. To indent, press the Tab key, which is marked ⇆.

Then, to run the program, you must compile it. Hold down Alt and press R. The following menu will appear:

```
Start        Shift+F5
Restart
Continue           F5
Modify COMMAND$...
-------------------------
Make EXE File...
Make Library...
-------------------------
Set Main Module...
```

As you press the cursor Up Arrow and cursor Down Arrow keys, a gray bar will highlight one of the three text lines. You can select that line by pressing Enter while it is highlighted.

In this case, you want to select the "Start" line, which will compile the program and then run it. You can do this by selecting the top line and pressing Enter, or by pressing Esc to dismiss the menu and holding down Shift and pressing the F5 key. This short cut is symbolized on the menu display by "Shift+F5".

When you select the top line or press Shift+F5 QuickBASIC will compile and execute the program. You will see the program execute and display the answer

```
The sum of  5.6  and  7.7  is  13.3
```

followed by the message

```
Press any key to continue
```

That's all there is to using QuickBASIC. It is as simple as any other BASIC, and much faster than older ways. In addition, you have a powerful text editor for arranging your text and making changes when you make typing mistakes or programming errors.

A PROGRAM TO READ IN TWO NUMBERS

Now let's write a more useful program that allows us to enter the two numbers at the keyboard and then adds them together:

```
'Program to read in two numbers and add them together
   PRINT "a=";
   INPUT a           'get value from keyboard
   PRINT "b=";
   INPUT b           'get value of B from keyboard
   c = a + b         'add A and B and put the result in C
     PRINT "The sum of "; a; " and "; b; " is "; c
 END
```

You can change the first program into this second program by simply deleting the top two statements and replacing them with the first four statements of this new program, or you can clear the screen and type in the program from scratch. Both ways are discussed below.

CLEARING MEMORY—THE NEW COMMAND

To clear the screen (and memory) of the current program, select the File menu by pressing Alt+F. QuickBASIC will display the following:

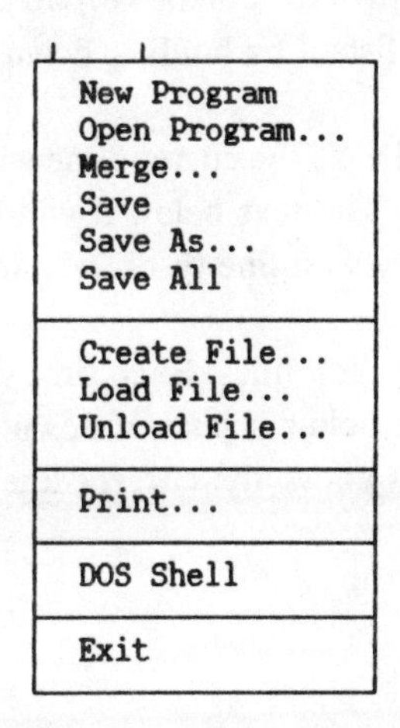

Press the cursor Down Arrow until "New Program" is highlighted and press Enter. QuickBASIC will display the message

```
One or more loaded files are not saved. Save them now?
Yes              No              Cancel
```

You have not saved the first program, and QuickBASIC is reminding you that you should do so before clearing memory. To do this, use the Tab key to move the highlight to the Yes box and press Enter. Selecting No does not save the files and selecting Cancel aborts the New operation.

EDITING THE CURRENT PROGRAM

To change program 1 to program 2, we simply need to delete the first two statements

```
a = 5.6             'assign 5.6 to variable A
b = 7.7             'assign 7.7 to variable B
```

and replace them with the statements

```
PRINT "a=";
INPUT a             'get value of A from keyboard
PRINT "b=";
INPUT b             'get value of B from keyboard
```

You can delete the two lines by moving the cursor to that line using the Up Arrow and Down Arrow keys of the cursor keypad and then pressing Ctrl+Y. Remember, this is accomplished by holding down the Ctrl key and pressing Y.

Each time you press Ctrl+Y, the current line will be highlighted for a moment and then be deleted. The text below it will then move up a line. The cursor will then be on the second line (b = 7.7) and pressing Ctrl+Y again will delete this line as well.

Now, just type in the four new lines. Each time you press Enter, a new line will be created and the text below it pushed down on the screen.

You can also insert lines above the current line using the Ctrl+N (Next) key.

CAPITALIZATION

Note that no matter what case you type PRINT and INPUT in, QuickBASIC will convert them to uppercase when you finish typing that line. This is true of all of the QuickBASIC instructions or keywords, and is intended to set off these keywords from the names of the variables and mathematical expressions.

RUNNING OUR SECOND PROGRAM

To compile our second program, we just press Shift+F5 again. The screen will be cleared, and the message

```
a=?
```

will be printed. This "a=" is the message from our PRINT statement. The question mark is printed by BASIC to indicate that it is waiting in an INPUT statement for you to type something in.

Type in a number, such as 6 followed by Enter, and the program will print

```
b=?
```

Type in another number, such as 7 followed by Enter, and the program will add them and print out:

```
The sum of 6 and 7 is 13
Press any key to continue
```

ERROR CHECKING AND HELP

As you type in each statement in QuickBASIC, it is compiled and checked for errors. If you make a typing mistake in a command, QuickBASIC will prompt you for a correction. QuickBASIC cannot catch all errors when you type them, and may not find them until you try to start the program. If it finds any then, it will highlight them on the display and show the following box on the screen:

```
Syntax Error
OK
```

Type Enter or Esc or point to the OK box with the mouse and press the left button and the box will disappear so you can correct the typing error. If it is not clear to you what the change should be, you can get on-line help for the entire QuickBASIC language by pressing F1 or Shift+F1.

When you press Shift+F1, QuickBASIC displays the syntax rules for the keyword currently pointed to by the cursor. When you press F1, the screen displays a summary of the editing commands and a line of commands along the bottom:

```
Next      Previous      Keywords           Cancel
```

You can select any of these boxes by moving the highlight to them with the Tab key or clicking on them with the mouse. If you select "Next," another summary screen showing the ASCII character codes will be displayed. If you select "Keywords," a complete list of all the QuickBASIC keywords will be displayed. If you select "Cancel," the screen will disappear.

On the Keywords screen, you can select any keyword with the cursor or Tab keys or with the mouse, and press Enter. QuickBASIC will display a one-screen summary of the rules for using that keyword. Meanwhile, the statement causing the error appears along the bottom line in the immediate window. You can edit the line there to get it to conform to the rules for that keyword while displaying the correct syntax in the box above.

EXITING FROM QUICKBASIC

Once you've finished with these examples, you may want to exit from QuickBASIC. To do this, select the File menu by pressing Alt+F. Then press the Up Arrow key once so that "Exit" is highlighted, and press Enter. QuickBASIC will display the same message as above, asking you to save the files.

Type in a name to store your program under, followed by Enter, or if you don't want to save the file, press the Tab key so that Cancel is highlighted and press Enter. QuickBASIC will then exit to DOS.

Now that you've seen how easy it is to write, compile, execute and change simple BASIC programs we'll go on to explain the language in detail in the chapters that follow.

2 Elements of the BASIC Language

In this chapter we will define some of the major features of the BASIC language and illustrate their uses in simple programs.

THE SHAPE OF A BASIC PROGRAM

A BASIC program consists of a number of *statements* and *remarks* or comments. Each statement should occupy a separate line. Every statement represents one operation to BASIC, such as

```
y = m * x + b
```

You can put several statements on the same line by separating them with colons (:), but this is a holdover from interpreted BASIC, where line numbers made splitting statements more difficult; it has no real advantage in QuickBASIC and in fact may make programs harder to read:

```
y = m * x + b : z = y - k
```

The maximum length of a QuickBASIC program line is 255 characters. You cannot continue a statement onto another line since there is no continuation character. If you create a QuickBASIC program using another editor and end lines with the underscore (_) character, QuickBASIC will combine the lines as it reads them in. In this case the maximum line length of 255 characters is relaxed.

Remarks or comments in QuickBASIC may be an entire line within a program or may start at the end of a line. Such remarks are used to improve your ability to read the program and figure out what you meant it to do when you review it later. You indicate that what follows is a remark by starting it with an apostrophe (').

All characters after the apostrophe are ignored by the QuickBASIC compiler:

```
'Equation for a straight line
y = m * x + b           'calculate the value of Y
```

You can also start remarks with "REM," but only at the beginning of lines:

```
REM This is another form of remark
```

In general we will use the apostophe form in this book as it seems to be more readable.

TYPES OF DATA IN QUICKBASIC

BASIC allows you to use five different kinds of values in your programs:

- Single precision floating point
- Double precision floating point
- Integer
- Long integer
- String

Most values that you handle in BASIC are *single precision* floating point. Variables of this type can take on values from -1.7×10^{38} to -2.9×10^{-39} for negative values and 2.9×10^{-39} to 1.7×10^{38} for positive values. The power of 10 is written following an "E", so these are represented as

```
-1.7E38 to 2.9E-39 and 2.9E-39 to 1.7E38.
```

Floating point means that the computer uses a fixed number of bytes (in this case 4) to store these values in an exponent–mantissa format so that the number of significant figures is constant regardless of the size of the number. These numbers are represented accurately to seven decimal places.

Double precision floating point numbers can vary from -1.797×10^{308} to -4.94×10^{324} and 4.94×10^{-324} to 1.797×10^{308} and are represented accurately to 15 significant figures.

Integers are values having no fractional part and may range from $-32{,}768$ to $+32{,}767$. They are kept in 2 bytes of memory (16 bits).

Long integers are 32-bit values which can take on values in the range of plus or minus two billion. They also occupy 4 bytes but have no fractional part. Calculations involving long integers are faster than those in floating point, and have greater range than those in normal integer mode.

Strings are sequences of characters. Strings are represented as sequences of characters inside quotation marks:

```
"A"
"Furd Burfle"
"1.2 x 10"
"A really long string with %$!@*&(^:'# lots of characters"
```

You may not include the quote (") character inside a string.

A string may have a length from 0 to 32767 characters in QuickBASIC. Many other versions of BASIC allow strings of only 255 characters in length.

VARIABLES IN BASIC

In our previous two program examples, we used the variable names A, B, and C to represent numbers which could take on different values. These are examples of single precision (floating point) variables. Variables names may be from 1 to 40 characters long, and may be made up of any combination of letters and numbers and decimal points. The first character of a variable name, however, *must* be a letter.

```
a = 6
ball.bat = 6.32
antidisestablishmentarianism = -1.2E6
```

Note that the underscore character (_) cannot be used in a variable name, since it has been used in previous versions of BASIC as a line continuation character.

CASE OF VARIABLE NAMES

Variable names may also be in uppercase or lowercase, but while you can use the case to improve readability, upper and lower case letters are treated as identical by QuickBASIC. Thus all of the following are treated as the same variable name:

```
SUMOFPAIRS
sumofpairs
SumOfPairs
```

In this book we will write BASIC's keywords in upper case. Within programs, we will write variable names in *lower case.* We do this because there is a feeling among programmers and human engineering specialists that lowercase letters are easier to read than upper case ones. When we discuss a variable in running text or comment lines, we will capitalize it to set it off from the surrounding text. However, to reiterate, BASIC is not *case-sensitive,* and you may write your programs either or both ways.

QuickBASIC does, however, remember the case in which you first type a variable name, and displays all other occurrences of that name in the same case.

RESTRICTIONS ON VARIABLE NAMES

Variable names may not be the same as any of the words BASIC uses to describe operations or define functions. These names are called *reserved words* and may only be used as the verbs and functions of BASIC define them. These reserved words are listed in Table 2.1.

In addition, you can't use a variable name which starts with the letters FN. These names are assumed to be *functions* which you have defined in your program. BASIC will always issue an error message if you try to assign a value to any variable whose name begins in FN.

TYPES OF VARIABLES

The five types of variables—integer, long integer, single, double, and string—are usually indicated in BASIC by the last character of the variable name:

TABLE 2.1 BASIC Reserved Words

ABS	DEF FN	INPUT	OPTION	
ACCESS	DEF SEG	INPUT$	OR	SPACE$
ALIAS	DEF USR	INSTR	OUT	SPC
AND	DEFDBL	INT	OUTPUT	SQR
ANY	DEFINT	INTEGER		STATIC
APPEND	DEFLNG	IOCTL	PAINT	STEP
AS	DEFSNG	IOCTL$	PALETTE	STICK
ASC	DEFSTR		PCOPY	STOP
ATN	DELETE	KEY	PEEK	STR$
	DIM	KILL	PEN	STRIG
BASE	DO		PLAY	STRING
BEEP	DRAW	LBOUND	PMAP	STRING$
BINARY	ELSE	LCASE$	POINT	SUB
BLOAD	ELSEIF	LEFT$	POKE	SWAP
BSAVE	END	LEN	POS	SYSTEM
BYVAL	ENDIF	LINE	PRESET	
	ENVIRON	LIST	PRINT	TAB
CALL	ENVIRON$	LOC	PSET	TAN
CALLS	EOF	LOCAL	PUT	THEN
CASE	EQV	LOCATE	RANDOMIZE	TIME$
CDBL	ERASE	LOCK	READ	TIMER
CDECL	ERDEV	LOF	REDIM	TO
CHAIN	ERDEV$	LOG	REM	TROFF
CHDIR	ERL	LONG	RESET	TRON
CHR$	ERR	LOOP	RESTORE	TYPE
CINT	ERROR	LPOS	RESUME	
CIRCLE	EXIT	LPRINT	RETURN	UBOUND
CLEAR	EXP	LSET	RIGHT$	UCASE$
CLNG		LTRIM$	RMDIR	UNLOCK
CLOSE	FIELD		RND	UNTIL
CLS	FILEATTR	MID$	RSET	USING
COLOR	FILES	MKD$	RTRIM$	
COM	FIX	MKDIR	RUN	VAL
COMMAND$	FOR	MKDMBF$		VARPTR
COMMON	FRE	MKI$	SADD	VARPTR$
CONST	FREEFILE	MKL$	SCREEN	VARSEG
COS	FUNCTION	MKS$	SEEK	VIEW
CSNG		MKSMBF$	SEG	
CSRLIN	GET	MOD	SELECT	WAIT
CVD	GOSUB		SETMEM	WEND
CVI	GOTO	NAME	SGN	WHILE
CVL		NEXT	SHARED	WIDTH
CVS	HEX$	NOT	SHELL	WINDOW
CVSMBF			SIGNAL	WRITE
	IF	OCT$	SIN	
DATA	IMP	OFF	SINGLE	XOR
DATE$	INKEY$	ON	SLEEP	
DECLARE	INP	OPEN	SOUND	

%	Integer
&	Long Integer
#	Double
$	String
!	Single
or	
(none)	Single

Thus A is a single precision variable, and A% is an integer variable. We see some more examples below:

```
Counter%  = 123               'integer
Fval&     = 12345678          'long integer
vertex    = 12.6432           'single precision
diagonal# = 16.473245682123   'double precision
name$     = "Alphonse"        'string
```

The same base variable name can actually be five different variables depending on the final type character.

```
xy  = 6.2             'single
xy% = 6               'integer
xy& = 100000          'long integer
xy# = 7.025634786     'double
xy$ = "Six"           'string
```

This is, of course, a terribly confusing practice and is not recommended.

WHY WE USE DIFFERENT DATA TYPES

The usual variable type in BASIC is single precision. Nearly all of the programs people write use only this type along with a few strings to print out names and messages.

We might use double precision in cases where high computational accuracy is required, or a large number of significant figures must be carried along. This sometimes happens in least-squares calculations or in diagonalizing matrices, where we must take the difference between two large numbers which differ only slightly.

The disadvantage of double precision is, of course, that it takes twice as much memory to store each number: 8 bytes instead of 4. More important, computations involving double precision numbers are twice as slow as single precision calculations, so use double precision only when you actually need it.

The integer data type, on the other hand, takes up only 2 bytes of storage. Manipulating integer data is much faster than single precision floating point data, because only a few actual computer instructions are required to carry out integer arithmetic, while the floating point routines take nearly twice as long to perform addition.

The long integer data type is for exact calculations that run somewhat faster than the same floating point values, where no fractional numbers are involved.

DEFINING TYPES BY LETTER

As a convenience to FORTRAN programmers, BASIC allows you to define the types of variables implicitly by the first letter of the variable name, using the following DEF statememts:

```
DEFtype letter-letter
```

where *type* is DBL, INT, LNG, SNG, or STR. Then, variable names beginning with the letter specified are automatically all of the type named:

```
DEFINT I - N        'variables starting with letters I - N
                    ' are integers
DEFDBL X,Z          'variables starting with X or Z
                    ' are double precision
```

While these appear to be a convenience at first, they can quickly become a nuisance, since variables should be named by the function they perform rather than by some arbitary first letter. However, if all variables in a program are to be integer, long, or real, this prevents having to append the characters %, &, or # to each instance of each variable.

NAMED CONSTANTS IN QUICKBASIC

QuickBASIC allows you to declare names for constants as well as for variables:

```
CONST pi = 3.14159, Temp = 273.16, Planet = "Earth"
CONST Maxdim = 100, Escape.key = 27
CONST Avogadro = 6.023E23
```

You can then use these constant names throughout the program wherever you would normally write a number. Constants are particularly useful for quantities that you may eventually change but which are fixed for a particular run of the program. It is preferable to use named constants over variables which have been assigned a particular value because QuickBASIC can generate more efficient code for constants. Constants are particularly useful in defining the dimensions of arrays, as we will illustrate in Chapter 5.

The type of a constant is determined by the value you assign to it rather than by the terminating type characters (%, $, or !). Thus, a string *constant* does not need to have a $ sign as part of its name. Further, the type of a constant is not affected by any DEF statements in effect.

DOING ARITHMETIC IN BASIC

BASIC allows you to do most computations very quickly and simply, using more or less the same symbols as you use in algebra:

+	Addition
−	Subtraction
*	Multiplication
/	Division
\	Integer division
MOD	Remainder after division
^	Exponentiation

Using these symbols, you could write the equation

$$y = mx + b$$

as

```
y = m * x + b
```

In a similar fashion, you could write the quadratic formula:

$$y = \frac{\sqrt{b^2 - 4ac}}{2a}$$

as

```
y = SQR ( b^2 - 4 * a * c)/(2 * a)
```

where the SQR function is used to obtain the square root of the expression in parenthesis.

INTEGER MULTIPLICATION AND DIVISION

Since integer values are stored in only 2 bytes of memory, the range of values that an integer can contain is limited to that range of numbers that can be held in 16 bits, or -2^{15} to $2^{15} - 1$. Consequently, the numbers that can be put in an integer variable are likewise limited.

Foremost, of course, is the fact that integer variables have no fractional parts. When you divide an integer by another integer, the result will be an integer. Thus, while

```
5 / 2
```

will produce 2.5,

```
5 \ 2
```

will produce 2 with no fractional part.

The MOD (modulo) function produces the remainder after an integer division. So

```
5 MOD 2
```

will produce 1 since $5/2 = 2$ with a remainder of 1.

The following program illustrates these features,

```
'Illustration of integer division
a = 5 'these are single precision floating point numbers
b = 2

PRINT "Using floating point variables:"
PRINT "Floating division "; a / b
PRINT "Integer division  "; a \ b

PRINT "Remainder = "; a MOD b
```

```
a% = 5 'these are already integers
b% = 2

PRINT
PRINT "Using integer variables:"
PRINT "Floating division "; a% / b%
PRINT "Integer division  "; a% \ b%

PRINT "Remainder = "; a% MOD b%

END
```

and when run it prints out the following answers:

```
Using floating point variables:
Floating division 2.5
Integer division  2
Remainder = 1
Using integer variables:
Floating division  2.5
Integer division   2
Remainder = 1
```

Note that it makes *no difference* whether the original variables are floating point or integer. The operations produce the same answers, since the result of any operation is always a floating point number. Thus, while dividing two *integers* 5 and 2 would produce a quotient of 2, the actual operations are done in floating point and have the same quotient as 5.0 and 2.0. The nature of the result depends on the operations (/ or \) rather than the type of the data (floating point or integer).

ORDER OF OPERATIONS IN AN ARITHMETIC EXPRESSION

Suppose we write the expression

```
y = 5 + 2 * 3 - 7 / 2
```

What answer will QuickBASIC produce? We should first note that no one should seriously write such an expression, since it is confusing to read. Any program should be readable as well as executable.

In fact, BASIC applies the same set of precedence rules that mathematics students are taught, the "My Dear Aunt Sally" rules. Multiplication and division are done before addition and subtraction, and operations of equal precedence are performed from left to right. Thus, the above expression evaluates the same as if it had been written as:

```
y = 5 + (2 * 3) - (7 / 2)
```

which is in fact the way it should have been written in the first place for readability.

There are in fact several more operators in the complete list:

Exponentiation	^
Negation	–
Multiplication and Division	* /
Integer division	\
Modulo	MOD
Addition and subtraction	+ –

You should seldom need to consult this list if you use parentheses to indicate the order of operations you really mean, as we did in the last example.

HOW BASIC CONVERTS BETWEEN TYPES

If you write an arithmetic expression containing constants and/or variables of different data types, QuickBASIC converts all the numbers to the highest precision of any variable in the expression. Then, after the calculation is performed, the result is converted to the type and precision of the resulting variable.

PRINTING OUT RESULTS

We have implicitly used the PRINT statement in this chapter and in Chapter 1 without formally describing it. As you have surmised, the PRINT statement prints the values of variables and strings to the terminal, meaning in this case, the screen of your PC.

You can print out one or more values in a single print statement:

```
PRINT "The answers are "; a; " and "; b
```

Variables separated by *semicolons* are printed out immediately following one another. Variables separated by *commas,*

```
PRINT "The values are", a, b
```

are printed in columns 15 spaces apart, in columns 1, 16, 31, 46, and 61. This provides a simple way to align data in columns.

If you terminate a PRINT statement with a semicolon or comma, printing continues on the same line in the next PRINT statement. This is illustrated in the following program,

```
'Showing the features of the print statement
a=5: b=3: c=7: d=2          'colon can separate statements

PRINT a, b,                 'list with commas
PRINT c, d

PRINT a; b;                 'list with semicolons
PRINT c; d

PRINT "the values are "; a; b;
PRINT " and the others are "; c; d
end
```

which produces the result:

```
5             3             7             2
5  3  7  2
the values are 5 3    and the others are 7 2
```

READING IN DATA—THE READ AND DATA STATEMENTS

QuickBASIC provides a simple way for you to write programs which operate on the same data every time they are run using the READ and DATA statements. The DATA statement contains a list of values to be read in, separated by commas, and usually is placed at the beginning of the program. DATA statements can contain mixtures of single or double precision data, integers, and string constants, as long as the program reads them in the order they are listed. String constants do not have to be surrounded with quotation marks as long as they don't contain commas, colons or spaces. Consequently a DATA statement can only be followed with a comment on the same line if it terminates with a colon.

```
DATA 1, 1.5, 33.4#, Fred
DATA 6, 6.3, 12.23, Jones: 'Here is a comment
```

You read the constants in a DATA statement into variables using a READ statement. READ statements consist of a list of variable names of any types separated by commas:

```
READ n%, x, db#, nm$
```

The READ and DATA statement combination is usually used in testing programs so that you don't have to keep entering the same test data, and in initializing a large number of variables efficiently. Truly useful programs allow you to enter values at the keyboard or from files when the program is run.

ENTERING DATA—THE INPUT STATEMENT

The companion statement to the PRINT statement is the INPUT statement, which we used in Chapter 1 to read in data from the keyboard.

```
INPUT a
```

QuickBASIC will print a question mark to indicate that it is waiting for data during an INPUT statement. It reads data up to the first carriage return (Enter key) or comma it finds. If you put several items in a list in an INPUT statement,

```
INPUT a,b,c
```

QuickBASIC reads data up to the first comma you type for the first value, the second comma for the second value, and the third comma or carriage return you type. This form of the INPUT statement is hardly "friendly" to the users of the program and it is not recommended.

PROMPTING MESSAGES DURING INPUT

You can print a message to the user as part of the INPUT statement by including a string in quotes before the variable name:

```
INPUT "Enter number of points"; n
```

This will print out

```
Enter number of points?
```

To suppress the question mark in such cases, follow the prompting message with a comma instead of a semicolon:

```
INPUT "Enter number of points", n
```

READING IN STRINGS

You can read in floating point, integer, or string variables using the INPUT statement. However, the same rules regarding the comma apply: QuickBASIC reads the string until it finds the first comma or carriage return character. Thus, if you want to enter the city and state as a single string with the usual comma,

```
INPUT "Enter City and state: ", address2$
```

and type in the answer,

```
Columbus, Ohio
```

the string ADDRESS2$ will only contain the city name "Columbus"; the comma and state will not be read.

There are two ways to get around this problem. One is to enclose the string you type in quotes. If you answer the question by typing

```
"Columbus, Ohio"
```

then the entire city, state, and comma will become part of the ADDRESS2$ string. This is somewhat inconvenient for the user, however.

THE LINE INPUT STATEMENT

The LINE INPUT statement was designed for reading in an entire line up to the carriage return. Commas and other punctuation characters are read as part of the string. The only allowed variable in a LINE INPUT statement is a single string variable. You cannot include numeric variables or lists of variables:

```
LINE INPUT "Enter City, State: ",address2$
```

CONTROLLING THE FORMAT OF PRINT STATEMENTS

The PRINT statement can also be written with the modifier USING followed by a string describing the format and spacing of the numbers and characters on that line. It has the following format

```
PRINT USING "string";v1,v2,v3
```

where "string" describes the format and spacing of the numbers, and V1, V2 and V3 are the single or double precision, integer, or string variables.

The format string can be written as follows:

####.### For the number of digits to the left and right of the decimal point
Exponential format, where the carets specify the number of spaces for the E+*nn* characters
Number of spaces for a string, including the spaces occupied by the backslashes themselves

REPRESENTING NUMBERS IN OTHER BASES

QuickBASIC allows you to represent numeric constants in bases other than 10, using the characters

```
&Hnnn          'for hexadecimal numbers and
&Onnn          'for octal numbers
```

where *nnn* is any series of digits legal for that number base. In the octal, or base 8 number system, there are only eight digits from 0 to 7. These digits are used to represent 3-bit groups in a single digit. These digits correspond to the following bit patterns:

0	000	4	100
1	001	5	101
2	010	6	110
3	011	7	111

The *hexadecimal* number system is the base 16 number system and is used to represent 4-bit groups in a single digit:

0	0000	8	1000
1	0001	9	1001
2	0010	A	1010
3	0011	B	1011
4	0100	C	1100
5	0101	D	1101
6	0110	E	1110
7	0111	F	1111

Thus, the expression

```
x1 = &h000a
```

assigns the value 10 (decimal) to the variable X1. Octal and hexadecimal constants are used primarily to refer to addresses in the PC's memory and bit patterns used to read or write to certain hardware registers. All numbers written in this form are assumed by QuickBASIC to be integers.

You can also print out numbers in octal or hexadecimal using the OCT$ and HEX$ functions:

```
PRINT hex$(141)           'prints out "8D"
PRINT oct$(127)           'prints out "177"
```

We will see in the next chapter how we can use these constants to test and set particular bits in words.

3 Making Decisions in BASIC

If BASIC could only perform simple arithmetic calculations such as those shown in Chapter 2, it would only be a rather inconvenient kind of pocket calculator. In fact, the power of BASIC (and many other computer languages) is its ability to make *decisions*.

THE FOR-NEXT LOOP

The FOR loop is the primary method of passing through a set of instructions a fixed number of times. It has the simple form

```
FOR variable = low TO high
      :
      statements
      :
NEXT variable
```

This statement means to

1. Set the variable to the low value.
2. Check to see that the low value is less than or equal to the high value.

3. Execute the statements.
4. At the NEXT statement, add 1 to the variable.
5. Go back to step 2.

The loop may be executed many times or not executed at all if the LOW values is greater than the HIGH value. The test for whether the variable is less than the high value takes place at the top of the loop.

For example, you might want to print out a list of numbers and their squares:

```
'print squares of numbers from 1 to 10

        FOR num = 1 TO 10          'top of squaring loop
            sq = num ^ 2           'calculate square
            print num, sq          'print number and square
        NEXT num                   'see if we're done yet
```

will produce the table:

```
1           1
2           4
3           9
4           16
5           25
6           36
7           49
8           64
9           81
10          100
```

THE FOR–NEXT–STEP LOOP

The complete form of the FOR loop includes the STEP modifier, which allows you to increment the variable by numbers other than 1, and in fact step in the negative direction if you wish:

```
FOR variable = first TO last STEP incr
      :
               statements
      :
NEXT incr
```

This form starts the variable at FIRST, executes the loop, adds INCR to the variable, and checks to see if it is still less than or equal to LAST. If it is, the loop is executed again, and if it is not, the program goes on. If the value of INCR is negative, the program tests to see if FIRST is greater than or equal to LAST rather than less than or equal it.

Let us suppose that we want to print out a table of Celsius vs. Fahrenheit temperatures for every half Celsius degree. We could do this with the following program:

```
'Print out a Table of Celsius vs Fahrenheit
FOR Celsius = 0 TO 40 STEP 0.5
        Fahr = (9/5) * (Celsius) + 32
        PRINT Celsius, Fahr
NEXT Celsius
END
```

QuickBASIC allows you to terminate a FOR loop with a NEXT statement which has no variable name associated with it:

```
FOR k = 1 TO n
   x(k) = x(k) + x(k - 1)
NEXT
```

The NEXT statement always terminates the current innermost FOR loop. However, these statements are much harder to read, since you must look back through the code to see which variable is changing, and this form of the FOR - NEXT loop is not recommended.

QuickBASIC also provides the EXIT FOR statement as a way to exit from a FOR - NEXT loop before the loop counter is satisfied. However, this is not a recommended statement, since it leads to unstructured programs where you cannot always tell how a program reaches a particular statement.

PROGRAMMING STYLE

You may have noticed that we have been indenting the code within a FOR loop. QuickBASIC allows you to lay out your statements anywhere on the page. In order to take advantage of this freedom, we recommend that you indent the code inside the FOR loops and leave the FOR and NEXT statements aligned and not indented in order to make the limits of the loop clear to the eye. This becomes more useful when you have several nested loops and need to keep track of where they begin and end.

THE WHILE - WEND LOOP

The second looping structure in QuickBASIC is the WHILE-WEND loop. It has the following form:

```
WHILE expression
    :
    statements
    :
WEND
```

The expression may be any logical statement that can be true or false. For example:

```
WHILE price < 9.99
          or
WHILE sum = 0
```

The complete list of comparison or *Boolean* operations that you can use in the WHILE expression are:

<	less than
<=	less than or equal to
=	equal to
>=	greater than or equal to
>	greater than
<>	not equal to

Note that the symbols "<", ">", and "< >" are two-character symbols. You may *not* separate them with a space, although you should preceed and follow them with a space for readability:

```
WHILE time >= 108.16      'this way
WHILE time>=108.16        'not this way
```

The WHILE loop is similar to the FOR loop in that it is possible for the expression to be false and thus the loop might *never* be executed. This happens because the program tests the expression *before* the loop is executed. By contrast, since FOR loops usually are set up around integer steps, they are usually executed at least once.

In the following sample program, we use the WHILE statement to decide when all of the numbers in a list have been entered so that the average can be calculated:

```
'Program to calculate the average of a list of numbers

count = 1                    'set counter to 1
sum = 0                      'set running sum to 0

INPUT num                    'get first number

WHILE num <> 0               'loop while the number entered is not
                             'zero
   sum = sum + num           'add number into running sum
   count = count + 1         'count the number entered
   INPUT num                 'get another number
 WEND

avg = sum / count            'calculate average

PRINT "The average of ";count; " entries is "; avg
END
```

CAUTIONS IN USING WHILE

One of the easiest mistakes to make in writing a loop with a WHILE statement is the error of the ***uninitialized variable.*** If we write

```
   WHILE num <> 0
```

we'd better be sure that NUM is in fact *not* zero when the loop begins or it will never be executed at all. Thus, it is not uncommon that there be one initial setting of that variable to some value before the loop begins. This is why there are two INPUT statements in the program above.

THE DO - LOOP STATEMENTS

QuickBASIC 4.0 has the additional DO - LOOP statements specified by the proposed ANSI BASIC standard. These statements have the following four forms:

```
DO                    DO
'statements           'statements
LOOP UNTIL expr       LOOP WHILE expr

DO UNTIL expr         DO WHILE expr
'statements           'statements
LOOP                  LOOP
```

These expressions do just what they appear to: in the left two examples the statements are executed only *until* the expression *expr* is true, and in the right two examples the statements are executed WHILE the expression *expr* is true. Note that the DO WHILE statement is identical in function to the WHILE–WEND statement:

```
i = 1                 i = 1
WHILE  i > 0          DO WHILE i > 0
   INPUT i               INPUT i
WEND                  LOOP
```

The DO–LOOP statements are considerably more versatile than the WHILE–WEND statement, because you can test for the condition at the beginning or at the end of any loop, and you have the ability to state your problem in terms of the condition to continue the loop (WHILE) or the condition to terminate the loop (UNTIL).

DIFFERENCES BETWEEN WHILE, FOR, AND DO

The WHILE statement differs from the FOR statement in that it is much more versatile. The FOR statement only allows you to pass through a loop a fixed number of times based on a counter. The WHILE statement allows you to execute a loop never, for a number of times to be calculated, or forever.

The loop "variable" in a FOR statement is called the *control variable.* While BASIC does not prevent you from changing the value of the variable within the loop, good programming practice suggests that you avoid this because it leads to a great deal of confusion, since the variable seems to change only at the NEXT statement. The control variable in a WHILE loop is whatever value is being compared in the expression following the WHILE statement. We *expect* that it will be changed within the loop or the loop will never finish.

DO statements differ from WHILE statements in that it is possible to check for whether a condition is true either at the beginning *or* at the end of the loop. The WHILE statement checks at the beginning of a loop and can lead to conditions where the loop is never executed. The DO WHILE - LOOP statement is identical in this regard.

The DO - LOOP WHILE statement differs in that the loop will always be executed at least once, and then the condition will tested to see if it should be executed again.

The DO UNTIL - LOOP and DO - LOOP UNTIL statements are really simply syntactical variants on the DO WHILE - LOOP and the DO - LOOP WHILE statements. You can always express a logical test in either the WHILE or UNTIL form, but one may be more readable than the other. For example, the following two loops usually produce identical results:

```
DO                       DO
 :                        :
LOOP WHILE x <> 0        LOOP UNTIL x = 0
```

COMBINING LOGICAL TESTS

It often occurs in writing BASIC programs that you need to perform a loop only if *two or more* conditions are satisfied. For example, you might want to restrict the number of values in a list of numbers to be averaged to no more than 20. You can do this by simply listing the two conditions connected by one of the logical operators AND or OR:

```
WHILE num <> 0 AND count < 20
```

You can make this more readable by enclosing the conditions in parentheses:

```
WHILE (num <> 0) AND (count < 20)
   sum = sum + num                  'add number into running sum
   count = count + 1                'count the number entered
   input num                        'get another number
WEND
```

The complete set of logical operators you can use in QuickBASIC are:

AND	Logical AND
OR	Logical OR
XOR	Exclusive OR
NOT	Logical complement
EQV	Logical equivalence
IMP	Logical implication

The *AND and OR operations* mean just what they seem to mean linguistically: AND means the result is true if *both* conditions are true, and OR means the result is true if *either* condition is true. This is sometimes expressed in a truth table, as follows:

AND	F	T
F	F	F
T	F	T

OR	F	T
F	F	T
T	T	T

The *XOR (Exclusive OR) operation* is less common in everyday use, but finds a few useful applications in programming. The result of an XOR is true if the two input values are *different*:

XOR	F	T
F	F	T
T	T	F

The EQV operation is simply the opposite of the XOR operation. It returns a result which is true if the two operators are the *same*:

EQV	F	T
F	T	F
T	F	T

The *implication operator* (IMP) is seldom used in programming and is included only for completeness. It is the only assymetrical operator, and depends on the order of the operands:

a	b	a IMP b
F	F	T
F	T	T
T	F	F
T	T	T

MAKING DECISIONS WITH THE IF – THEN STATEMENT

While the ability to loop through statements can produce a powerful program, the real decision-making power of QuickBASIC lies in the IF – THEN statement, which allows you to perform certain statements if and only if some expression is true. It has the simple form:

```
IF expression THEN statement
```

and the expanded form in QuickBASIC:

```
IF expression THEN
        :
        statements
        :
END IF
```

The upper one-line form exists in all implementations of BASIC, but the much more powerful block-structured lower form is unique to QuickBASIC (and a few other expanded BASIC systems). We will use the lower form exclusively; it is more readable and powerful, since you can execute any number of statements if the expression is true, while you are limited to a single line's worth of statements in the upper form.

Suppose that we wish to write a program to convert back and forth between degrees Celsius and Fahrenheit, but we don't know which way we might wish to convert at any given time. We can read in a temperature and a letter to indicate which way to convert and perform one conversion or the other:

```
'Convert back and forth between Celsius and Fahrenheit

INPUT "Enter temperature: ", temp
INPUT "Enter 'C' or 'F': ", scale$
```

```
IF UCASE$(scale$) = "C" THEN 'convert to Fahrenheit
        newtemp = (9 / 5) * temp + 32
        PRINT temp; " degrees C equals "; newtemp; " degrees F"
END IF

IF UCASE$(scale$) = "F" THEN 'convert to Celsius
        newtemp = (temp - 32) * (5 / 9)
        PRINT temp; " degrees F equals "; newtemp; " degrees C"
END IF

END
```

THE IF-THEN-ELSE STATEMENT

The IF-THEN statement has a more general form as follows:

```
    IF expression THEN
            statement1
    ELSE
            statement2
    END IF
```

In this form, *statement1* is executed if the expression *expression* is true, and *statement2* is executed if *expression* is false. For example, you could test for even and odd numbers by checking to see if an integer is the same after being halved and doubled:

```
INPUT num%
IT ( (num% \ 2) * 2) = num% THEN        'integer division
        PRINT num%;" is even"           'print this if true
ELSE
        PRINT num%;" is odd"            'print this if false
END IF
```

THE IF-THEN-ELSEIF MULTIPLE STATEMENT

In BASIC, the problem often arose when there were more than two possible cases to consider as to how to program this clearly. A special syntax was provided in BASIC for these cases where the IF-THEN statement is terminated with ELSEIF to indicate that more choices are to be considered. For example:

```
IF (scale$ = "C") THEN
    newtemp = (9/5) * temp + 32

ELSEIF (scale$ = "F") THEN
    newtemp = (5/9) * (temp - 32)

ELSEIF (scale$ = "K") THEN
    newtemp = (9/5) * (temp - 273.16) + 32

END IF
```

This syntax is now seldom used, as it has been supplanted by the SELECT CASE statement.

THE SELECT CASE STATEMENT

QuickBASIC provides an even more efficient way to specify choices from a list. If a variable can take on a number of values, whether integer, real, or string, the SELECT CASE statement can be used economically to specify the choices in a simple, elegant fashion.

In the following example, the variable C is compared against the constants in the various CASE selectors. If they match, the statements following that CASE are executed. You can also use CASE ELSE to indicate actions to be taken if none of the other cases match:

```
SELECT CASE c
CASE 1
        statements1
CASE 2,3
        statements2
CASE 5 TO 8
        statements3
CASE ELSE
        statements4

END SELECT
```

In fact, CASE ELSE should be part of every SELECT CASE list, even if there is no statement following it. This prevents errors if an unusual value occurs.

In this example, *statements1* are executed if C has the value 1, *statements2* are executed if C is either 2 or 3, and *statements3* executed if C lies anywhere from 5 through 8. If C has any other value, *statements4* are executed. Note that the CASE lists may only contain constants: named variables are not allowed.

You can also use string variables, as is illustrated in the revised version of the temperature conversion program:

```
'Print out values in degrees Celsius, Fahrenheit, or Kelvin
'Exit if a Q is typed
quit = 0                                'initialize to 0

WHILE (quit = 0)
    INPUT "Enter temperature: ", temp
    INPUT "Enter scale (C,F,K,Q): ", scale$

SELECT CASE scale$
   CASE "C", "c"
       newtemp = (9 / 5) * temp + 32
       PRINT temp; " Celsius equals "; newtemp; "Fahrenheit"

   CASE "F", "f"
       newtemp = (5 / 9) * (temp - 32)
       PRINT temp; " Fahrenheit equals "; newtemp; "Celsius"

   CASE "K", "k"
       newtemp = (9 / 5) * (temp - 273.16) + 32
       PRINT temp; " Kelvin equals "; newtemp; "Fahrenheit"

   CASE "Q", "q"
       quit = 1                                  'exit if q typed
   CASE ELSE
   END SELECT

WEND
```

RELATIONAL OPERATORS IN SELECT CASE STATEMENTS

You can also specify cases where an expression involving a relational operator is used:

```
    CASE IS >= "Z"
    CASE IS < 0
```

These serve to provide additional ways to limit the extremes of possible values that might occasionally occur.

HOW TO USE *AND* AND *OR* FOR EXAMINING BITS

While the primary use of AND and OR in QuickBASIC is for logical statements regarding a number of conditions, you can also use AND, OR, and XOR to examine and set bits in variables used to set or reset bits or hardware registers.

For example, suppose that the variable REGSTAT% contains some value which you want to be sure has bit 3 set regardless of the setting of the other bits. You can do this with the OR operations:

```
regstat% = regstat% OR &h8          'set bit 3 (1000)
```

This actually will work correctly, even if the variable is not an integer variable,

```
regstat = regstat OR &h8          'set bit 3 (1000)
```

because QuickBASIC converts the value of any variable to an integer before applying the logical operation.

In the same way, if the variable CONFIG contains the bits representing the current configuration of your PC, and you want to see the value of bits 4 and 5, you can write

```
video = config AND &h18
```

and find that VIDEO contains the values of just those bits.

4 Handling Strings and Using Functions in BASIC

LIBRARY FUNCTIONS IN BASIC

In Chapter 2 we used the SQR function to obtain the square root of an expression. BASIC has quite a number of built-in or library functions for performing useful calculations. A complete list of these is shown in Table 4.1. All of them are discussed in detail in the QuickBASIC Compiler handbook.

CLASSIFICATION OF FUNCTIONS

Arithmetic Functions

The following functions return a floating point value:

ABS	Absolute value	RND	Random number
ATN	Arctangent	SGN	Sign of expression
COS	Cosine	SIN	Sine
EXP	Exponential	SQR	Square root
FIX	Truncated integer	TAN	Tangent
INT	Largest integer less than or equal to a number	VAL	Numerical value of string
LOG	Natural log		

TABLE 4.1 Standard Functions in QuickBASIC

Function	Description
ABS(x)	Absolute value
ASC(x$)	Numeric value of the first character of string X$
ATN(x)	Arctangent of X
CDBL(x)	Converts X to double precision
CHR$(x)	Converts numeric value X to an ASCII character
COMMAND$	Returns the string used to call the QuickBASIC program
COS(x)	Cosine of X, where X is in radians
CSNG(x)	Converts X to single precision
CSRLIN(x)	Returns the line position of the cursor
CVD(x$)	Converts numeric bytes from record file to double precision
CVI(x$)	Converts numeric bytes from record file to integer
CVL(x$)	Converts numeric bytes from record file to long integer
CVS(x$)	Converts numeric bytes from record file to single precision
DATE$	Returns a string containing the date
EOF(n)	Returns true if file *n* is at end of file
ENVIRON$	Returns the command string used to call the program
ERDEV	Returns the error code from the last device to get an error
ERL	Returns the line number of the last error
ERR	Returns the number of the last error
EXP(x)	Returns *e* raised to the power X
FIX(x)	Returns the truncated integer value of X
FRE(-1)	Returns the number of free bytes of memory remaining
FREEFILE	Returns the next free file number
HEX$(x)	Returns the hexadecimal string representing the value of X
INKEY$	Returns a character if the keyboard was struck or a null if not
INSTR(i, s1$, s2$)	returns the position of s2$ in s1$ after position i
INP(n)	Returns a value from I/O port n
INPUT$(n, #f)	Returns n bytes from file #f
INT(x)	Returns the largest integer less than or equal to X
LBOUND(a,i)	Returns the lowest array index for dimension in the array A
LCASE$(s$)	Returns string S$ in lower case letters
LEFT$(s$,n)	Returns a string of the N leftmost characters of S$
LEN(s$)	Returns the length of string S$
LOC(f)	Returns the current position in file F
LOF(f)	Returns the length of file number F in bytes
LOG(x)	Returns the log to base e of X
LPOS	Returns the current position of the printer print head
LTRIM$(s$)	Returns string S$ with leading blanks removed

TABLE 4.1 Standard Functions in QuickBASIC—Continued

Function	Description
MID$(s$,n,l)	Extracts a string from S$ of N characters starting at position l
MKD$(x)	Returns an 8-byte string equivalent to the bytes in X#
MKI$(x)	Returns a 2-byte string equivalent to the bytes in X%
MKL$(x)	Returns a 4-byte string equivalent to the bytes in X&
MKS$(x)	Returns a 4-byte string equivalent to the bytes in X!
OCT$(x)	Returns a string which consists of the octal value of X
PEEK(n)	Returns the byte read from memory location N
PEN(i)	Returns light-pen coordinates
PLAY(n)	Returns the number of notes in the background music queue
PMAP(x,n)	Converts logical to physical coordinate, according to N
POINT(x, y)	Returns the color number of the pixel at X,Y
POINT(n)	Returns the current physical or logical coordinate
POS(n)	Returns the current horizontal position of the cursor
RND(x)	Returns a random number between 0 and 1
RTRIM$(s$)	Returns a string with trailing blanks removed
SADD(s$)	Returns the address of string S$
SCREEN(row,col)	Returns the character on the screen at ROW, COL
SEEK(f)	Returns the current file position
SGN(x)	Returns the sign of expression X (1, 0, or -1)
SIN(x)	Returns the sine of X, where X is in radians
SPACE$(n)	Returns a string of spaces of length N
SPC(n)	Skips N spaces in a PRINT statement
SQR(x)	Returns the square root of X
STR$(x)	Returns a string expression representing the value of X
STRING$(m,s$)	Returns a string of length M all of whose characters are equal to the first character in S$
TAB(n)	Moves the print position to column N
TAN(x)	Returns the tangent of X, where X is in radians
TIME$	Returns the current time as a string
TIMER	Returns the number of seconds since midnight
TROFF	Turn error tracing off
TRON	Turn error tracing on
UBOUND(a,i)	Returns the upper bound of array A in dimension I
UCASE$(s$)	Returns the string S$ in upper case letters
VAL(s$)	Returns the numeric value of the number stored as a string in S$
VARPTR(x)	Returns the offset address of variable X in the current data segment

Integer Functions

The INT and FIX functions differ in the way they handle the integer part of a negative number. INT returns the first negative integer less than X, and FIX returns the first negative integer greater than X.

Random Numbers

The RND function returns a random number between 0 and 1. This is a pseudorandom number generator which will always return the same sequence of random numbers each time the program is run unless you *reseed* the random number generator by calling the RANDOMIZE function. The random number seed is then used as the basis for calculating new random numbers.

The most common way to generate new random numbers is using the TIMER function to seed the generator:

```
RANDOMIZE(TIMER)
```

String Functions

The following functions operate on and/or return strings:

ASC	ASCII value of character
CHR$	Character having ASCII value
COMMAND$	Command line
DATE$	Current date
ENVIRON$	Current environment string
HEX$	Hexadecimal value of number
INKEY$	Key just struck
INPUT$	Number of bytes from file
LCASE$	Lower case string
LEFT$	Left *n* characters of a string
LTRIM$	String with leading blanks removed
MID$	Middle *n* characters of a string
OCT$	Octal value of a number
RIGHT$	Right n characters of a string
RTRIM$	String with trailing blanks removed
SPACE$	String consisting of the requested number of spaces
STR$	String representing value
STRING$	String of all one character
TIME$	Current time
UCASE$	Upper case string

All strings of characters are in fact arrays of bytes containing numbers between 0 and 255, which are the codes for each of the characters in the character set your PC can print. These character codes are called *ASCII codes* or *ISO codes*, where ASCII stands for the American Standard Code for Information Interchange, and ISO stands for the International Standards Organization.

Most printing characters have values between 32 and 127: those below 32 are the special printer and communications control characters such as Carriage Return, Linefeed, Tab, Space and Formfeed. Some of these are

Bell	7
Backspace	8
Tab	9
Linefeed	10
Formfeed	11
Carriage Return	13
Escape	27
Space	32
Delete	127

The characters for printing numbers start at ASCII 48:

0	48
1	49
⋮	⋮
9	57

In other words, to print the character "7" on the screen or a printer, you do not send the *number* 7 but the number 55. This is handled internally by BASIC for nearly all operations.

The ASCII codes for the letters of the alphabet are also of interest to us:

A	65	a	97
B	66	b	98
C	67	c	99
⋮	⋮	⋮	⋮
Y	89	y	121
Z	90	z	122

Note that there are separate codes for uppercase and lowercase letters, and that the codes for the whole uppercase or lowercase alphabet are continuous from A to Z. Thus, the difference between the code for "A" and the code for "a" is the same as the difference between any other two uppercase and lowercase letters.

Converting between Lowercase and Uppercase

This leads to a simple method of converting any lowercase character to uppercase by simply subtracting the constant difference between the two alphabets. While we can see by inspection that this difference is 32, we don't need to know this to write the program:

```
'program CASECHANGE
'converts any lowercase character to uppercase
'uppercase characters are unchanged
'strings longer than one character are rejected

a$ = ""                                'null length string
WHILE LEN(a$) <> 1
   INPUT "Type one character:"; a$   'get a character
WEND

IF ("a" <= a$) AND (a$ <= "z") THEN 'if the char is lower case...
        a$ = CHR$(ASC(a$) + (ASC("A") - ASC("a")))
END IF

PRINT "The character is: "; a$       'print converted character
END
```

In this example program, a string of one character is read in using the INPUT statement inside a WHILE loop that only exits if the entered string is only one character long. This character is then compared with the strings "a" and "z". If it lies between them, it is converted to uppercase by adding to its ASCII value the difference between the ASCII values of "A" and "a". The converted character is then printed out.

Actually, we note that QuickBASIC 4.0 provides functions for performing these conversions automatically: UCASE$ and LCASE$.

DEFINING NEW FUNCTIONS IN BASIC

QuickBASIC allows you to define new functions that operate just like the library functions, returning integers, single precision, or double precision numbers or strings. There are three ways that you can define a function:

1. As a one-line DEF FN*xxx* statement.
2. As a multiline DEF FN*xxx* statement.
3. As a FUNCTION subprogram.

The most modern and versatile of these techniques is the last, the FUNCTION subprogram, and we will use it here.

FUNCTION SUBPROGRAMS

QuickBASIC keeps each function and procedure in a separate logical compartment in memory. To create a new function, then, you must tell QuickBASIC you want to do this by selecting this item from the Edit menu. When you press Alt+E, you will see that one of the selections is

```
Make FUNCTION ...
```

If you select this item, QuickBASIC will ask you for a function name. Type in a name followed by Enter. QuickBASIC will clear the screen and display an empty function. If we called the function FODD, it would display

```
FUNCTION FODD
END FUNCTION
```

You can then type in any arguments to the function enclosed in parentheses and then type in the function statements. For example:

```
FUNCTION FODD(x)                 'returns 1 if X is odd
                                 'and 0 if even
   half = INT( INT(x)/2 )
   If half * 2 = x THEN
           FODD = 0              'not odd, return 0
   ELSE
           FODD = 1              'odd if half*2 is not = original
   END IF
END FUNCTION
```

The variable X is the argument of the function FODD and is referred to as the *dummy variable.* It is replaced by the value in the call to the function, such as

```
j = FODD(temp)
```

The value of TEMP is passed to FODD and is used in the calculation of the return value.

VIEWING AND COMPILING FUNCTIONS

Once you have finished typing in your function, you can go back to view the main calling program by pressing Shift+F2. This key circulates among all the currently available functions and procedures. You can also select View from the menu.

To compile and run, press Shift+F5 as before, and all the routines will be compiled, and the program will execute as usual.

VARIABLES USED INSIDE A FUNCTION

Variables named inside a function have values only inside that function. In general, you do not want variables such as HALF in the FODD function above to affect the value of any other use of the name HALF outside of the FODD function. Thus, you could have a variable named HALF in the main program whose value would not be affected by the fact that you call the FODD function, and make use of an internal variable also called HALF.

CONVERTING AN ENTIRE STRING TO UPPERCASE

In the program below, we define the function FUPPER$ to scan an entire string and convert any characters which were lowercase to uppercase. Spaces, punctuation, and characters already upper case are unaffected. The function works by determining the length of the string using the LEN function and then extracting, examining, and changing each character using the MID$ function:

```
'Program UCSTR
'Uses the function FUPPER to convert an entire string
'to uppercase letters
```

```
DECLARE FUNCTION fupper$ (st$)

INPUT "Enter a string: "; s$               'read in the string
s$ = fupper$(s$)                           'call the function
PRINT "The new string is: "; s$            'print out the answer
END
'----------------------------------------------------------------
FUNCTION fupper$ (st$)
'function to convert all the characters in a string
'from  lower to uppercase

      FOR i = 1 TO LEN(st$)        'up to the length of the string
      c$ = MID$(st$, i, 1)         'get each char in the string
      IF ("a" < c$) AND (c$ <= "z") THEN
        c$ = CHR$(ASC(c$) + ASC("A") - ASC("a"))
        MID$(st$, i, 1) = c$
      END IF
     NEXT i                        'go through all characters
fupper$ = st$                      'return new string

END FUNCTION
```

Note the use of the DECLARE statement at the top of the program. This statement is generated automatically by the compiler as it compiles the function FUPPER$. This tells the compiler that the function FUPPER$ exists and has one string argument. This make it possible for the compiler to check each call to FUPPER$ to make sure that it has the correct number and type of arguments and returns the correct variable type.

5 Using Arrays and Files in QuickBASIC

ARRAYS

BASIC allows you to handle data as single values and as arrays of values. An *array* is simply a list of numbers of the same type referred to by their position in the list

x_1, x_2, x_3, etc.

You might use such arrays to keep a list of measurements at different times, or a list of names for a mailing list or scoring sheet. You can define an array of 10 or fewer elements by simply referring to it by a variable name followed by parentheses followed by an array index value:

```
b(2)            'the 2nd element of real array B
c$(5)           'the 5th element of string array C$
x(i)            'the ith element of array X
```

QuickBASIC will allow you to create arrays in this fashion as long as you don't refer to elements above 10. If you need to handle larger arrays, you must tell QuickBASIC their size by *dimensioning* them using the DIM declaration. For example:

```
DIM x(200), c$(30)
```

The first array has 200 single precision elements and the second array 30 string elements. You can list any number of arrays on the same line of a DIM declaration, but, if you have more than one line of arrays, each line must begin with a new DIM declaration. We call DIM a *declaration* rather than a statement because it simply tells the QuickBASIC compiler how much space to leave for each array. It doesn't actually cause a program to *do* anything.

However, if you leave the DIM declaration out of a QuickBASIC program, it will execute until a reference is made to a location above 10. Then, a ***run-time error*** will occur, and the program will stop, displaying the message:

```
Subscript out of range
```

The QuickBASIC program will be displayed with the cursor on the reference to the array that caused the error. Consider the following simple program:

```
'Store 12 squares in array X(I) and print them out
FOR i= 1 TO 12
x(i) = i^2        'x equals i squared
PRINT i, x(i)     'print out i and its square
NEXT i
END
```

This program will compile correctly, but when you execute it, it will print out I values from 1 to 10 along with the squares; it will then stop and print the out-of-range message. When you press any key, the cursor will be on the beginning of the second line.

LIMITS ON ARRAYS

You can keep quite a large number of values in a single array. However, in QuickBASIC 4.0, no single array can occupy more than 64K bytes (65,536 bytes). This limits the dimensions of arrays as follows:

Single precision	16,382
Double precision	8,190
Integer	32,766
Long integer	16,382
String	16,382

String arrays can be this large because the actual array contains a 32-bit *pointer* to where each actual string is kept.

MULTIDIMENSIONAL ARRAYS

Arrays can have more than one dimension. In fact, in QuickBASIC you can have an array with up to 63 different indexes. The most common case, of course, is a two-dimensional array:

```
DIM x(10,3)
```

Two-dimensional arrays are generally used to keep related values together. For example, you could write a program to keep the values of $\sqrt{x}$, x^2, and x^3 in an array:

```
'store the square root, square, and cube of X in an array
      CONST SQRT = 1, SQUARE = 2, CUBE = 3
      DIM x(10,3)
      FOR i = 1 TO 10
          x(i,SQRT) = SQR(x)
          x(i,SQUARE) = x<2
          x(i,CUBE) = x<3
      NEXT i
END
```

As before, you can refer to arrays where each dimension is less than 10 without using the DIM statement. This will, however, lead to a warning message when you compile the program, and it is usually safer to dimension each array specifically.

Multidimensional arrays may not in total occupy more than 64K bytes of data. That is, the product of all the dimensions must be less than 64K bytes.

USING CONST STATEMENTS FOR DIMS

The CONST statement is ideal for dimensioning a group of arrays to the same size using a named constant dimension which you can easily change as your program's needs grow:

```
CONST AMAX = 30              'define array bounds
DIM x(AMAX), xy(AMAX,AMAX)   'use in DIM statements
```

LIMITS ON ARRAYS USING THE /AH SWITCH

If you start QuickBASIC with the /ah switch following the program name,

```
qb /ah
```

you are not limited to the previously mentioned dimension restrictions. Multidimensional arrays may be much larger, up to the limits of available memory, but no single dimension can be larger than 32,766 elements. These larger arrays are only available if they are *dynamic arrays* rather than static arrays. Dynamic arrays are generated when the dimensions are variables rather than actual or named constants:

```
max = 32766        'variable dimension
DIM x(max)         'dynamic array
```

SPECIFYING DIFFERENT SUBSCRIPT RANGES

In order for an array to correspond more closely to the physical reality it may represent, you can specify a different subscript range than the usual one of 0 to the maximum dimension value. For example, you might have an array of measurements taken at temperatures from −20 to +40 and wish to store them in corresponding array index values. You can dimension an array for this purpose using the *lower* TO *upper* syntax:

```
DIM meas(-20 TO 40)
```

Then you can store the measurement for −20 degrees in element MEAS (−20).

USING THE DIM STATEMENT TO SPECIFY TYPE

You can specify the type of any variable you dimension as part of the DIM statement:

```
DIM fred(1 TO 20) AS INTEGER
```

This makes the array FRED an integer array despite any DEF statement in effect and even though no % sign is appended to the array.

More important, you can declare the type of any individual nonarray variable in the same way:

```
DIM i AS INTEGER, temp AS DOUBLE
DIM FirstName AS STRING, profit AS LONG
```

This is a considerable improvement over having to type in awkward punctuation marks such as %, $, &, and # each time you use a variable.

USING TEXT FILES IN QUICKBASIC

In addition to reading from the keyboard and printing on the printer, BASIC allows you to read and write to disk files just as simply. The only difference is that you must first tell BASIC the *name* of the file you wish to read from or write to. You do this using the OPEN statement:

```
OPEN "file.txt" FOR INPUT AS #1    'open to read in
      OR
OPEN "file.txt" FOR OUTPUT AS #1   'open to write out
      OR
OPEN "file.txt" FOR APPEND AS #1   'open to add to end
```

The file number following the # sign must be an integer value or variable whose value is between 1 and 255.

- If you open a file for *input,* this means it already exists on the disk or diskette and that you want to read from it. If it doesn't exist, a run-time error will occur.
- If you open a file for *output,* this means that you wish to begin writing to a file that did not previously exist. If that file does exist, it is *deleted.*
- *If you open a file for append,* you are going to write to a file that may or may not already exist. If it does, any new information is added to the end of the file. If it doesn't exist, a new file of that name is created.

WRITING TO A DISK FILE

In order to write to a disk file, you use the PRINT#n, statement, where *n* is the number you choose in the OPEN statement. Since these numbers can be variables, we will choose variable names describing the nature of the file and assign small whole-number values to the file variable names. In the following program, we open the file SINES.DAT, and write 512 sines into it, and use the variable name SINEFILE to hold the file number which we arbitrarily select as 2. Remember that you can choose any number between 1 and 255 for a file number, but that each file that is open simultaneously must have a different number.

```
'Program to write 513 sines into a file
CONST SINEFILE = 2                              'arbitrary file number
CONST PI = 3.141593                             'the constant pi
CONST MAXSINES = 512

OPEN "sine.dat" FOR OUTPUT AS #SINEFILE 'open the file

FOR i = 0 TO MAXSINES
        PRINT #SINEFILE, SIN(i * PI / (2 * 512))
NEXT i

CLOSE #SINEFILE
END
```

CLOSING A FILE

Note that whenever we open a file for output, we must also close it before that file exists on disk in its final form. While QuickBASIC automatically closes files when you exit from a program, it is good practice to do it yourself, since you cannot read data back from that file within your program unless it has first been closed. The syntax is that shown in the example above

```
    CLOSE #f            'where f is the number used
                        ' when you opened the file
```

FORMAT OF A TEXT FILE

Files written by PRINT# statements are *text files,* and are therefore just the characters that would have appeared on the screen had you used the PRINT statement instead of printing to a file. If you exit to DOS from QuickBASIC and use the TYPE command to print out the contents of such a file, you will see exactly the text, including new lines and spaces, that you specified with the PRINT# command. This can be useful in reading that data back in, since you need only use the complementary INPUT# statement.

FINDING FILE NUMBERS

As noted, files are referred to in these statements by number. In the previous program we arbitrarily picked numbers for the files when we opened them. However, in a complex program it may not be easy to decide which file numbers are already in use and which are still available. QuickBASIC provides the FREEFILE function for that purpose. Any call to FREEFILE returns the next free file number, so you never have to know what file number is in use or available:

```
sindat = FREEFILE           'get file number
OPEN "sines.dat" FOR  OUTPUT AS #sindat
```

READING FROM A TEXT FILE

To read data from a text file, you must first OPEN the file for input. You can then read data in using the INPUT# statement just as you could from the terminal. The following small program reads in the 513 sines written into the file SINE.DAT by the previous program:

```
'Program to read in the data in SINES.DAT
DIM x(513)                                'dimension array X
sindat = FREEFILE                         'file number
OPEN "sine.dat" FOR INPUT AS #sindat      'open the file

FOR i = 0 to 512
   INPUT #sindat, x(i)                    'read in each sine
   PRINT x(i)                             'and print it
NEXT i
CLOSE #sindat                             'close the file when done
END
```

THE LINE INPUT STATEMENT AND TEXT FILES

Recall that the INPUT statement reads data up to the first comma, and not necessarily to the end of the line. Thus, if you write out a text file containing strings of information with embedded commas, the INPUT# statement will stop at each comma. Using the LINE INPUT# statement, you can read a whole line at a time from the text file.

DETECTING THE END OF A FILE

The previous program will read in the 513 values in the SINE.DAT file and print each of them out as it reads them. This method works fine in our case, since we know how many values there are in the file to start with. However, in many cases, we don't know how many values there are in a file, and we need to loop through the file read-in statements until we run out of data. We can do this in BASIC using the *EOF (end-of-file) function* to detect whether the end of a file has been reached.

In the following revised program, we read in data while EOF is not true. When it becomes true, the loop is no longer executed.

```
'Program to read in the data in SINES.DAT until end of file
CONST maxsines = 513
DIM x(maxsines)                                'dimension array X

sindat = FREEFILE
OPEN "sine.dat" FOR INPUT AS #sindat           'open the file

i = 0                                          'start with I at 0
WHILE NOT EOF(sindat)                          'read until end of file
    INPUT #sindat, x(i)                        'read in each sine
    PRINT x(i)                                 'and print it
    i = i +1                                   'on to next I-value
WEND

END
```

DELETING AND RENAMING FILES

BASIC allows you to delete and rename files without returning to DOS using the KILL and NAME statements. In order to delete a file, it must not be currently open, and you can delete it by simple giving the command

```
    KILL "SINES.DAT"          'delete the file SINES.DAT
```

or using a variable name

```
FS$ = "SINES.DAT"          'set string variable equal to filename
KILL FS$                   'and delete the file
```

The NAME statement allows you to give a file a new name. It has the form

```
NAME oldname$ AS newname$          'rename OLDNAME to NEWNAME
       or
NAME "sines.dat" AS "sines.old"   'rename SINES.DAT to SINES.OLD
```

The file you are renaming must not currently be open, and there cannot be a file already having the new name, or a run-time error will occur.

BINARY FILES

The most convenient method of handling files is the text file method we describe earlier. However, text files are not particularly compact and take up relatively large amounts of disk space, since each character in each number takes up one byte. You can also store data in files using a binary format using the GET and PUT statements. These are described in detail in Chapter 14.

6 More on Editing and Compiling Programs

In Chapter 1 we saw how to get started in QuickBASIC by typing in simple programs and executing them using a minimum number of commands and keystrokes. By now, you have probably discovered a number of other features of the editor and would like to know more about the compiler's features. In this chapter we will tell you how to use the editor efficiently and how to compile programs you can save on disk and run without starting QuickBASIC.

HELP IN QuickBASIC

In this chapter we will be discussing a number of keys and functions you can use to edit and compile a program. While we show them listed in a series of tables in the text, you can get a summary of these functions on the screen at any time by pressing the function key F1. A full screen list of the keys used to select the menu, move the cursor, edit, and compile will appear on the screen. You can make this Help screen disappear and return to editing by pressing Enter.

You can also go on to the second and third screens by selecting "Next" from the boxes at the bottom of the display. These two screens show the entire alphabet and all the symbols of the ASCII character codes.

By selecting "Keywords" you get a display of the entire list of the keywords in QuickBASIC. If you select one of these and press the mouse button or press Enter, a display describing that keyword appears on the screen.

THE SMART EDITOR

As you type in text in QuickBASIC, the program checks the syntax, capitalizes keywords, and issues error messages if you leave out a part of a statement. If you have a question about any keyword, position the cursor on it and press Shift+F1. A display about that keyword will appear in the top part of the screen and the statement will appear at the bottom, where you can edit it while reading the description.

PARTS OF THE QuickBASIC SCREEN

When you start QuickBASIC, you see the following displayed on the screen:

- A command bar containing the menu commands

  ```
  File   Edit   View   Search   Run   Debug   Calls
  ```

  which you can select by pointing to them with the mouse, or by holding down Alt and pressing the first letter of any of the commands.
- A program window containing the current program, or the word "Untitled" if you have started typing in a program which has not yet been saved.
- An immediate window, where you can type in any QuickBASIC statement and have it executed immediately. Statements in this window can be executed individually: successive lines are not related, and only the line with the cursor on it is executed when you press Enter or double-click the mouse. The purpose of the immediate window is to allow debugging of statements which you will then insert in your program. To hop back and forth between immediate and program windows, press Shift+F6. To expand or contract this window, press Alt+Plus, or Alt+Minus. You can keep up to 10 statements in the immediate window, but only the one with the cursor on it is executed when you press Enter.

Variables in the immediate window are the same as those in the program window. Thus, if you type "PRINT x" in the immediate window, the current value of X will be displayed.

- The information bar, which gives you current message information, including the purpose of any of the commands in the menus as you select them.
- The scroll bar along the right side, which allows you to move up and down through the text by clicking at various points on the bar with the mouse. There is no alternate use of the scroll bar without a mouse; if you are not using a mouse, you can remove the scroll bar from the screen by selecting Setup from the View menu and indicating that you do not wish to display the scroll bar.
- The Up Arrow in the upper right corner of the screen. It can be clicked on with the mouse to make the Immediate Window disappear so you can display program text on the entire screen. Clicking on it again makes the Immediate Window return.

EDITING

Whenever you are not running a program or compiling, you are in the editor and can change any part of your program to improve its content or readability.

As you have probably discovered, if there are any characters to the right of the cursor when you type a character, all of the characters on that line move over each time you enter a new character. This is the same as the insert mode of interpretive BASIC. QuickBASIC also allows you to switch to an editing mode where you can type over existing characters and replace them by pressing the Ins (Insert) key. When you do this, the cursor changes in shape from a half block to an underline character, and any characters you type replace the current characters. You can switch back to insert mode by pressing Ins again: the cursor changes back to a block. You can also delete characters in one of four ways:

Backspace	Deletes the character before the cursor
Shift+Backspace	Deletes the character after the cursor

Delete	Deletes the character on the cursor
Ctrl+Y	Deletes the whole line containing the cursor

MOVING THE CURSOR AROUND

On the right side of the PC keyboard, there is a matrix of 12 important keys:

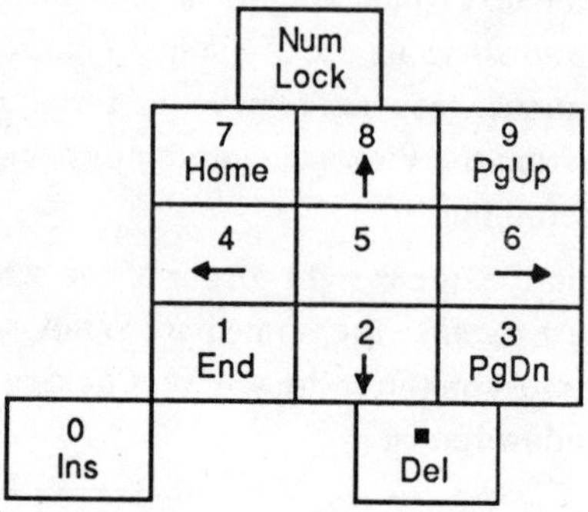

	Num Lock	
7 Home	8 ↑	9 PgUp
4 ←	5	6 →
1 End	2 ↓	3 PgDn
0 Ins		■ Del

These keys are used to control cursor movement if NumLock is off and to enter numbers if NumLock is on. On standard PCs, you can't tell whether it has been pressed or not except by trying it. However, when you are running QuickBASIC, it tells you if NumLock has been depressed by displaying "N" in the lower right corner of the screen. If "N" is displayed, pressing the right arrow key will produce a "6" on the screen; if "N" is not displayed, the cursor will move one place to the right. You can move the cursor Up, Down, Right, or Left on the screen using the four cursor keys marked with the up, down right and left arrows on the numeric keypad.

You can also move the cursor a word at a time across the screen by holding down the Ctrl key and pressing the Right or Left Arrow keys. If you press the PgUp or PgDn keys, your view of the program's text will scroll up or down by one page. You can move to the beginning or end of the text by pressing Ctrl+PgUp or Ctrl+PgDn, and to the top or bottom of the screen by pressing Ctrl+Home and Ctrl+End.

These functions are:

Up Arrow	Moves cursor up one line
Down Arrow	Moves cursor down one line

Right Arrow	Moves cursor right one character
Ctrl+Right Arrow	Moves cursor right one word
Left Arrow	Moves cursor left one character
Ctrl+Left Arrow	Moves cursor left one word
Home	Moves cursor to left end of line
Ctrl+Home	Moves cursor to top of screen
End	Moves cursor to end of line
Ctrl+End	Moves cursor to bottom of screen
PgUp	Moves cursor up one screen of text
PgDn	Moves cursor down one screen of text
Ctrl+PgUp	Moves cursor to top of file
Ctrl+PgDn	Moves cursor to bottom of file

SPLITTING AND COMBINING LINES

By now you may have discovered that if you press the Enter (Return) key while the cursor is in the middle of a line of text, you will split the line in half at that point. This feature is designed to allow you to split up long lines to improve readability. Conversely, you can also combine two lines by presssing Home to place the cursor at the left side and then pressing Backspace to delete the previous character. This deletes the preceding Enter character and makes two lines become one. For example you might have the statement:

```
IF (xsum-ysum) = 0 THEN ■ PRINT "The difference is zero"
```

The ■ character after the THEN represents the position of the cursor. If you press Enter with the cursor at that point, QuickBASIC will split the line into

```
IF (xsum-ysum) = 0 THEN
■ PRINT "The difference is zero"
```

To complete the change to the multiline IF statement, you need only move down one line by pressing the Down Arrow key and type "END IF"

```
IF (xsum-ysum) = 0 THEN
  PRINT "The difference is zero"
END IF
```

ADDING AND REMOVING LINES

You can create a new line just below the current one by pressing Enter when the cursor is at the right end of a line, or by using the following special characters:

Ctrl+N	Insert a line above the current line
Ctrl+Y	Delete the current line
End Enter	Insert a line below the current line

If you accidently add a line in the wrong place, you can always delete it with Ctrl+Y.

THE UNDO FUNCTION

If you accidently type the wrong thing on a line and want to put it back to what it was before, you can use the undo command:

```
Alt+Bksp        Undo changes in current line
```

This will restore the current line to the form it had before you began typing characters. Undo *only* works as long as your cursor has not been moved to another line, since QuickBASIC only remembers the unchanged version of the line with the cursor on it.

MOVING AND DELETING BLOCKS OF CHARACTERS

The QuickBASIC editor provides you with a way to mark a group of characters, a word or a line or group of lines and copy them, move them or delete them. You do this by highlighting the characters or lines you wish to operate on and then pressing

Ctrl+Ins	To copy them into the clipboard
Shift+Del	To copy them in the clipboard and delete them

and then pressing

Shift+Ins	To copy the contents of the clipboard to a new position in the text.

To highlight a text area, put the cursor on the beginning of the area to be highlighted; then hold down the Shift key and press one of the arrow keys to mark the area of interest:

Shift+Right Arrow	Marks characters to the right
Shift+Left Arrow	Marks characters to the left
Shift+Down Arrow	Marks current line and moves down
Shift+Up Arrow	Marks current line and moves up
Ctrl+Shift+Right Arrow	Marks next word to the right

A marked area is shown in another color or in reverse video, depending on the display card in your computer. These areas stay marked only until you move the cursor without the Shift key depressed. Thus, you can start over and mark another area by pressing any arrow key and moving to the start of the region you wish to mark.

Once you have marked the words or line of interest, you can copy it into a storage area called the *clipboard*. This happens when you press Ctrl+Ins. There is no visible indication that you have copied anything, but pressing Ctrl+Ins does indeed copy the current highlighted region into the clipboard. You can then move the cursor to where you want to move the text and then press Shift+Ins to insert this text at the new position.

If you want to move the text from one location to the other so that there are not two copies of the text in your program, you can highlight an area, press Shift+Del to delete the highlighted region, move the cursor, and press Shift +Ins to copy it. You can also use this feature to delete a block even if you don't want to copy it.

DELETING AND SAVING TEXT

The Ctrl+Y command deletes a single line from the program text, highlighting it first. This highlighting followed by deletion actually copies that line into the clipboard area and then deletes it from the text. When this happens, the previous contents of the clipboard are lost.

In a similar fashion, if you mark an area and delete it with the Shift+Del key, it is copied into the clipboard area. You can then move the cursor to the new position and press Shift+Ins key to copy the text from the clipboard back into the program.

Copying text from the program into the clipboard is destructive: the previous contents of the clipboard are lost. Copying text from the clipboard back into the program is nondestructive: the contents of the clipboard are remembered for further copying operations.

THE MENUS AND EDITING

The top line of the QuickBASIC display contains the menu items

```
File Edit View Search Run Debug Calls
```

You can select each of these menus by pressing the Alt key followed by the first character of the menu:

```
Alt+F  Alt+E  Alt+V  Alt+S  Alt+R  Alt+D  and  Alt+C
```

If you select the Edit menu by pressing Alt+E, you will get the following popup display:

```
Undo    Alt+Backspace
Cut         Shift+Del
Copy         Ctrl+Ins
Paste       Shift+Ins
Clear             Del
---------------------
New SUB...
New FUNCTION...
---------------------
√ Syntax Checking
```

This simply summarizes the commands described above. If you have changed the current line since the cursor has been moved to it, the Undo line will be intensified. If there is text in the clipboard, the Paste line will be intensified. You can select any of these lines by pressing the Up Arrow or Down Arrow keys to highlight one of the four lines, and then pressing Enter. This is equivalent to pressing the shortcut keys described earlier.

You can make any menu disappear by pressing the Escape key, and you can switch directly to another menu by pressing the Left or Right Arrow keys.

DISABLING THE SMART EDITOR

The Syntax Checking line is normally "checked" with the "√" sign, indicating that the syntax checking feature of the QuickBASIC smart editor is turned on. To turn this feature off, select this line of the menu and either press Enter or click the mouse button. The check will disappear and the syntax checking will no longer be active. The editor will then function like any text editor: it will not capitalize BASIC keywords, and it will not check for illegal syntax in each statement as you enter it. This is used for entering text or data to be processed by QuickBASIC programs. For actual program code, you should always leave the smart editor turned on.

NEW FUNCTIONS AND SUBS

Selecting either of these lines allows you to begin entering a new function or procedure. As we noted earlier, QuickBASIC keeps each of these routines in separate logical compartments, emphasizing that each of them is compiled separately, with no reference to variable names outside that function or procedure. We have already discussed creating functions in Chapter 4, and we will discuss the creation of procedures (SUBs) in the chapters that follow.

SEARCHING FOR TEXT

If you select the Search menu by pressing Alt+S, the following menu will appear:

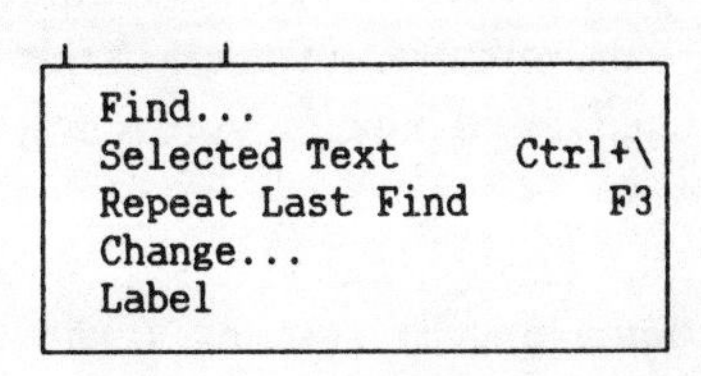

These commands are used to search for any text in the program and replace any text in the program. If you select "Find...," the following display appears:

```
Find What: [                                        ]

 ┌ Search ──────────────────┐   [ ] Match Upper/Lowercase
 │ ( ) 1. Active Window     │   [ ] Whole Word
 │ (•) 2. Current Module    │
 │ ( ) 3. All Modules       │
 └──────────────────────────┘        OK        Cancel
```

To search for any text, just type it in at the cursor, and press Enter to begin the search. QuickBASIC will search for the first occurrence of this text after the current position of the cursor and highlight it for you. You can then edit at this position as usual.

If there are several instances of this text, you can select "Repeat Last Find" from the menu or press the shortcut key F3 and the next instance of this text will be found.

Normally, Find searches the current module for the text you specify. To have it search all subroutines and functions in addition to the current program, select option 3, All Modules. The Label search command tells QuickBASIC to look for the currently selected text followed by a colon. Since we do not recommend using labels and their accompanying GOTO statements, we will not be using this option.

CASE SENSITIVITY IN SEARCHES

You can select two options as part of searches, which are highlighted if turned on. To select these options, press the Tab key until they are highlighted and then press the Space Bar to turn them on or off. The first of these is the Match Upper/Lowercase option. QuickBASIC normally matches text whether it is in upper- or lowercase or any mixture. If you select this Match Upper/Lowercase option, text is matched if and only if it agrees exactly in position of capital and lowercase letters.

The Whole Word search feature is used to search for a string of text only when it is *not* embedded in a longer text string. If you select "Whole Word", the text will be found only when it is surrounded by spaces or other conventional punctuation characters. Thus, searching for "int" would *not* find the name "integral" if the Whole Word option is selected.

CHANGING TEXT

Selecting the Change... option from the Search menu causes the following display to pop up:

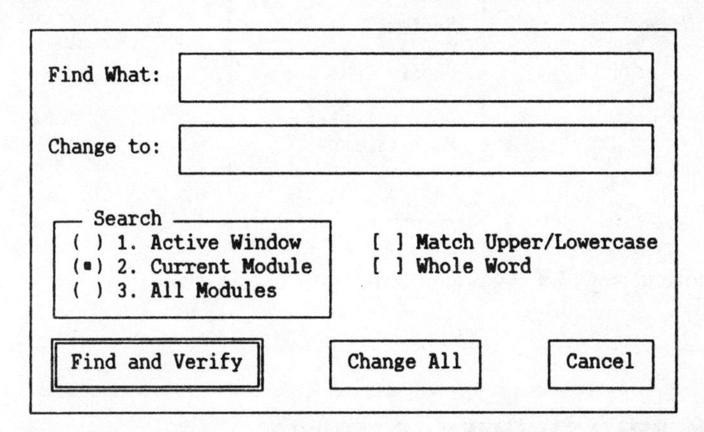

This command allows you to search for one text string and replace it with another. To do this, type in the text to find in the upper box, press the Tab key to move to the lower box, type in the new text it is to be changed to, and then type Enter to execute the search-and-replace. QuickBASIC will search for the text to replace, highlight it, and then display the menu selections

with the Change block highlighted. To change it, just type Enter. To skip to the next occurrence without changing it, press Tab to highlight "Skip" and then press Enter.

You can also change *all* occurrences of one text string to another by selecting both text strings as above, and then pressing the Tab key to highlight "Change All". Then, pressing Enter will cause all occurrences of the text to be changed.

COMPILING PROGRAMS

So far we have begun compiling programs by typing Shift+F5, which initiates compiling and if successful begins the execution of the program as well. When you type Alt+R to get the compilation menu, the following display pops up:

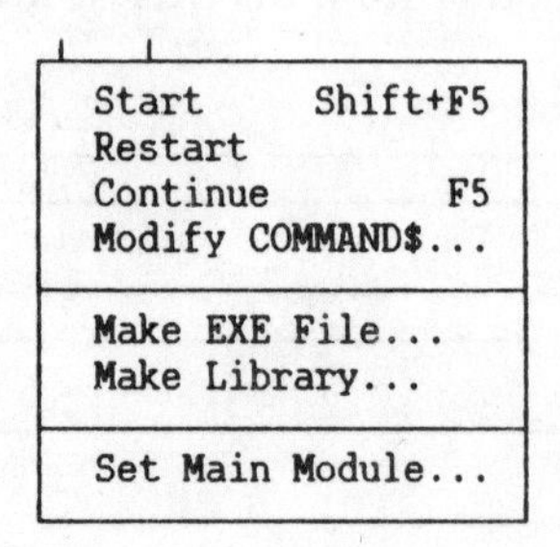

The shortcut key Shift+F5 selects the Start option.

THE INCREMENTAL THREADED COMPILER

You may have already noted that even though QuickBASIC is a *compiler,* there does not seem to be any compilation delay between the time you press Shift+F5 and the time your program begins executing. This is because QuickBASIC compiles each line of the program as you type it in or as it is read in from disk. The significance of this is that you can make changes in your program without having to wait for it to recompile: QuickBASIC is always ready to run your program. This allows QuickBASIC to check the syntax of each statement as you type it in and issue error messages as needed. Most important, you can stop a running program, make many kinds of changes to the code and continue executing without having to restart the program! This is a great help in debugging programs where a problem occurs in the middle of a long computation. If you make a change which requires QuickBASIC to alter the storage allocated for variables, you may get the message that you will have to restart the program after that change. You can always undo the change with Alt+Backspace if you do not wish to restart the program.

WAYS OF COMPILING YOUR PROGRAM

So far, all of our programs have been compiled into memory so that they execute from within QuickBASIC but cannot be executed by themselves. There are actually three ways of compiling a QuickBASIC program which you can use:

Memory The threaded compiled code is generated in memory by the compiler and can only be executed by starting QuickBASIC and loading the program. This is the fastest way to create and debug a program.

EXE Requiring BRUN40.EXE An executable file is created and written to disk having the filename of the original BASIC file, but with an .EXE extension. You can then run this file from DOS without starting QuickBASIC at all. However, this file looks for the file BRUN40.EXE and must find and load it for the program to run. This BRUN40.EXE file must be in the current subdirectory or in an subdirectory listed in the current PATH list.

Stand Alone EXE File The compiler compiles the program and generates a file with an .OBJ extension which is then linked using the LINK program. Such a file is completely stand-alone and requires no other files to run.

THE BC COMPILER

QuickBASIC actually consists of two compilers, the QB.EXE program we have been discussing and the BC.EXE program. QB is designed to be an easy-to-use interactive environment for development and debugging. BC is a compiler which produces stand-alone code which will run when linked to BRUN40.OBJ or BCOM40.OBJ. When you select "Make EXE File..." from the Run menu, you are presented with the following display:

```
EXE File Name: [                                        ]

Produce:
    (•) EXE Requiring BRUN40.EXE     [ ] Produce Debug Code
    ( ) Stand-Alone EXE File

     [ Make EXE ]   [ Make EXE and Exit ]   [ Cancel ]
```

If you select the upper option, QuickBASIC invokes the BC compiler automatically, and generates a program which will run with the BRUN40.EXE run-time library. If you select the Stand-Alone EXE File option, QB will call BC and the LINK program generating a somewhat larger program which will run without the BRUN40.EXE file being present. The main reason for choosing the first option is that if you are developing a suite of related programs, you can put them on the same diskette with one copy of the BRUN40.EXE file and all of them will run. If you are developing or distributing a single program, the Stand-Alone EXE File option may be the better choice.

For small programs, the difference in size between a file linked to run alone and one to run with BRUN is rather dramatic. For the simple four-line program to print out 10 values of x and x^2, the sizes in bytes are:

Size in Bytes of Squares Files

	.BAS File	.OBJ File	.EXE File
BRUN	120	913	3,229
STAND ALONE	120	913	24,221
BRUN40.EXE			76,816

DETECTING COMPILATION ERRORS

If QuickBASIC detects any errors when it starts to run a program, it will show them in a message box, with the cursor positioned on the error it found.

You can correct the error on the spot using the editor's commands and then continue executing by pressing function key F5. Occasionally, such a change will require you to restart the program, but many errors can be corrected while you are running through the program.

In the following simple program, we have included two errors to illustrate QuickBASIC's error-handling capabilities:

```
'Simple program with two errors

FOR i = 1 TO 12
   PRINT i,SQRT(i)
NEXT j
```

If we type in this program and press Shift+F5 to compile it, we will get the error message

```
NEXT without FOR
```

and the cursor will be positioned on the line

```
NEXT j█
```

Obviously, the statement was supposed to be

```
NEXT i
```

so we correct it by pressing Backspace to delete the "j" and typing an "i".

Now, if we restart the program and run it by pressing Shift+F5 we will get the answers

```
1       0
2       0
3       0
4       0
5       0
6       0
7       0
8       0
9       0
10      0
11
```

and then the error message

```
Subscript out of range
```

These zeros are clearly not the square root of I, and the subscript error message suggests that QuickBASIC is treating the SQRT(i) expression as an array. If we press Shift+F1 while the cursor is on SQRT, we will get a listing of all QuickBASIC keywords, rather than an intepretation of the SQRT function. In fact, by looking at the list, we discover that the correct name of the function for the square root is SQR. We simply delete the T and restart the program, which then gives the expected answers.

Table 6.1 lists the special keys used by the compiler and editor.

USING A MOUSE TO SELECT MENUS IN QuickBASIC

If you have a mouse attached to your PC or PS/2, you can use it with QuickBASIC by first running the driver program so that the mouse can be detected

TABLE 6.1 Summary of Special Keys Used by the Compiler and Editor

Key	Function
F1	Display Help
Shift+F1	Display information about keyword at cursor
F2	Display list of all modules
Shift+F2	Display next module in window
F3	Repeat last find
F4	View output screen
Shift+F5	Start program
F5	Continue program execution
F6	Jump to next window
Shift+F6	Jump to previous window
F7	Execute program to cursor position
F8	Single step program
Shift+F8	History back
F9	Set/remove breakpoint
F10	Step past procedure
Shift+F10	History forward
Alt+Bksp	Undo changes in current line
Ctrl+Y	Delete current line; copy into clipboard
Del	Delete highlighted area
Shift+Del	Delete highlighted area; put in clipboard
Ctrl+Ins	Copy highlighted area into clipboard
Shift+Ins	Insert clipboard text at cursor
Ctrl+\	Search for another copy of highlighted text
Ctrl+N	Insert blank line above cursor
Alt+Plus	Expand current window
Alt+Minus	Contract current window

by QuickBASIC. For example, with the Mouse Systems mouse, you must run the program MSMOUSE.COM before starting QuickBASIC. This program allows the Mouse Systems mouse to emulate the calls used by the Microsoft mouse. QuickBASIC is designed to run with the Microsoft mouse. If you have this mouse, you can run QuickBASIC without further installation.

If your mouse is recognized by QuickBASIC, you will see a rectangular cursor on the screen which moves around when you move your mouse. QuickBASIC uses only the left-most button of the mouse for selecting all functions.

To select a menu using the mouse, move the mouse cursor to point to one of the words in the menu bar and press the left mouse button. The menu will drop down just as if you had pressed Alt followed by one of the menu letters.

To select an item from the menu, move the mouse down to that line and press the left button again. QuickBASIC will immediately execute this function. To make the menu disappear without selecting any function, simply move the mouse cursor outside the menu and press the left button.

HIGHLIGHTING AREAS USING THE MOUSE

You can select words or lines to highlight for deletion or copying into the clipboard using the mouse. Point to the line where you want to start. Then drag the mouse to the right, down, up, or left while keeping the left button depressed. You highlight part of a line by moving right or left, and one or more lines by moving up or down. You can also highlight exactly one word by pointing to it and pressing the left button twice. Copying and deletion are accomplished as usual with the Ctrl+Ins and Ctrl+Del keys.

READING IN AND SAVING PROGRAMS

If you press the Alt+F key or select "File" with the mouse, you will get the following menu:

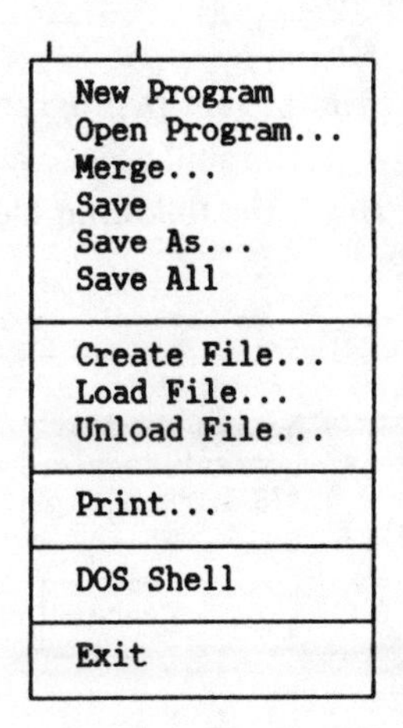

If you select "Open Program...," QuickBASIC will display a menu of all files in the current subdirectory with the .BAS extension. You can point to the one you want with the mouse or cursor keys and load the one you wish.

The Save option allows you to store the current file on disk as described in Chapter 1. The Save As... selection will allow you to enter a new filename for your program.

LOADING AND MERGING FILES

The Merge... command allows you to insert the contents of another file at the current cursor position. The same filename display as appeared for the Open command now appears, but the text becomes part of the current file. Subprograms (SUBs) and functions are put into separate modules in the same way they would be if they were part of the original main file.

By contrast, the Load command reads in a file of QuickBASIC SUBs and functions and keeps track of the fact that they came from a separate file. When you select "Save All Modules", the modules are put back into the files they were loaded from. QuickBASIC also makes a special file with the .MAK extension containing a list of the files which were loaded. The next time you load the main program, all of these modules will be loaded automatically. This file list is also used if you compile and make an .EXE file.

PRINTING YOUR PROGRAM

The Print... command will print the entire program, the current module, the currently displayed window, all modules, or the highlighted text on the printer. After you select "Print", the following menu appears:

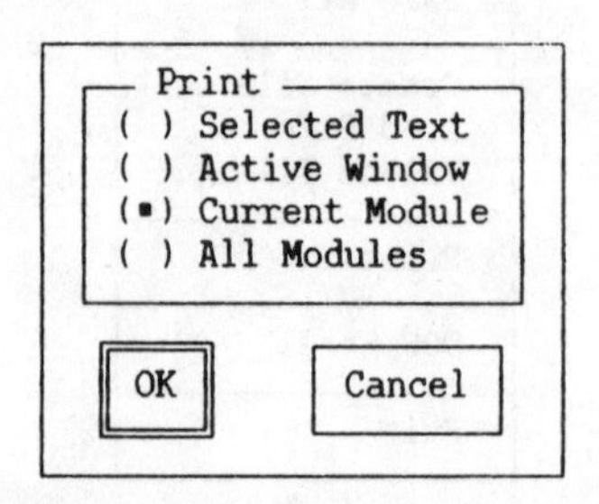

You can either print the entire file, the current module, or, if a region is highlighted, that highlighted region. Select the correct option by moving to it with the Tab key and select it with the Space Bar.

CHANGING DISPLAY PARAMETERS

If you select the View menu, you have the following choice of:

```
SUBs...              F2
Next SUB       SHIFT+F2
Split
-----------------------
Next Statement
Output Screen        F4
-----------------------
Include File
Included Lines
-----------------------
Options...
```

As we have noted earlier, QuickBASIC separates all functions and procedures into separate units or *modules,* and only one of these modules can be displayed at a time. Pressing F2 displays a list of all the modules presently in memory, and pressing Shift+F2 causes QuickBASIC to display the next one in the list each time.

The Output Screen selection allows you to view the current output from the program on the screen. Pressing any key returns to the display of the current module.

Selecting "Options" displays the following menu:

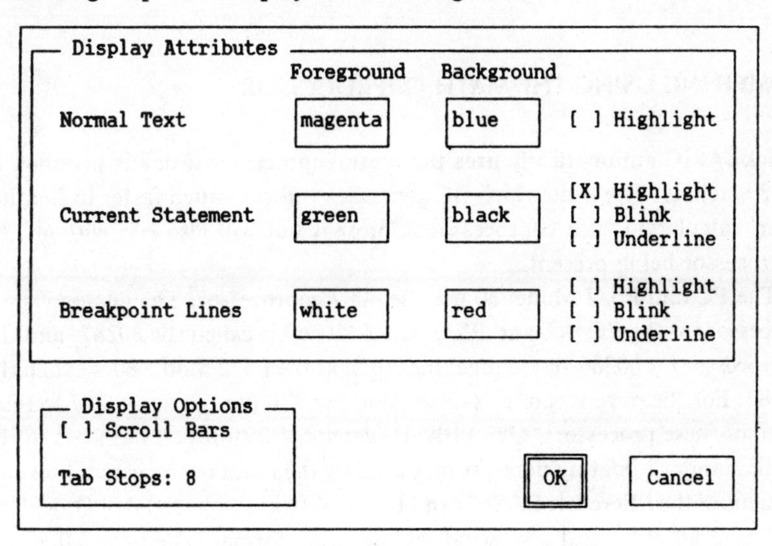

You can turn on and off the scroll bars and can change the tab stops and foreground and background colors.

The scroll bars are arrows on the bottom and right border. They show the relative position of the current display in the file. If you have a mouse you can point at these borders to move to a position in the file or shift the display right and left.

To select a new foreground and background color on a color display or enhanced color display point to the box and press the cursor arrow keys to cycle through allowed colors:

Black
Blue
Green
Cyan
Red
Magenta
Yellow
White

To keep these changes, select "OK." Otherwise, you can exit by pressing Escape or selecting "Cancel."

COMPILING USING THE MATH COPROCESSOR

QuickBASIC automatically uses the math coprocessor if one is installed in your machine. The code which BC generates will run much faster in floating point calculations if a coprocessor is present but will also run without the coprocessor being present.

The PC and PS/2 Model 30 use the 8087 coprocessor. The analogous coprocessor for the PC/AT and PS/2 Model 50–60 is called the 80287, and the coprocessor for 80386-based machines such as the PS/2 Model 80 is called the 80387. For the purposes of this discussion, we will use the term 8087 to refer to all of these processors. QuickBASIC version 4.0 stores all numbers in the IEEE standard floating point format used by the math coprocessor. Previous versions of the Microsoft BASIC (and BASICA) interpreters and of QuickBASIC used an older and somewhat less accurate format called the Microsoft Binary Format (MBF).

If you are writing and running programs which read old data stored in MBF format, you can start QuickBASIC using the /MBF switch, which causes the compiled program to read MBF numbers and convert them to IEEE format internally.

If you want to switch permanently to the new format, you can use the special functions CVSMBF, CVDMBF and MKSMBF$, and MKDMBF$ to convert old data files to the new format. Unless you have written files in record or binary format, this will seldom be a problem. Further, you should note that this new format applies only to single and double precision variables. Integer and string variables are unchanged.

7 Debugging Using QuickBASIC

Since QuickBASIC is a threaded interpreter, you can stop and examine any variable or set of variables by simply pressing Ctrl+Break, hopping to the immediate window by pressing Shift+F6, and executing a PRINT statement to examine the values of the variables in question.

However, the debugging options available under QuickBASIC are considerably more versatile than that, allowing you to step through the program, watch variables change, and set up to eight *breakpoints.* If you select "Debug" from the menu, you will get the following display:

```
Add Watch...
Watchpoint...
Delete Watch...
Delete All Watch
--------------------------------
Trace On
History On
--------------------------------
Toggle Breakpoint          F9
Clear All Breakpoints
Set Next Statement
```

The *watchpoint* commands allow you to watch the values of variables change in the watch window while your program executes. You can also enter entire expressions as watchpoints and watch their value change. The Watchpoint command allows you to enter the name of a variable whose value is to be displayed as the program executes. The Add Watchpoint command allows you to enter a variable *relation* which will cause the program to halt if it becomes true. For example, you might enter

```
i >= 20
```

to indicate that if the variable I ever becomes greater than or equal to 20 you want the program to halt so you can find out why.

The *single step* key (F8) executes a single program statement each time it is pressed. The *procedure step* key (F10) executes a line containing a procedure call without jumping to the procedure and executing each of its lines individually.

If you select "Trace On," your program will execute a step at a time with each expression highlighted as it is executed. In addition, a *history table* is kept of the last 20 statements executed; you can stop the program, step *backwards or forwards* through these statements, and watch the effects on various variables.

Finally, the Toggle Breakpoint command (F9) turns a breakpoint on or off at the current line. This allows you to set points where a running program will stop so you can examine the values of variables. QuickBASIC allows you to keep up to eight breakpoints active at one time.

A SIMPLE DEBUGGING EXAMPLE

Let's consider the following incorrect program. It reads in the file TEST.DAT a line at a time until a zero line is found. The actual file we will be using contains the lines

```
6
5
2
7
4
0
```

The program is

```
tfile = FREEFILE                              'get next file number
OPEN "test.dat" FOR INPUT AS #tfile           'open file on disk
WHILE (x(i) > 0)                              'read in values
  INPUT #tfile, x(i)
  i = i + 1                                   'increment counter
WEND                                          'until zero value read
CLOSE #tfile                                  'close the file
max = i - 1                                   'save the count
PRINT "max ="; max                            'print it out
END                                           'and stop
```

There are actually at least two mistakes in this program, and we will try to find them by using the features of the debugger.

We first run the program as usual and find that it prints out

```
max = -1
```

and stops. There are no errors in execution, so the file is apparently opened correctly, but no data are read in. We start our debugging process by selecting "Add Watchpoint", and in answer to the question we enter the variable name "i". The screen changes so there is a small window at the top, called the *debugging* or *watchpoint window*, and the module name followed by the variable name is displayed:

```
deb: i =
```

where "deb" is the name of this file.

SINGLE STEPPING THROUGH THE PROGRAM

The debugging function keys are

F4	View output screen
F7	Execute to cursor
F8	Single Step
F9	Set/reset breakpoint
F10	Procedure step
Shift+F10	History forward
Shift+F8	History backward

Then, to see what happens when the program runs, we press F8. The program starts and highlights the first line:

```
tfile = FREEFILE                              'get next file number
```

Each time we press F8, the highlight moves to the next line to be executed, and we find that the order of the execution of program steps is:

```
1    tfile = FREEFILE                         'get next file number
2    OPEN "test.dat" FOR INPUT AS #tfile      'open file on disk
3    WHILE (x(i) > 0)                         'read in values
       INPUT #tfile, x(i)
       i = i + 1                              'increment counter
4    WEND                                     'until zero value read
5    CLOSE #tfile                             'close the file
6    max = i - 1                              'save the count
7    PRINT "max ="; max                       'print it out
8    END                                      'and stop
```

and that the watchpoint display in the debugging window continually shows

```
deb: i = 0
```

Obviously, none of the file input steps is ever executed. It is also fairly plain that the value of I was never set to anything, and while we might have expected to start I at 1, QuickBASIC initializes all variables to 0 when it starts. This is a classic programming error which, as we will see, has occurred more than once in this program.

We might then set a new watchpoint to look at X(I), and see that the following situation occurs:

```
deb: i = 0
deb: x(i) = 0
```

We now see that X(0) is never set to any value and since QuickBASIC sets all variables to zero when it starts, the WHILE statement is immediately satisfied, with X(0) being zero from the start. we now revise the program to include the following initialization steps:

```
i = 1               'start index at 1
x(i) = 1            'make sure first value is not zero
```

Now, when we execute the program, we are able to read data from the input file, but we find that the result of the program is

```
max = 1
```

Since we know that there are clearly five nonzero values in our text file, we still need to do some debugging. Leaving the same two watchpoints set, we again step through the program and see that the following steps are executed:

```
i   x(i)   step#
1    0       1      i = 1
1    1       2      x(i) = 1
1    1       3      OPEN "test.dat" FOR INPUT AS #tfile
1    1       4      WHILE (x(i) > 0)
1    6       5        INPUT #tfile, x(i)
2    0       6        i = i + 1
2    0       7      WEND

2    0       8      CLOSE #tfile
2    0       9      max = i - 1
```

In other words, while we have initialized X(1), when I becomes 2, we again have the condition that X(I) = 0 and the WHILE loop is satisfied. The program thus drops through the WHILE loop after only one iteration. In order to correct this, we again rewrite the program so that the data are read into a single variable which is checked each time.

```
tfile = FREEFILE                         'get next file number
OPEN "test.dat" FOR INPUT AS #tfile      'open file on disk
i = 1                                    'start index at 1
temp = 1                                 'make sure it is not zero
WHILE (temp > 0)                         'read in values
  INPUT #tfile, temp
  x(i) = temp
  i = i + 1                              'increment counter
WEND                                     'until zero value read

CLOSE #tfile                             'close the file
max = i - 1                              'save the count
PRINT "max ="; max                       'print it out
END
```

Now, when we execute the program, we get the answer

```
max = 6
```

This is certainly more satisfying than −1 or 1, but it is still *wrong!* If we wish to have MAX represent the total number of nonzero values, it should be 5 not 6.

USING THE IMMEDIATE WINDOW

To find out why this is happening, let's first use the immediate window to see what is in the X array. To move the cursor down to the immediate window, we press F6. Recall that any single line statement is executed in the immediate window without relation to any other line. So, to print out the contents of the array, we type in the simple one-line loop:

```
FOR i = 1 TO 6: PRINT i; x(i) : NEXT i
```

QuickBASIC will switch to the output screen and print out

```
1    6
2    5
3    2
4    7
5    4
6    0
```

showing that X(6) is 0. Now, we could solve this right here, but let's use the breakpoint feature to get right to the problem.

SETTING A BREAKPOINT

First we move the cursor back to the program window by pressing F6 again, and then move the cursor to the line where the CLOSE statement is located. Then we restart the program by pressing Shift+F5. The program will execute and pause with the CLOSE line highlighted. In fact, we could regard the breakpoint as a CLOSE pin.

The program is now in the state where MAX is to be calculated from I. If we look in the debugging window above the program we will see:

```
deb: i = 7
deb: x(i) = 0
```

Thus the final bug is that I is incremented after it is used in the WHILE loop and is thus *two* counts ahead of the last nonzero value in the X array. The last change we need to make to the program is then

```
max = i - 2      'set max from the index I
```

To undo all of our debugging probes, we put the cursor back on the CLOSE line and press F9. The line is now no longer highlighted. Then we select "Delete All Watch" from the debug menu, and the debugging window disappears.

CONCLUSIONS ABOUT DEBUGGING

This section has illustrated the powerful nature of QuickBASIC's integral debugger. It has also illustrated some important concepts about debugging.

1. Always have a test case for which you know the answer when you are ready to debug a program.
2. Be careful that all variables are properly initialized.
3. Beware of "end effects." The value of the index is often not equal to the value of the last useful number stored in an array.

8 Subroutines and Subprograms

It doesn't take very long in writing programs to discover that you need to use some operation over and over again, with different variables to accomplish some simple repetitive task. BASIC allows you to write sections of code that can be called from several parts of the program and that return to the following statement after the call.

In this chapter, we will see how to write subroutines and the more powerful subprograms. We will also see how to break up a program into modules that can be compiled separately.

SUBROUTINES

The simplest of these program units is the *subroutine.* Subroutines are sections of the program which are set off from the main line of the program and are called using the GOSUB statement. You exit from a subroutine with the RETURN statement:

```
'main program
   :
GOSUB subr1              'call to subroutine
   :
END                      'end of main program
```

```
subr1:                          'beginning of subroutine
     :
   'some statements
     :
   RETURN                       'exit from subroutine
```

In QuickBASIC, subroutines are usually named rather than numbered with line numbers as Ur-BASIC required.

In the following program, we use the simple subroutine SETNLQ to send the characters "Esc" and "G" to the printer, setting it to near letter quality mode.

```
'Program to set printer to near letter quality
'and print a message
LPRINT "This is the current printer mode"     'print message
GOSUB setnlq                                  'set near let qual
LPRINT "This is the nlq printer mode"
END                                           'and quit
'=================================================================
'sets Proprinter to near letter quality
setnlq:
     LPRINT CHR$(27); "G";                    'escape G
RETURN
```

ARGUMENTS IN SUBROUTINES

For simple cases, the advantages of subroutines are obvious: you can call a useful operation from any place in a program. The problem occurs when you have to pass a subroutine data to operate on and have a subroutine pass a result back to the calling program.

Let's consider a simple routine to get a single precision number from the keyboard. It should print out the current value of a variable, allow entry of a new value and keep the old one if the new value entered is only the Enter key without any value. This gives us the ability to print a value and confirm it by pressing Enter or to change it by entering a new value followed by Enter. Such a program is shown in the following example:

```
'Enter number of datapoints
'Program to get a number of datapoints
datapoints = 128                         'default value
```

```
df = datapoints                              'df is default value
PRINT "Enter number of datapoints: ";        'ask for number of pts
GOSUB getreal                                'get new value in "real"
datapoints = real                            'copy into datapoints

PRINT "New value ="; datapoints              'print out value
PRINT "s$="; s$
END                                          'and quit
'=================================================================
getreal:
       PRINT df; " ";          'print out default value
       INPUT s$                'read in new value as string
       IF LEN(s$) > 0 THEN     'if a value was entered
           real = VAL(s$)      'convert it
       ELSE
           real = df           'otherwise return default value
       END IF
       RETURN
```

In this program, we start by setting DATAPOINTS equal to a default value of 128 and then set the DF variable to the current value of DATA-POINTS. Then we call the subroutine GETREAL, which reads in a string S$. If the length of S$ is zero, then no characters were typed and only the Enter key was pressed. This means that the user wants to leave the current value of the variable alone and the value of DF is returned in the variable REAL when the subroutine exits. If the length of S$ is not zero, it is converted to a number whose value is returned in REAL.

The problem with a subroutine that handles arguments such as the default value of a single precision number or the value actually entered is that you must (1) establish variable names that the subroutine will use for these purposes (DF, REAL), (2) assign values to them before calling the subroutine, and (3) read values from them after the subroutine:

```
df = datapoints                           'DF is default value
GOSUB getreal                             'get new value in "real"
datapoints = real                         'copy into datapoints
```

This is extremely awkward, especially for two or more variables, and can lead to confusion about what value a variable should hold at a given time. For example, GETREAL uses a string variable S$ which changes within GE-TREAL. Thus, if S$ had some value from elsewhere in the program, that value would be lost by calling GETREAL. We say that all of the variables used in a subroutine are *global* since they exist and have the same values throughout the main program and all subroutines.

SUBPROGRAMS

The method of handling variables in subroutines described in the previous section is so awkward that we will not use it further in this text. Instead, we will use the subprogram method, which is unique to QuickBASIC.

Subprograms are totally independent routines which start with the SUB declaration and end with END SUB. They have arguments like functions, but unlike subroutines, their variables exist only *locally* within the subprogram, even if they have the same names as ones in the main program.

```
'Main program
        :
CALL subp1(a,b,c)
        :
END

'beginning of subprogram
SUB subp1(x,y,z)
        :
'statements
        :
END SUB
```

If we rewrite the subroutine in the previous section using this convention, we see that both the subprogram and the main program are actually simpler:

```
'Enter number of data points
'Program to get a number of data points
datapoints = 128                           'default value

PRINT "Enter number of datapoints: ";      'ask for number of points
CALL getreal(datapoints)                   'get new value in "real"

PRINT "New value = "; datapoints           'print out value
PRINT "S$="; S$                            'show value of S$
END                                        'and quit

' ===================================================
SUB getreal (x)
  PRINT x; " ";                            'print out current value
  INPUT s$                                 'get new string
  IF LEN(s$) > 0 THEN                      'check its length
         x = VAL(s$)                       'if not zero convert
   END IF
END SUB                                    'exit subprogram
```

In this program, the value of DATAPOINTS is passed as an *argument* to the subprogram GETREAL. Inside GETREAL, this variable is referred to as X. In other words, just as in functions, X is a *dummy variable* whose value is replaced when GETREAL is called. Further, unlike a function, this subprogram operates on X and returns a value in it if the length of string S$ is not zero.

Note that all subprograms must start with a SUB statement followed by the subprogram name and argument list.

When we run this program, it has the same general effect as the previous one, although it is simpler to write and to read. However, when the program is run, it prints out the following:

```
Enter number of datapoints: 128   145
New value = 145
S$ =
```

The old value, 128, is printed out and the new one, 145, is typed in. The string "145" is converted to the single precision number 145 and returned in DATAPOINTS and printed out.

The program then prints out the contents of the string S$ as blank. Since the value of S$ within GETREAL was "145", this is somewhat surprising. This leads to the following conclusions:

- Variables within a subprogram are always *local*. They have no existence outside of the subprogram, and variables of the same name in other parts of the program are totally separate.
- A subprogram is a separately compiled unit with its own variables. Unless you specifically indicate that variables from outside the subprogram are to be used, the variables are entirely independent.

In other words, the S$ in GETREAL and the S$ in the main program are totally separate variables, and only the S$ within GETREAL has the value "145".

This feature of totally separate compilation of subprograms is extremely useful, since it prevents you from accidently changing the value of a variable in the main program which happens to have the same name.

STATIC VARIABLES IN SUBPROGRAMS

Normally, QuickBASIC allocates space for variables in a subprogram at the time it is called. All such variables are initialized to zero. However, such variables are not "remembered" from one call to the next. If you declare your subprogram to be *STATIC*, then all local variables remain unchanged in memory from one call to the next. The syntax of this feature is:

```
SUB getreal(r) STATIC   'all variables are remembered
```

ARGUMENTS IN SUBPROGRAMS

In addition, you can pass several arguments to a subprogram and return several arguments. This is an extremely powerful way to write your programs in modular form, where each subprogram performs functions that can be used in a number of situations. For example, you could turn our Fahrenheit-to-Celsius converter into a subroutine with three arguments: INPUT.TEMP, OUTPUT.TEMP, and TEMP.TYPE$. Then, within the subprogram, you could decide which operation to perform based on whether TEMP.TYPE$ is "F" or "C" and then return the converted temperature in OUTPUT.TEMP:

```
'calling program for convert.temp
PRINT "Input temperature: ";    'ask for temperature
INPUT temp
PRINT "C, F, or K:";            'get scale
INPUT Ctype$
CALL Convert.temp(temp, Outtemp, Ctype$)  'call subprogram
PRINT "Convert = ", Outtemp               'print results
END
' ================================================================

SUB Convert.temp (input.temp, output.temp, temptype$)
'converts input.temp to a value returned in output.temp
'depending on the character in temp.type$

SELECT CASE temptype$
   CASE "C", "c"
        output.temp = (9 / 5) * input.temp + 32
    CASE "F", "f"
        output.temp = (5 / 9) * (input.temp - 32)

    CASE "k", "k"
        output.temp = (9 / 5) * (input.temp - 273.16) + 32
```

```
    CASE ELSE
        output.temp = -1000       'set to this if temp.type$ is
                                  'not C, F, or K
    END SELECT
END SUB
```

This example illustrates the fact that any variable in a variable list in the call to a subprogram may be *changed* within the subprogram, as the variable OUTPUT.TEMP is here. In this case the actual memory address where the data value is stored is passed to the subprogram, and the subprogram can thus change this location directly. This is referred to in computer jargon as *calling by reference* since the subprogram *refers* to the actual variable location in the subprogram-calling statement. QuickBASIC also allows you to pass arguments to the subprogram *by value* by enclosing them in parentheses.

```
    call Convert.temp( (temp1), outvalue, "F")
```

In this example, the value of the variable TEMP1 is copied to a temporarary location which is passed to the subprogram CONVERT.TEMP so that any changes or operations on the first variable within CONVERT.TEMP do not affect the value of TEMP1 in the main program. Note that if you enclosed OUTVALUE in parentheses in this call, its value would not change and you would not be able to use the converted value in the main program.

ARGUMENT TYPES IN SUBPROGRAMS

It is important that you make clear to QuickBASIC what type of variable you expect to have passed to the subprogram. This can be done by using the type definition characters:

```
    SUB conv(a, b%, c$)
    or by using the AS modifier:
    SUB conv(a AS SINGLE, b AS INTEGER, c AS STRING)
```

The second method obviates the necessity for carrying along the awkward punctuation throughout a complicated subprogram, but the first method may make the code more readable at a glance.

PASSING ARRAYS TO SUBPROGRAMS

You can pass whole arrays to subprograms in the CALL statement by listing the array's name followed by one set of parentheses without anything inside them:

```
DIM x(15,20)
call snerd( x() )
```

You indicate to the subprogram that the argument is an array by showing the same empty parentheses.

```
SUB snerd ( z() )
```

Previous versions of QuickBASIC required that you put the number of dimensions to the array inside the parentheses of the SUB statement. In this case, the two-dimensional array X would have been defined in the SUB statement with the number 2 to indicate the two dimensions:

```
SUB snerd ( z(2) )
```

This unattractive syntax is still allowed but is no longer necessary.

WRITING SUBPROGRAMS

In QuickBASIC, each subprogram and function is stored as a separate logical unit within a program. If you press function key F2, you will get a display of the names of all the currently loaded functions, and by selecting one of these names you can display and edit that function.

To enter a new function, you must select the New Function line from the Edit menu, and to create a new subprogram you select the New Subs line from the Edit menu.

One thing you will discover is that QuickBASIC inserts a DECLARE statement at the top of the module for each subprogram or function in that module. For example, for the subprogram CONVERT.TEMP, QuickBASIC inserts the line

```
DECLARE SUB Convert.temp (input.temp!, output.temp!, temptype$)
```

which tells QuickBASIC that the name CONVERT.TEMP refers to a subprogram which has three arguments: two single precision and one string. These DECLARE statements are automatically generated and should be left in any single- module program you are writing. When you write multiple-module programs, you will have to copy these DECLARE statements into modules which call subprograms in other modules.

DIFFERENCES BETWEEN SUBROUTINES, SUBPROGRAMS, AND FUNCTIONS

We have now seen that there are three methods of putting parts of your program into small units that can be called from elsewhere: the subroutine, the subprogram, and the function.

Subprograms and functions are both classed as *procedures* in QuickBASIC 4.0, by analogy with similar statements in Pascal. The QuickBASIC manuals refer to SUB procedures and function procedures as well as to subprograms and functions. These have identical meanings. We review their properties in the accompanying table:

	Subroutine	Subprogram	Function
Pass arguments			
By reference	No	Yes	Yes
By value	No	Yes	Yes
Return values	No	Yes	One only
Global variables	Yes–only	Shared	No
Use of COMMON	Yes	Yes	Yes
may call GOSUBs	Yes	Only local	Only local
may CALL subprograms	Yes	Yes	Yes
Must be in same module	Yes	No	No

In summary, we see that subprograms and functions are much more versatile than subroutines and that subprograms have, in fact, supplanted the GOSUB subroutine structure in QuickBASIC.

REFERRING TO VARIABLES IN SUBPROGRAMS

There are two ways to communicate variables between the main program and subprograms: arguments and COMMON blocks. Arguments are simply the list of variables in parentheses in the call to a subprogram. *COMMON blocks* are lists of variables which can be referred to by any subprograms which have COMMON statements. COMMON blocks are like a separate group of arguments which can be listed at the beginning of a module in addition to those in the call.

In QuickBASIC, you can indicate that a group of COMMON variables is to be shared among all the subprograms in a given program module by following the declaration COMMON with the modifier SHARED. Then, all subprograms in that source file can access these variables even though they are only declared in one place:

```
DIM x(200)                   'X is an array
COMMON SHARED x(), y, z      'put X,Y and Z in common
'main program
    :
END
'---------------------------------------------------
SUB subr1                    'can also access x, y and z
    :
END SUB
'---------------------------------------------------
SUB subr2                    'this also can access x, y and z
    :
END SUB
```

Note that, as shown in this example, you can put whole arrays in COMMON as well as individual variables. In order to put an array in COMMON, you must first dimension it as shown, and then indicate in the COMMON statement that it is an array by following its name with left and right parentheses with nothing between them.

You can also divide groups of variables into separate COMMON blocks by giving the block names. These COMMON blocks can then be referred to by name in other modules.

```
COMMON SHARED /mats/ x( ), y(), z()
COMMON SHARED /scalars/ size, sweep.width, norm.constant
COMMON SHARED /proc/ line.broad, zerophase, threshold
```

Then, any other module can refer only to the set of parameters it needs, rather than to all of them.

SHARING PARAMETERS WITH ONE SUBPROGRAM

The COMMON declaration causes all subprograms in that program module to have access to all of the variables in that COMMON block. You can tell a single subprogram that it is to access the variables of the main program by using the SHARED statement:

```
width = 5000                'variables in main program
sweeps = 32
norm.constant = 2
     :
END
'------------------------------------------------------------
SUB sub1
SHARED width, sweeps        'access to 2 variables in main
                            'program
   :
END SUB
'------------------------------------------------------------
SUB sub2
SHARED norm.constant        'access to 1 variable in main
                            'program
   :
END SUB
```

RECURSIVE FUNCTIONS AND SUBPROGRAMS

QuickBASIC 4.0 allows you to write subprogram and functions which call themselves. Such routines are referred to as *recursive.* The concept of a routine which calls itself may seem a paradox, but for a certain class of problems, it can be quite valuable. Whenever a problem can be expressed in terms of another problem of the same type involving fewer steps, recursion is a possible solution. Many of these problems occur in computer science, but one standard mathematical problem amenable to a recursive solution is the calculation of a factorial.

The factorial of a positive integer is that number multiplied by all integers less than itself but greater than zero. The exclamation point is generally used to symbolize the factorial:

$$4! = 4 \times 3 \times 2 \times 1$$
$$n! = n(n - 1)(n - 2) \cdots (1)$$

We also define

0! = 1

Now we note that the factorial of any number is that number times the factorial of the next smaller number:

4! = 4 x 3! = 4 x 3 x 2!, etc.

and we have the conditions for a recursive solution to the problem.

We will write the function FACTR so that it calls itself as long as the factorial to be calculated is greater than 1. If the factorial is of 1, it will exit with the value as the solution.

The reason that recursion works is that each instance of the FACTR function has its own values of the calling variables and any internal variables which are kept in any area of memory called the *stack*. The return pointers for each call of the function are also kept on this stack and when the function calls itself again, the current values are preserved on the stack as new values and passed to the next instance of the function. When the function finally reaches the value of 1, it exits from that instance. Then each previous instance exits, each time multiplying its answer times the previous answer, until all instances have exited and the final value of the factorial is returned from the first call to FACTR.

There is, of course, no "free lunch" about this method. Each call to a recursive function or subprogram uses up stack memory, and a sufficient number of calls to such a function will cause an error exit when memory is exhausted. In the case of this program, however, the largest factorial that can be held in a single precision is 10^{37}, which turns out to be 36 factorial.

```
'program to calculate the factorial of any entered number
DIM num AS INTEGER, x AS SINGLE

DO
   INPUT "Enter number: "; num  'get number
   IF (num >= 0) THEN           'if not negative
     x = factr(num)             'calculate the factorial
     PRINT num; "! = "; x       'print out the result
   END IF
LOOP UNTIL num < 0              'loop back until negative value
'=================================================================
FUNCTION factr (num%)

'function to calculate the factorial of num%
```

```
IF (num% > 0) THEN                       'if > 0 then
   factr = num% * factr(num% - 1)        'calculate recursively
ELSE
   factr = 1                             '0! = 1
END IF
END FUNCTION                             'end of function
```

MAKING LIBRARIES AND QUICKLIBRARIES

You can put any number of commonly used subprograms into different modules and compile them separately using QuickBASIC. This is an extremely useful way to break up the parts of a program which are being developed from those parts which are already working. You can also make sets of useful routines which any of your programs can call in this way.

Once you have compiled these modules, you can combine them into a library file which you can load every time you start QuickBASIC. Then, any new programs you write can call these routines just as if they were present in the current program. QuickBASIC supports two types of libraries: Quicklibraries (.QLB files) and standard libraries (.LIB files). You can load one *Quicklibrary* when you start QuickBASIC and call these routines from within any new programs you run during that session. *Standard libraries,* on the other hand are to be linked with modules produced by the BC compiler outside the QB environment. QuickBASIC makes a library of each kind when you call the Make Library command from the Run menu.

To make a library, write the subprograms (*not* subroutines) as a group without any main program:

```
'General subroutine library GENGET

      SUB getreal(r)
         :
      END SUB

      SUB getint(k%)
         :
      END SUB

      SUB setprinter(p)
         :
      END SUB
```

Give this group of routines a filename, such as GENGET. WHen you store this file, it will be called GENGET.BAS. Then compile these routines using the Make Library menu selection. QuickBASIC will call BC and make a file GENGET.OBJ, and then will call the LIB to make a .LIB file and the LINK program to make a .QLB file.

LOADING A QUICK LIBRARY

QuickBASIC allows you to load one file as a Quick library when you start it from the command line by using the /L option switch. If you type

```
qb file/l
```

QuickBASIC will load the file QB.QLB if it can find it. You can also load your own Quick library having any name, by specifying that library name following the /L option:

```
qb file/l genlib
```

which loads the Quicklibrary GENLIB.QLB. Then you can call any of the routines in the library directly while running any new program within QB.

KEEPING VARIABLES IN COMMON STORAGE BETWEEN MODULES

If you put variables in a storage area called COMMON, they can be referred to from any subprogram that is part of your program.

```
DIM x(100), y(30)
COMMON a, blub, crud, x(), y()
```

If you have ever written programs in the FORTRAN language, you should note that the COMMON statement in QuickBASIC is quite different from the COMMON statement in FORTRAN. In QuickBASIC, there can only be one group of COMMON statements per module, and they must come before any *executable* statements. In QuickBASIC, only the following statements are not executable:

DEF type	To define which variable names are integer
DIM	For fixed-dimension arrays
REM	For comments starting on new lines
COMMON	To list variables in COMMON block

All other statements must come after COMMON. This means that a subprogram at the end of your module can*not* contain another COMMON statement. Therefore you must tell QuickBASIC that all subprograms in the module must be able to share these variables. You do this using the SHARED modifier to the COMMON statement:

```
DIM x(100), y(30)
COMMON SHARED a, blub, crud, x(), y()
'
        :
'main program
'
        :
END

SUB furd                    'can also access SHARED COMMON
'
        :
END SUB
```

You can put COMMON statements in subprogram groups in separate modules, but again,

1. There can be only one group of COMMON statements in the module,
2. They must contain the SHARED modifier, and
3. They must come before any executable statements.

In fact, the only case where you use COMMON statements without the SHARED modifier is in new programs that you load by chaining. In QuickBASIC, the CHAIN statement loads and executes another .EXE file, which could refer to the same COMMON block as the original program. This is a holdover from earlier forms of BASIC and is not a particularly elegant way to fasten modules together. It does, however, allow you to write exceptionally large programs as a series of separate programs which are loaded in succession.

THE SHARED STATEMENT

Another way for a subprogram to gain access to a few variables in the main program is to use the SHARED statement in that subprogram, without putting any variables into a COMMON block in the main program:

```
DIM x(200), y(10)
z = x(i) + y(j)
    :
END

SUB math
SHARED x(), y(), z
    :
END SUB
```

The SHARED statement only works within a single compiled module, however. It cannot be used when several modules are linked together. The SHARED statement must appear within a subprogram. It cannot appear at the beginning of a module containing several subprograms, but outside those subprograms. In contrast, the COMMON SHARED statement must appear outside the subprograms, at the beginning of a module.

USING LIBRARIES TO MAKE STAND-ALONE PROGRAMS

To illustrate the utility of making up a library of commonly used functions, we here present the small library GENLIB.BAS:

```
' -------------User library  GENLIB.BAS------------------
DECLARE FUNCTION yesno! (ans!)
DECLARE FUNCTION uppercase$ (s$)
'*******************************************************
'get a real number from the keyboard
SUB getreal (r)

        PRINT r;          'default value
        INPUT " ", s$     'get new value
        IF LEN(s$) > 0 THEN
                r = VAL(s$)
        END IF
END SUB
'*******************************************************
'get a string
SUB getstring (a$)
        PRINT a$;
        INPUT " ", s$
        IF LEN(s$) > 0 THEN
           a$ = s$                  'new value if nonzero length
        END IF
END SUB
'*******************************************************
```

```
'set printer to 12 cpi
SUB set.elite
'set 12 cpi
LPRINT CHR$(27); ":"
END SUB
'*********************************************************
'set printer to near letter quality
SUB set.nlq
LPRINT CHR$(27); "G";
END SUB
'*********************************************************
'get yes or no
FUNCTION yesno (ans)
'get Y or N and return 1 or 0. The argument may be 1 or 0
'and causes the prompt to print Y or N on entry
a = -1                          'must be 0 or 1 to exit
IF (ans > 0) THEN
        PRINT "Y ";             '1 means print Y for Yes
ELSE
        PRINT "N ";             '0 means print N for No
END IF
WHILE a < 0         'get either Y or N
        INPUT "Y or N:", s$
        s$ = UCASE$(s$)         'could be upper or lowercase
        IF MID$(s$, 1, 1) = "Y" THEN a = 1
        IF MID$(s$, 1, 1) = "N" THEN a = 0
        IF (a < 0) THEN
                PRINT "Please answer Y or N"
        END IF
WEND
yesno = a

END FUNCTION
```

First we must compile and link the library GENLIB. To do this we load GENLIB and select "Make Library and Exit" from the Run menu. QuickBASIC will compile the program using BC, and produce the Quick Library GENLIB.QLB using LINK and the normal library GENLIB.LIB using LIB. Then we restart QuickBASIC using the /L switch to load the Quicklibrary:

```
qb /l genlib
```

Note that QuickBASIC has generated two DECLARE statements for two of the functions in the library. These DECLARE statements need to be available to other modules that call the routines in this library so that the argument count and type can be checked properly. You can do this most conveniently by simply making up a file of these DECLARE statements and then including it in every program which makes calls to the GENLIB library. To do this,

1. Open the GENLIB.BAS file.
2. Mark the two DECLARE lines using the cursor and Shift keys.
3. Press Ctrl+Ins to copy these lines into the clipboard.
4. Select New from the File menu to clear memory.
5. Press Shift+Ins to copy the lines back from the clipboard.
6. Select "Save As" from the File menu.
7. Give the file the name GENLIB.BI (for BASIC Include).
8. Select "Save in Text Format" and press Enter.

Now let us write a program using these library functions. In order to include the two DECLARE statements in our program we could merge them with our program using the File Merge menu item, or we could *include* the file GENLIB.BI in our program using the $INCLUDE: metacommand.

INCLUDING ANOTHER FILE

One of the most useful features of QuickBASIC is this ability to include another file in the middle of one you are compiling. The $INCLUDE: command is termed a *metacommand* since it is not a program command but a command telling the compiler how to proceed. These commands are part of comments starting either with the apostrophe or REM. The first non-blank character must be a dollar sign, followed by the metacommand, a colon, and a filename, enclosed in apostrophes (single quotes):

```
' $INCLUDE: 'genlib.bi'
```

Note the colon after $INCLUDE: and note that the filename is enclosed in *single quotes.* Our simple example program for calling this library is

```
' Program to illustrate using calls to GENLIB

' $INCLUDE: 'genlib.bi'
```

```
s$ = "fred"                'assign a value to a string
CALL getstring(s$)         'get a new value for the string
PRINT s$                   'print out the new value
ans = 1                    'assign a value to the answer
ans = yesno(ans)           'get a new answer
END
```

MAKING STAND-ALONE PROGRAMS WITH LIBRARIES

If you elect to make an .EXE file out of a program which uses a loaded user library, QuickBASIC will automatically generate the commands needed by the BC compiler and by LINK so that the library GENLIB.LIB is linked with the calling program.

If you load several modules into memory to develop your program, QuickBASIC will construct a file with the extension .MAK which contains a list of all the files you loaded, so that they can all be compiled and linked if you select the Make EXE file command. Note, however, that if you merge these files into memory, then they are copied into your main program file permanently and no .MAK file is generated or necessary.

9 Using the Keyboard and Display

All of the examples we have seen so far make use of the features of QuickBASIC, but no particular use of the features of the keyboard and display of the IBM PC.

THE INKEY$ FUNCTION

The INKEY$ function can be used to see if a key has been pressed, and whether the key is a printing character or a function or cursor key. The INKEY$ function always returns a string as follows:

```
s$ = INKEY$          'get a key
```

String Length	Meaning
0	No key has been pressed.
1	S$ contains a printing character or space.
2	A function or cursor key has been pressed.

INKEY$ does not wait for any key to be struck, but returns immediately with a string of length 0, 1, or 2. The usual usage for this function is

```
SUB getkey(k$)
'subroutine to wait for a key to be struck
'and return with the character in k$
DO                            'zero length string
  k$ = INKEY$                 'read key
LOOP WHILE LEN(k$) = 0        'until character struck
END SUB
```

If the length of the string returned by INKEY$ is 1, a normal key has been pressed. All printing characters return single values. In addition, the following special characters return a single ASCII value:

Esc	27
Enter	15
Tab	07
Backspace	08

This GETKEY subprogram will be called by various programs throughout the rest of the text without being specifically reprinted.

READING FUNCTION AND CURSOR KEYS

The function and cursor keys return a two-byte string whose first byte is zero and whose second byte has the following decimal value:

F1	59	Home	71
F2	60	End	79
F3	61	PgUp	73
F4	62	PgDn	81
F5	63	Up Arrow	72
F6	64	Down Arrow	80
F7	65	Left Arrow	75
F8	66	Right Arrow	77
F9	67	Ins	82
F10	68	Del	83

The 5 key on the numeric keypad has no character code in non-numeric mode, and sends a 5 in NumLock mode. The following keys cannot be read by INKEY$:

Ctrl
Shift
Alt
NumLock
CapsLock
ScrollLock
Ctrl+Break — Stops the program if compiled with DEBUG on
Ctrl+Alt+Del — Warm start of computer system
Shift+PrtScrn — Prints character contents of screen
Ctrl+NumLock — Causes the program to pause if printing

However, the Ctrl, Alt and Shift keys can be used to modify the Function keys and produce new key codes as follows:

	No Modifier	Shift	Ctrl	Alt
F1	59	84	94	104
F2	60	85	95	105
F3	61	85	96	106
F4	62	87	97	107
F5	63	88	98	108
F6	64	89	99	109
F7	65	90	100	110
F8	66	91	101	111
F9	67	92	102	112
F10	68	93	103	113
F11	133	135	137	139
F12	134	136	138	140

Note that these are the *values* of the second byte, not the character in the second byte. To get the value of a byte in a string, we use the ASC function to convert an ASCII character to an integer, and the RIGHT$ function to get the second byte out of the string.

```
kval = ASC(RIGHT$(s$,1))  'key value of 2nd byte
```

This is illustrated in the following INKEY program, which shows how to take action on a particular function key press:

```
'How to read function keys

'=================================================================

'    set constants equal to function key values
'    so we don't have to remember them
CONST F1 = 59, F2 = 60, HOME = 71

'=================================================================

k$ = ""                           'set string length to zero
WHILE k$ <> "Q"                   'exit if "Q" struck
   CALL getkey(k$)                'wait for key to be pressed
   IF LEN(k$) = 2 THEN            'if 2 a function key was pressed
     kval = ASC(RIGHT$(k$, 1))    'get scan code

     SELECT CASE kval             'check for desired function keys
         CASE F1
                  PRINT "Function Key 1"
         CASE F2
                  PRINT "Function Key 2"
         CASE HOME
                  PRINT "Home Key"
         CASE ELSE
                  'do nothing
     END SELECT
   END IF
WEND
END
```

POSITIONING THE SCREEN CURSOR

The next character to be written on the display is written at the current cursor position. If you clear the screen with a CLS command, the cursor is moved to the upper left corner: row 1, column 1. You can, however, put the cursor anywhere you want with the LOCATE command:

```
LOCATE row,col,cursor
```

where ROW is a value between 1 and 25, COL is a value between 1 and 80, and CURSOR is 1 if you want to display the flashing cursor and 0 if you do not want to display a cursor there.

Row 25 is special: it does not scroll with the rest of the screen, but stays at the bottom of the screen so it can be used as a message or information line.

SCREEN CHARACTER COLORS

You can select the color of any character or characters to be printed using the COLOR statement:

```
COLOR fore,back
```

where FORE has values between 0 and 15 and BACK has values between 0 and 7 as follows:

Color	Monochrome	Color
0	Black	Black
1	Underlined	Dark blue
2	Green	Dark green
3	Green	Dark cyan
4	Green	Dark red
5	Green	Dark magenta
6	Green	Brown
7	Green	White
8		Gray
9		Intense blue
10		Intense green
11		Intense cyan
12		Intense red
13		Intense magenta
14		Yellow
15		White

If you have a monochrome card, any color except 0 is treated as being on. Colors 1 - 7 are of low intensity and 8 - 15 of high intensity. If you set the foreground to black (0, 8, 16 or 24), then you can set the background to 7 and achieve *reverse video.*

If you have a standard Color Graphics Adapter (CGA), the colors above are shown. If you have an Enhanced Graphics Adapter (EGA), or PS/2 VGA, you can use the PALETTE statement to change the colors to any of 64 possible hues.

You can add 16 to any of these colors and get a flashing color. Flashing colors apply only to the foreground.

GRAPHICS CHARACTERS ON THE DISPLAY

In addition to the usual alphabetic and numeric characters, all IBM PCs and most compatible systems allow you to draw a number of block graphics characters on the screen and printer. They are called *block graphics characters* because they are used mainly for drawing rectangular boxes to outline parts of text on a screen. Tables of these are available in most PC and printer manuals.

To type the characters into a program, you simply hold down the Alt key, and type the character's ASCII value on the numeric keypad. (This will *not* work with the numbers on the row above the letter keys, only with the numeric keypad.) However, to type these characters, you have to know their ASCII codes. The usual printing characters—letters, numbers, and punctuation—lie in the range from 0 to 127, and the graphics characters between 128 and 255.

If you know any character's ASCII code (a value between 0 and 255), you can use the CHR$ function to convert that value to a one-character string. We illustrate this in the following program, which prints out the block graphics characters on the screen or printer as a table of values:

```
'print out the enhanced graphics characters

OPEN "blockgr.asc" FOR OUTPUT AS #1
c = 120                    'start with character 120

'-----------------------------------------------------

'  print table header
PRINT #1, "Table of IBM Graphics Characters"
PRINT #1,
PRINT #1,

'-----------------------------------------------------

FOR j = 1 TO 7                    'print index values along the side
  PRINT #1, USING "###  "; c;
FOR i = 0 TO 9                    'print actual characters
    IF (c + i) < 256 THEN
        PRINT #1, CHR$(c + i); "  ";
    END IF
```

```
    NEXT i
    PRINT #1, USING "     ###  "; c + 70; 'print#1, 2nd column numbers

    FOR i = 70 TO 79                'and 2nd column characters
      IF (c + i) < 256 THEN
        PRINT #1, CHR$(c + i); "  ";
      END IF
    NEXT i
    PRINT #1, : PRINT #1,
  c = c + 10
  NEXT j
  CLOSE #1
  END
```

This will produce the following table:

Table of IBM Graphics Characters

120	x	y	z	{	|	}	~	⌂	Ç	ü	190	╛	┐	└	┴	┬	├	─	┼	╞	╟
130	é	â	ä	à	å	ç	ê	ë	è	ï	200	╚	╔	╩	╦	╠	═	╬	╧	╨	╤
140	î	ì	Ä	Å	É	æ	Æ	ô	ö	ò	210	╥	╙	╘	╒	╓	╫	╪	┘	┌	█
150	û	ù	ÿ	Ö	Ü	¢	£	¥	₧	ƒ	220	▄	▌	▐	▀	α	ß	Γ	π	Σ	σ
160	á	í	ó	ú	ñ	Ñ	ª	º	¿	⌐	230	µ	τ	Φ	Θ	Ω	δ	∞	φ	ε	∩
170	¬	½	¼	¡	«	»	░	▒	▓	│	240	≡	±	≥	≤	⌠	⌡	÷	≈	°	•
180	┤	╡	╢	╖	╕	╣	║	╗	╝	╜	250	·	√	n	2	■					

These characters will enable you to make boxes on the screen to enclose messages:

You can also use combinations of these to create "shadows" around boxes:

While it is possible to look up the values for any graphics characters you need, it is more common to give names to the ones you will use most and put them in a file which you then include with any program that uses these characters:

```
' $INCLUDE: 'boxdef.bas'  'includes this file
```

or

```
REM $INCLUDE: 'boxdef.bas'
```

Following is a typical definitions file:

```
'define box character constants
CONST LEFT.UPPER$ = " ", RIGHT.UPPER$ = " "
CONST LEFT.LOWER$ = " ", RIGHT.LOWER$ = " "
CONST HORIZ$ = "-", VERT$ = "|"
CONST DBL.LFT.UP$ = " ", DBL.RGT.UP$ = " "
CONST DBL.LFT.LWR$ = " ", DBL.RGT.LWR$ = " "
CONST DBL.HORIZ$ = "=", DBL.VERT$ = "||"
```

Then you can write a simple program to draw a box on the screen:

```
'Main program to illustrate call of drawbox
CALL drawbox(5, 10, 12, 15)
END
'*************************************************************
SUB drawbox (row%, col%, wdth%, length%)
'-------------------------------------------------------------
'subprogram to draw a box starting at position "row,col"
'of width wdth% and height length%

' $INCLUDE: 'boxdef.bas'--include the definition file here
'-------------------------------------------------------------
LOCATE row%, col%, 0        'posn of left corner
PRINT LEFT.UPPER$;

FOR i = 1 TO wdth%          'draw horizontal line
  PRINT HORIZ$;
NEXT i

PRINT RIGHT.UPPER$;         'right upper corner

FOR i = 1 TO length%        'draw vertical sides
  LOCATE row% + i, col%, 0
  PRINT VERT$;
  LOCATE row% + i, col% + wdth% + 1, 0
  PRINT VERT$;
NEXT i
```

```
LOCATE row% + length% + 1, col%, 0 'draw bottom corner

PRINT LEFT.LOWER$;

FOR i = 1 TO wdth%           'draw bottom line
  PRINT HORIZ$;
NEXT i

PRINT RIGHT.LOWER$;          'right lower corner
END SUB                      'drawbox
```

USING THE KEYBOARD AND GRAPHICS CHARACTERS

A number of popular commercial programs, including QuickBASIC itself, allow you to display information in a number of fields, and move between these fields using the cursor arrow keys, and highlight the current field in reverse video. For example, in a simple names-and-addresses file, you might enclose each field in boxes and allow change of any field by selecting it with a cursor:

```
Fred

Farkle

123 Furd St

W Yellowstone     MT     59758     717-632-1122
```

First we define a table giving the row, column, and width of each of the seven fields in the address file and use the READ statement to read them in:

```
'Program to display name and address boxes on the screen
' and allow changes to boxes using the cursor keys.
' Each box is highlighted in reverse video when
' it is selected for change.
DEFINT A-Z              'all variables are integer

'arrays used for positions of boxes on the screen
CONST fields = 7, WHITE = 15, BLUE = 1

DIM row(fields)  AS INTEGER, col(fields)  AS INTEGER
DIM fldlen(fields)  AS INTEGER, name$(fields)
'Display and allow highlighted changes of name-address records
```

```
'The following DATA statements describe the screen position
'and size of each field

DATA 2,2,20        :'first name, last name, address
DATA 5,2,20
DATA 8,2,25
DATA 11,2,15       :'City, State and Zip and Phone
DATA 11,25,2
DATA 11,32,5
DATA 11,42,15

'Text used in display
DATA Fred,Farkle, 123 Furd St, W Yellowstone,
DATA MT,59758,717-632-1122

'read in values for screen positions
FOR i = 1 TO fields
  READ row(i), col(i), fldlen(i)
NEXT i

FOR i = 1 TO fields     'read in default name and address
  READ name$(i)
NEXT i
```

Note that we can't put the comments on the same line with the DATA statements unless preceded by a colon. We will assume that the text for the address files is read in and converted to the array NAME$(I) before these routines are called.

Then we draw the boxes on the screen and print the strings from the NAME$( ) array in each of them:

```
'draw boxes for fields and write strings in them
FOR i = 1 TO fields
  CALL drawbox(row(i) - 1, col(i) - 1, fldlen(i) + 2, 1)
  CALL drawtext(WHITE, BLUE, name$(i), row(i), col(i), fldlen(i))
NEXT i
```

Note that the DRAWBOX routine is called starting at row 1, column 1, so that the box starts above and to the left of the text line, and that the boxes' width is FLDLEN% + 2, so that, when drawn, the box continues on one character past the text field.

The DRAWTEXT routine draws the text using the foreground and background colors specified in the first two arguments and the row, column, and length coordinates specified in the last three arguments:

```
'*****************************************************************
'Print text inside a box
'*****************************************************************
SUB drawtext (fore, back, text$, row, col, fldlen)

   LOCATE row, col, 0
   COLOR fore, back

   'convert to format string, by adding first and last "\"
   sformat$ = SPACE$(fldlen)
   MID$(sformat$, 1, 1) = "\"     'convert to format string
   MID$(sformat$, fldlen, 1) = "\"

   'print out the string with trailing spaces using the format
   calculated
   PRINT USING sformat$; text$;
END SUB
```

The crucial part of this logic is the highlighting of a field in reverse video. Each time through the WHILE loop, the last highlighted field is redrawn in normal video if the variable OLDX is not zero. This occurs only if a cursor key has been pressed which increments or decrements the index I to the array of coordinates and names. Then the new field is redrawn in reverse video.

```
cquit = 0                   'set to 1 if Esc key pressed
i = 1                       'index of box being highlighted
oldx = 0                    'last box that was highlighted
WHILE cquit = 0
    IF oldx <> 0 THEN   'draw old one back if needed
       CALL drawtext(WHITE, BLUE, name$(oldx), row(oldx),
       col(oldx), fldlen(oldx))
    END IF
   CALL drawtext(BLUE, WHITE, name$(i), row(i), col(i), fldlen(i))
   CALL enterval(name$(i), i, row(i), col(i), fldlen(i), fields,
   oldx, cquit)
WEND
```

Finally, we show the subprogram ENTERVAL. In it, each key is read and tested for whether it is a function or cursor key. If it is, the subprogram exits with any changes to date in NAME$ and an increment or decrement of the index. If it is a normal character, and it is the first normal character the current field is *erased* to blanks and the first character printed. If it is a normal character after the first, it is just printed in the field.

The routine handles backspace characters itself by simply moving the cursor back one place, writing a space over the current character, and moving back to that space for the next character.

```
'**************************************************************
'Enter a new value in field index
'**************************************************************
SUB enterval (name$, index, row, col, fldlen, fields, oldx, cquit)

'This subprogram displays a highlighted box on a field with the
'contents in the variable NAME$ and having a position defined by
'the index position in arrays from 1 to fields of ROW, COL
'and of length FLDLEN
'The arrow keys can be used to move to the next or previous box

'include key definitions file:
' $INCLUDE: 'keydefs.bas'

'begin keyboard loop
change = 0              '1 if any printing character was entered
cquit = 0               '1 if we want to quit entry of all values
quit = 0                '1 to quit entry of current value
oldx = 0                'value of position in index array on entry
s$ = ""                 'initialize final string

WHILE (quit = 0)
'wait for a key to be struck
   k$ = ""
   WHILE LEN(k$) = 0
        k$ = INKEY$
   WEND
oldx = 0
  IF LEN(k$) = 2 THEN
     code = ASC(RIGHT$(k$, 1))  'get keyboard scan code if
                                'function or arrow key
     oldx = index               'remember current index position
     oldrow = row(index)
     'arrow key quit entry and move to new field
     SELECT CASE code
        CASE RIGHT.ARROW
                     index = index + 1: quit = 1
        CASE LEFT.ARROW
                     index = index - 1: quit = 1
        CASE F10
                     quit = 1: cquit = 1     'F10 means exit
                                             'and save
        CASE ELSE                            'do nothing FOR
                                             'other cases
     END SELECT
```

```
    IF index < 1 THEN index = 1                   'keep index in
                                                  'range 1-fields
    IF index > fields THEN index = fields
'if length = 1 then not a function key:
  ELSE
  SELECT CASE k$
    CASE ESC$
        quit = 1: change = 0: cquit = 1         'Esc means exit
                                                'no changes
    CASE TAB$
        oldx = index: index = index + 1: quit = 1
    CASE CR$
        quit = 1: change = 1
    END SELECT
    nopr = 0                           'non printing character flag

    'handle backspaces by backing up, printing a space, and
    backing up again
    IF k$ = BSP$ THEN
       nopr = 1
       IF LEN(s$) > 0 THEN
          LOCATE row, col + LEN(s$)             'back up
          PRINT " ";                            'print space
          LOCATE row, col + LEN(s$)             'back up again
          s$ = MID$(s$, 1, LEN(s$) - 1)         'remove last
                                                'character from
                                                'string
          END IF
       END IF
     'if there is no change so far then blank out current field
     IF (change = 0) AND (quit = 0) THEN
        CALL drawtext(WHITE, BLUE, "", row, col, fldlen)
        LOCATE row, col
        change = 1
     END IF
     'print new character if it is a printing character
     IF (quit = 0) AND (nopr = 0) THEN
        PRINT k$;
        s$ = s$ + k$                   'concatenate new char to string
     END IF
END IF
WEND
COLOR WHITE, BLUE              'reset colors on exit
IF change = 1 THEN             'save new value if change = 1
   name$ = s$
END IF
END SUB
```

THE NUMLOCK AND CAPSLOCK KEYS

On the original IBM PC, the state of the NumLock key and the CapsLock key could only be determined by typing a character and seeing if it was a capital or lowercase character, or a number or cursor movement key. This was remedied in the PC/AT and the Personal System/2 with indicator lights for CapsLock and NumLock. However, it is possible for your program to examine the memory location where this information is stored to find out and indeed *change* the state of these keys.

In standard DOS machines, location 40:17 (Hex) contains the following information:

Bit	
7	Insert on
6	CapsLock on
5	NumLock on
4	ScrollLock on
3	Alt key depressed
2	Ctrl key depressed
1	Left Shift key depressed
0	Right Shift key depressed

You can access this location with the PEEK command after setting the current segment to &H40:

```
DEF SEG = &H40          'set current segment to 40
key = PEEK(&H17)        'read location 40:17
DEF SEG                 'reset segment to current
```

Then, to read the bits in this word, simply use the AND instruction to examine the bits you are interested in. Recall that the result of a logical AND is 1 (true) if an only if both of the inputs are 1 (true). Thus, you can AND together constant values with the value of the key byte to see if these bits are set. This is illustrated in the following program:

```
'This program waits for any character to be struck,
'and meanwhile monitors the state of the NumLock and CapsLock
keys
s$ = ""                         'set string to null
flag% = -1                      'initialize flag so it will be set
```

```
WHILE LEN(s$) = 0
  s$ = INKEY$                   'wait for key to be struck
  CALL checkeys(flag%, 1, 70)   'display key state in row 1, col 70
WEND
END

'****************************************************************
SUB checkeys (flag%, row%, col%) STATIC
'if flag byte state has changed, change display of NumLock and
'CapsLock

NUMLOCK = 32                'bit 5
CAPSLOCK = 64               'bit 6
DEF SEG = &H40              'set current segment to 40

 f% = PEEK(&H17)            'read byte from memory
 IF f% <> flag% THEN        'if the flag byte is now different,
                            'change display
    LOCATE row%, col%, 0
    flag% = f%
    IF (flag% AND NUMLOCK) THEN
       PRINT "Num ";              'display "Num"
    ELSE
       PRINT "    ";              'erase "Num"
    END IF
    IF (flag% AND CAPSLOCK) THEN
       PRINT "Caps";              'display "Caps"
    ELSE
       PRINT "    ";              'erase "Caps"
    END IF
 END IF
 DEF SEG                          'reset segment to current value

 END SUB                          'and exit
```

10 Memory Handling in QuickBASIC

In most cases, QuickBASIC manages your PC's memory for you, without your having to become concerned as to what physical memory locations are being used for data storage. You do need to become concerned, however, when your program begins to exceed the available limits of the memory in your computer system.

DYNAMIC AND STATIC ARRAYS

Any array that is dimensioned using the DIM statement followed by a constant value (an integer number) or a named constant rather than a variable name is dimensioned as a *static array*. Static arrays occupy a fixed amount of memory determined when the program is run. *Dynamic arrays*, on the other hand, occupy variable amounts of memory depending on the current value of the dimensioning variable:

```
DIM X(100)            'Static array-400 bytes reserved

fsize = 40
DIM Y(fsize)          'Dynamic array-160 bytes set aside

fs2 = 300
REDIM Y(fs2)          'Dynamic array-1200 bytes set aside
```

```
ERASE Y                 'No space allocated for Y
DIM Y(fsize)            'now 160 bytes set aside again
```

THE ERASE COMMAND

The ERASE command deallocates the memory for all the dynamic arrays in the list that follows:

```
ERASE x y z             'deallocate memory for X, Y, and Z
```

After an array is erased, it cannot be used again without error until it is dimensioned with a DIM or REDIM statement.

If you ERASE an array which is static (dimensioned with a constant value), the memory is not deallocated, but all elements of the array are set to zero.

RULES OF DYNAMIC AND STATIC ARRAYS

The previous examples illustrate the following rules:

1. Static arrays may be dimensioned once with DIM and a *constant* size. Their size may not be changed by any statement.
2. Dynamic arrays are identified by the variable name used in the DIM statement.
3. You can change the size of a dynamic array using the REDIM statement or by using the ERASE statement followed by another DIM statement.
4. If you apply the ERASE statement to a static array, the storage is not deallocated, but the elements of the array are set to zero.
5. You can dimension a dynamic array the first time using either DIM or REDIM.
6. Only a dynamic array can take on a dimension greater than 64K bytes total. These dimensions are only possible if you start QB with the /AH switch. In this case any array bound can be up to 32,767 units.

DYNAMIC AND STATIC METACOMMANDS

The compiler metacommands $DYNAMIC and $STATIC are used to override the definitions given in the previous list. You can make all arrays dynamic, and thus redimensionable, if you include the metacommand:

```
'$DYNAMIC-all arrays that follow are dynamic
```

Likewise, you can override this and make all arrays with constant dimensions static again, by including the metacommand:

```
'$STATIC-all arrays that follow are static
```

These commands quickly allow you to convert all arrays to one type or the other.

The advantage of dynamic arrays, of course, is that you can reuse storage when memory is almost used up in a system, by dimensioning only those arrays that a particular part of a program actually uses.

The advantage of static arrays is primarily speed: QuickBASIC needs to make fewer calculations to determine the actual location of a static array element than a dynamic array element.

If you do not dimension an array at all using either DIM or REDIM, QuickBASIC assumes that it has a maximum dimension of 10. Such arrays are always assumed to be static regardless of any metacommands you may use.

ERROR CHECKING

If you compile your program with error checking on, as is the usual case, QuickBASIC will cause a run time error if you attempt to address an array element larger than the maximum dimension declared in the DIM statement. If error checking is not turned on, the program may crash or behave strangely.

Normally, QuickBASIC assumes that the minimum subscript of any array is zero. You can change the index range by using the form

```
DIM x(2 TO 30), y(-50 TO 50)
```

FINDING THE LOWER AND UPPER BOUNDS OF AN ARRAY

When you call a subprogram where one or more of the arguments is an array, the subprogram does not know the size of the array. The LBOUND and UBOUND statements can be used to find out the minimum and maximum indexes of an array:

```
SUB bounds (x(), y())          'x is one dimensional, y is two
                               'dimensional
lowx = LBOUND(x(1))            'get lower bound of array x
highx = UBOUND(x(1))           'get upper bound of array x
highy1 = UBOUND(y(1))          'get first  upper index
highy2 = UBOUND(y(2))          'get second upper index
END SUB
```

ACCESSING MEMORY LOCATIONS DIRECTLY

For the most part, you do not need to find out the contents of any specific memory locations while you are running QuickBASIC programs, and even more seldom do you need to change any. However, certain specific memory locations are used by certain interface cards, and these can be accessed using the PEEK function and POKE statement. These have the form

```
value = PEEK(address)          'get the value in byte address
POKE address, value            'put VALUE in byte address
```

SEGMENT ADDRESSES

The 8088 and 8086 microprocessor chips used in IBM PCs and Personal System 2/30 systems have 16-bit address registers, which allow the microprocessor to address 2^{16} bytes (or 65,536 bytes) without changing any other registers. It is this limitation that makes QuickBASIC and many other programs limit arrays to 64K bytes of data.

The other registers that can be changed are called *segment registers,* and they are used in conjunction with the address registers to address all of the possible 1 megabyte of memory that a PC could hold. In actual fact, only 640K of the possible 1024K are *memory,* and the rest are addresses used by various displays and other interface hardware.

You can change these registers in QuickBASIC using the DEF SEG statement:

```
DEF SEG = nnnn        'set current data segment to nnnn
DEF SEG               'reset to current data segment
```

The DEF SEG statement affects the addresses referred to by the next PEEK, POKE, BLOAD, BSAVE, or CALL ABSOLUTE statement. It does not affect references to any QuickBASIC variables or arrays.

We saw in Chapter 9 how you could use these statements to look at address 40:17 where the information on the NumLock and CapsLock keys is stored. You can also actually change these bits and affect the status of, say, NumLock using the POKE statement:

```
DEF SEG = &H40          'change segment to 40
key% = PEEK(&H17)       'read current value

key% = key% OR 32       'set bit 5 on-NumLock On

POKE &H17,key%          'put result back
DEF SEG                 'reset to current data segment
```

You can also use DEF SEG to access the display memory, as we will see in Chapter 12.

11 Screen Graphics in QuickBASIC

In this chapter, we discuss the methods for drawing lines and curves on the screen. It is not possible to draw anything except the block graphics characters if you only have a monochrome adapter card, but if you have either the standard Color Graphics Adapter (CGA), the Enhanced Graphics Adapter (EGA), or the Video Graphics Array (VGA) of the PS/2, you can draw graphic images on the screen.

In this chapter we are going to illustrate the use of the following BASIC graphics statements:

```
SCREEN n                  'set graphics mode 1 or 2
LINE (x1,y1)-(x2,y2)      'draw line from (x1,y1) to (x2,y2)
COLOR ,n                  'set RGB or B&W color palette
PAINT (x,y),color         'fill figure at (x,y) with color
CIRCLE (x,y),rad,color    'draw a circle with center x,y
                          'and radius rad
PSET (x,y),color          'set pixel (x,y) to color
WINDOW (x1,y1)-(x2,y2)    'redefine screen coordinates
PALETTE number,color      'set EGA palette color
```

THE CGA

The CGA display allows you to draw 25 lines of 80 characters in any of 16 colors, or 25 lines of 40 wide characters. In graphics modes you can draw four color graphic images in 320 × 200 dot resolution or two-color images in 640 × 200 dot resolution. Each dot in the display is referred to as a *pixel* or sometimes as a *pel.* These separate display *modes* are set in QuickBASIC using the SCREEN instruction

```
SCREEN mode
```

where MODE has the following values:

	Text			Graphics		
Mode	Rows	Columns	Colors	Rows	Columns	Colors
0	25	80	16	—	—	—
1	25	40	4	200	320	4
2	25	80	2	200	640	2

To summarize, then, you can draw characters in 16 colors in text mode, but you can draw lines and curves in graphics modes in lower resolution and fewer colors.

THE COLOR STATEMENT

We have already seen the COLOR statement used for text mode characters in the form

```
COLOR fore, back
```

where

FORE is 0 to 15 for foreground colors;
adding 16 to any color makes it blink.
BACK is 0 to 7 for background colors.

In graphics mode 1, COLOR has a different interpretation:

```
COLOR back, palette
```

where

BACK	is 0 to 15, the background color of the entire screen.
PALETTE	is 0 for colors black, green, red, yellow; 1 for colors black, cyan, magenta, white.

In graphics mode, you can choose between a palette made up of green, red, and yellow or cyan, magenta, and white. Generally the latter palette is more restful to the eye, and the former a bit more intense for emphasis.

THE LINE STATEMENT

The LINE statement can be used to draw a line or a box from one *(x, y)* point to another in modes 1 or 2. It has the form

```
LINE (x1,y1) - (x2,y2), color, opt, style
```

where

X1,X2	are values from 0 to 319 in mode 1 or 0 to 639 in mode 2.
Y1,Y2	are values from 0 to 199.
COLOR	is a value from 0 to 3 for green, red, yellow or cyan, magenta, white.
OPT	is blank, B, or BF: blank, draw line B, draw box BF, draw filled box
STYLE	is a 16-bit integer describing a pattern for a dashed, dotted line: &HFFFF is a solid line. &HF0F0 is a large dashed line. &HAAAA is a dotted line.

The following simple program draws a diagonal green line, a filled red box, and a hollow yellow box:

```
'Draw a filled red box, a hollow yellow box, and a green line
CONST GREEN = 1, RED = 2, YELLOW = 3     'define names for colors

SCREEN 1                                 '320 x 200 graphics
COLOR , 0                                'yellow, red, green
LINE (10, 10)-(50, 90), RED, BF          'filled red box
LINE (100, 70)-(200, 100), YELLOW, B     'hollow yellow box
LINE (0, 140)-(300, 90), GREEN           'diagonal green line
END
```

DRAWING A STRAIGHT LINE ON AXES

The program below displays the Cartesian coordinate axes with X and Y varying from −10 to +10, and after asking for the slope and intercept, displays a straight line in magenta against the axes in white. The tick marks from −5 to +5 are displayed on the axes. Since the actual dimensions of the screen are 320 × 200, the factors XSCALE and YSCALE are used to convert axis coordinates to screen coordinates, and the constants XOFF and YOFF are used to move the origin (0,0) to the center of the screen.

```
'draw Y = MX + B line in magenta on white Cartesian coordinates
CONST CYAN = 1, MAGENTA = 2, WHITE = 3

SCREEN 1  '320 × 200              define resolution
COLOR , 1                         'and colors

yscale = 200 / 20                 '+/-10 divisions in Y direction
xscale = 320 / 20                 '+/-10 divisions in X direction
xoff = 160                        'half of X scale
yoff = 100                        'half of Y scale

'get the slope and intercept from the keyboard
CLS
LOCATE 5, 2
INPUT "Slope = "; m
INPUT "Intercept = "; b

CLS

LINE (0, 100) - (319, 100), WHITE  'draw X axis
LINE (160, 0) - (160, 200), WHITE  'draw Y axis
```

```
'draw X tic marks
FOR x = -10 TO 10
  xpos = x * xscale + xoff
LINE (xpos, yoff + 2) - (xpos, yoff -  2), white
NEXT x

'draw Y-axis tic marks
FOR y = -10 TO 10
  ypos = y * xscale + yoff
LINE (xoff + 2, ypos) - (xoff - 2, ypos), white
NEXT y

ylow = m * (-5) + b             'calculate max and min values of Y
yhigh = m * 5 + b

x1 = -5 * xscale + xoff          'calculate 2 points
y1 = ylow * yscale + yoff        'to draw the line through
x2 = 5 * xscale + xoff
y2 = yhigh * yscale + yoff

LINE (x1, y1) - (x2, y2), magenta  'draw colored line

CALL getkey(s$)              'wait for key to be struck and exit
END
```

In this above example, we define a Y-offset and an X-offset equal to half the screen coordinates and use them to calculate the actual pixel values from our arbitrary coordinate system ranging from −10 to 10 in both the X and Y directions. You can also use the WINDOW statement to get QuickBASIC to calculate these values for you. If you issue the statement

```
WINDOW (-10, -10) - (10, 10)      'screen varies from -10 to +10
                                  ' in both dimensions
```

you can then plot your lines directly in this coordinate system:

```
ylow = m * (-10) + b                    'calculate Y min and Y max
yhigh = m * 5 + b

LINE (-10, ylow) - (10, yhigh), MAGENTA  'draw colored line
```

The resulting plot for slope = 1.5 and intercept = 2 is shown in Figure 11.1.

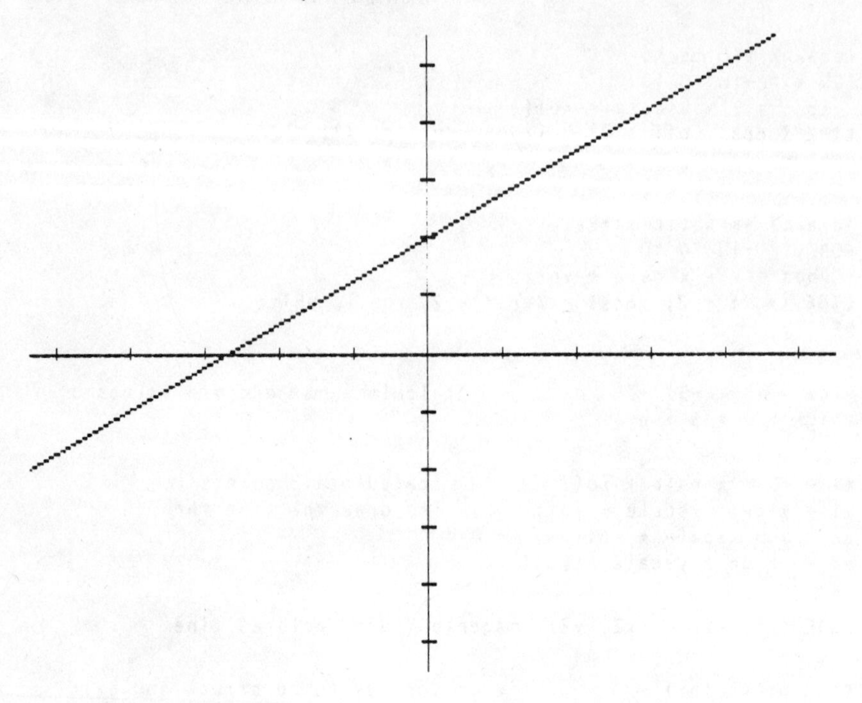

Figure 11.1 Display produced by setting slope = 1.5 and intercept = 2 in the $y = mx + b$ display program.

DRAWING CIRCLES

You can draw circles on the screen using the CIRCLE statement, which has the form

```
CIRCLE (x,y), radius, color
```

or arcs as parts of circles using

```
CIRCLE (x,y), radius, color, start, end
```

where START and END are in units varying from -2π to 2π.

RELATIVE DRAWING

You can indicate the coordinates of a new line or circle in terms of the distance from the most recently plotted point instead of in absolute pixel values by including the STEP modifier with the statements:

```
LINE STEP (x1,y1) - STEP (x2,y2)

CIRCLE STEP (x,y), radius, color
```

FILLING IN FIGURES USING PAINT

As noted in the section "The LINE Statement" earlier in this chapter, you can fill a box drawn by the LINE statement by including the argument BF:

```
LINE (x1,y1) - (x2,y2), color, BF
```

You can also fill in any enclosed figure in a solid color by using the PAINT statement. PAINT fills the figure which *encloses* its starting coordinates. Therefore, the point you select must be inside or outside the figure and not on its border:

```
PAINT (x,y), color, bordercolor
```

This statement paints a solid color up to the place where it encounters the border color specified. PAINT also allows you to fill a figure with a tiled pattern made of up bytes describing which bits to turn on and off. Up to 64 such bytes may make up the pattern:

```
PAINT (x,y), CHR$(arg1) + CHR$(arg2) + · · · + CHR$(argn)
```

COLORS IN THE EGA AND VGA DISPLAYS

The EGA (Enhanced Graphics Adapter) display provides significantly higher resolution and more colors for the PC display. The VGA (Video Graphics Array) is the standard display of the PS/2 product line, although VGA boards are also available for the PC line. In addition, the PS/2 Models 25 and 30 provide a display called the MCGA, which has the same modes as the CGA, and an additional 256-color mode which is ideal for shaded illustrations, although of less utility for line graphics.

QuickBASIC provides additional SCREEN statements for setting these display modes. If you do not have the proper hardware, you will get an error message when you try to execute these statements.

SCREEN 9	Set EGA to 640 × 350 graphics
SCREEN 11	Set VGA or MCGA to 640 × 480 in two colors
SCREEN 12	Set VGA to 640 × 480 in 16 colors
SCREEN 13	Set VGA and MCGA to 256-color mode

The Enhanced Graphics Adapter allows you to choose 16 out of 64 colors for graphics as well as character drawing. For each of the three color guns, there are two outputs set by bits in a color register:

	secondary			primary		
	R	G	B	R	G	B
bit:	5	4	3	2	1	0

You can thus set a dark blue by selecting color 000001 and an intense blue by selecting color 001001. Since only 16 colors can be selected out of the possible 64, a table of 16 6-bit values must be created, where each of these values is then selected when that color is picked with the COLOR statement. The colors that the EGA card selects by default are designed to mimic those of the CGA, and much more brilliant and interesting colors can be selected. This table is selected using the PALETTE statement as illustrated in Table 11.1. We use the *octal* representation of the bit patterns here because it conveniently groups the bits into threes. Following is a program for setting the palette and drawing the color bars:

```
'program to set the EGA or VGA palette in graphics mode
DIM p(17) as integer, i as integer
'    black, blue, blue-magenta, magenta, magenta-red, red
DATA 0,      &o1, &o15,         &o55,    &o45,        &o44
'    orange, yellow
DATA &o046,  &o066
```

```
'    yellow-green, green, green-cyan, cyan, light blue
DATA &o72,        &o22,      &o23,     &o33,     &o11
'    dark gray, light gray,
DATA &o70,       &o07
'    white and border black
DATA &o077,       &o0

FOR i = 1 TO 17                  'read in palette colors
  READ p(i)
NEXT i
SCREEN 9                         'set 640 x 350 EGA mode
PALETTE USING p(1)               'set new palette
CLS
FOR i = 1 TO 15
  COLOR i, 0                     'write numbers in colors
  PRINT i;
NEXT i

FOR i = 1 TO 15
  LINE (0, i * 12) - (30 * i, i * 12 + 10), i, BF 'draw color bars
NEXT i

END
```

TABLE 11.1 Suggested EGA and VGA Graphics Palette

Color	Color Number	Bits Set	Octal Representation
Black	0	000000	0
Blue	1	000001	&o1
Blue-magenta	2	001101	&o15
Magenta	3	101101	&o55
Magenta-red	4	100101	&o45
Red	5	100100	&o44
Orange	6	100110	&o46
Yellow	7	110110	&o66
Yellow-green	8	111010	&o72
Green	9	010010	&o22
Green-cyan	10	010011	&o23
Cyan	11	011011	&o33
Light blue	12	001001	&o11
Dark gray	13	111000	&o70
Light gray	14	000111	&o07
White	15	111111	&o77

ACCESSING THE SCREEN MEMORY OF THE DISPLAY DIRECTLY

In addition to the standard QuickBASIC commands for writing characters and drawing lines, you can access the memory of the displays directly for much faster drawing. The memory address segments of the three displays are as follows:

	Display Memory Starting Addresses	
	Character	Graphics
Monochrome	&Hb000	—
CGA	&Hb800	&Hb800, &Hba00
EGA	&Hb800	&Ha000

The monochrome display can display only characters; it has no graphics capability using the standard IBM monochrome graphics card. The two color cards have the ability to display either characters or graphics. In the two modes, display memory is used differently.

MONOCHROME DISPLAY CHARACTER MEMORY

The monochrome display stores alternating bytes of attributes and ASCII character codes. The attribute byte can have one of the following values:

00	Normal character
01	Underlined character
02	Blinking character
03	Reverse video character

Thus, each character can independently be set to normal, underlined, blinking, and inverse depending on the preceding attribute byte.

DECIDING WHICH DISPLAY IS INSTALLED

You can decide which displays are installed by examining location 40:10. Its bits have the following meanings:

0	DOS diskette in drive a:
1	Math coprocessor
4,5	Initial video mode:
	01, color card
	11, monochrome card
6,7	Number of diskette drives
9,10,11	Number of RS-232 cards
13	Internal modem card
14,15	Number of printers

CGA AND EGA DISPLAYS IN CHARACTER MODE

The display memories for the CGA and EGA are both organized in the same fashion in character modes: an attribute byte followed by an ASCII character code byte. The attribute bytes have the following format:

	background				foreground			
	blink	R	G	B	intens	R	G	B
bit:	7	6	5	4	3	2	1	0

The foreground can be set to any of eight colors (including black), seven of which can be intensified by setting bit 3. The background can be set to any of eight colors, and the blinking bit can be on or off.

While writing directly to the screen memory is at least three times faster than using the QuickBASIC calls to the PC's ROM program for handling the characters, it is cumbersome for all but the most highly optimized cases. One place where it is necessary to read and write to display memory is when you want to display a popup window on top of the current data.

Popup windows contain messages which appear and disappear, leaving the text "behind" them intact. Practically, this means that you must save the contents of the screen area where the window is to be displayed and rewrite this saved data to the display memory when the window is to be removed. This is very simple to do in QuickBASIC by using an integer array large enough to save a window area, and an array of strings to be written in the window. This is illustrated in the POPUP program:

```
'Popup demonstation program
DEFINT A-Z                          'all are integers
DIM st$(5), sv(200) AS INTEGER
CONST BLUE = 1, RED = 12, WHITE = 15
COLOR WHITE, BLUE
```

```
a$ = "A"                                'start with letter A
FOR i = 1 TO 24                         'fill screen with characters
LOCATE i, 1
  FOR j = 1 TO 80
  PRINT a$;
  NEXT j
a$ = CHR$(ASC(a$) + 1)                          'A through W
NEXT i

st$(1) = " Hello "                          'text for popup menu
st$(2) = " From  "                          'here each 7 characters wide
st$(3) = " Outer "
st$(4) = " SPACE "

s$ = ""
WHILE (s$ <> "Q")                               'repeat until "Q" pressed
  CALL popup(10, 20, 7, 4, st$(), sv())  'display menu
  CALL getkey(s$)                               'wait for any key
  COLOR WHITE, BLUE                             'reset screen color
  CALL restore.pop(10, 20, 7, 4, sv())  'restore screen
  CALL getkey(s$)                               'wait for any key
WEND

END

'*************************************************************
SUB popup (row%, col%, wd%, rows%, st$(), sv())

DEFINT A-Z
'pop up one menu size wd% + 2 by rows% +2
'surround text with box
' $INCLUDE: 'keydefs.bas'  'include key definitions for box chars

DEF SEG = &HB800             'address of CGA screen memory
offset = (row% - 1) * 160 + (col% - 1) * 2

'save characters in this space
i = 1                        'index into saved character array
FOR k = 1 TO (rows% + 2)
   FOR j = 1 TO (wd% + 2)
      sv(i) = PEEK(offset)                      'save attribute
      i = i + 1
      offset = offset + 1
      sv(i) = PEEK(offset)                      'and character
      i = i + 1
      offset = offset + 1
   NEXT j
offset = offset + 160 - (wd + 2) * 2    'next row
NEXT k
```

```
'write in new characters from string arrays
COLOR RED, WHITE
LOCATE row%, col%, 0

PRINT LEFT.UPPER$;                    'draw left corner
FOR i = 1 TO wd%
   PRINT HORIZ$;                      'draw upper box line
NEXT i
PRINT RIGHT.UPPER$                    'draw right corner
row% = row% + 1

FOR j = 1 TO rows%                    'draw text
   LOCATE row%, col%, 0
   PRINT VERT$; st$(j); VERT$;        'and vertical lines
   row% = row% + 1
NEXT j

LOCATE row%, col%, 0
PRINT LEFT.LOWER$;                    'draw left corner
FOR i = 1 TO wd%
   PRINT HORIZ$;                      'draw lower box line
NEXT i
PRINT RIGHT.LOWER$                    'draw right corner

DEF SEG                               'restore segment pointer
END SUB

'*****************************************************************
SUB restore.pop (row%, col%, wd%, rows%, sv())
'restore saved screen memory area

DEF SEG = &HB800          'address of CGA screen memory
offset% = (row% - 1) * 160 + (col% - 1) * 2
'restore characters in this space
i% = 1                    'index into saved character array
FOR k% = 1 TO (rows% + 2)
   FOR j% = 1 TO (wd% + 2)
      POKE offset%, sv(i%)      'put attribute back
      i% = i% + 1
      offset% = offset% + 1
      POKE offset%, sv(i%)      'and character back
      i% = i% + 1
      offset% = offset% + 1
   NEXT j%
offset% = offset% + 160 - (wd% + 2) * 2
NEXT k%

DEF SEG           'restore segment pointer
END SUB
```

READING AND WRITING MEMORY IN GRAPHICS MODE

In graphics mode (screen 1 and 2 for the CGA, screen 9 for the EGA, and screen 11 - 13 for the VGA), you can read and write bytes of memory to represent the actual pixels which are turned on. Each pixel on the screen is one or two bits of a byte in the graphics display adapter. These words are organized differently depending on whether you are in screen 1 or screen 2 mode or using the EGA.

Memory for the CGA starts at DEF SEG = &Hb800. In screen 1 mode (320 × 200) each byte represents the color state for 4 pixels:

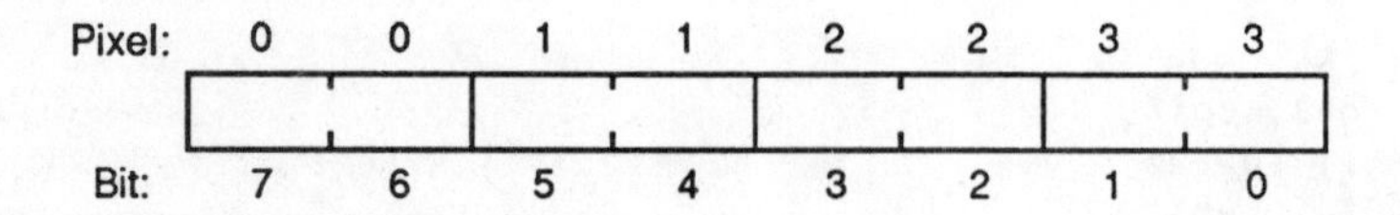

Each two bits has the value 00, 01, 10, or 11 depending on which of the four colors is to be displayed: black, cyan, magenta, or white; or black, green, red, or yellow.

In screen 2 mode (640 × 200), each bit of each byte represents a pixel which can be either white or black.

Memory in the CGA is organized so that alternate lines on the screen start at different addresses. All of the even row numbers, starting with 0, start at segment address &Hb800. The odd rows start at address &Hba00. Thus, to draw consecutive lines, you must draw them alternately from a segment base of B800 and a segment base of BA00. The following program draws a vertical line in byte 40 (column 160), halfway across the screen. Since it turns on bits 10101010 (&haa) the color is magenta. Alternate rows are handled by added &h2000 to every other address.

```
'draw a 4-pixel-wide magenta vertical line
DEF SEG = &HB800
SCREEN 1
row% = 40  'in center of screen

FOR i% = 1 TO 100                 '100 rows * 2
   POKE row%, &HAA                'draw 4 bits in even row
   POKE &H2000 + row%, &HAA       'draw 4 bits in odd row
   row% = row% + 80               'on to next row
NEXT i%
END
```

Writing directly to the screen memory can be somewhat faster when drawing complex data than using the LINE statement. You can also draw lines considerable faster by calling specifically written assembly language routines, as illustrated in the last chapters of this text.

GRAPHICS MODE FOR THE EGA CARD

You can use the SCREEN 9 mode and the LINE command to draw higher-resolution 16-color graphics on the EGA display. You can also write directly to the hardware registers of the EGA card using the QuickBASIC OUT instruction, which has the form

```
OUT port, value
```

where PORT is an address between 0 and &h3FF and VALUE is an 8-bit value to be sent out that input/output (I/O) port. The 8088 microprocessor used in the IBM PC has a set of these I/O ports which are specifically attached to particular devices.

All of the EGA registers are addressed in two steps: one in which a register selector address is specified and one in which the actual register is loaded. These addresses are part of the input-output address space, rather than actual physical memory address, and are addressed using the OUT instructions either in QuickBASIC or in assembly language. The relevant addresses are:

3c4	sequencer register select
3c5	selector value
0	reset
1	clocking mode
2	write map mask
3	character map select
4	memory mode select
3ce	graphics controller register select
3cf	selector value
0	set/reset
1	enable set/reset
2	color compare
3	data rotate and write mode
4	read map select
5	mode register
8	bit mask

In graphics mode, the EGA memory starts at address A0000 or segment &Ha000 and address 0. There can be up to 256K bytes of memory on the EGA, 128K of which is used in graphics mode for each of two graphics pages. Each *page* can hold an entire screen of graphics information. These pages are made up of four *planes*, all of which appear to be at address A0000, but are accessed in different ways depending on the write mode selected. By contrast in the VGA modes with resolutions of 640 × 480, there is only one page of graphics memory, since two pages would require more than 256K bytes of memory.

In the most common EGA and VGA high-resolution graphics mode, write mode 0, you select the combination of planes to write to by setting the *map mask register*. This selects the color you are going to write. Then, all of the bits that you set will appear in the color selected by this mask register, since only the planes whose bits were selected in the map mask register are affected.

For example, if the four planes have the value 1001 for a particular bit position,

the EGA will look in palette table location 1001 (9_{10}) and find the color green, value 010010, if the palette is set as shown previously. The following example draws a horizontal green line about one-third of the way down the screen:

```
' draw a line on the EGA display in  write mode 0
SCREEN 9                    'set 640 x 350 16-color graphics
DEF SEG = &Ha000            'address of EGA memory

OUT &h3c4,2        'select map mask register
OUT &h3c5,19       'combination of planes for green

FOR i = &H2000 TO &h2000 + 80
   POKE i,&Hff                   'set all 8 bits in each byte
NEXT i
END
```

SAVING SCREEN IMAGES TO FILES

You can create a screen image using a complex series of QuickBASIC graphics statements and save that image as a disk file using the BSAVE statement. This statement has the form

```
BSAVE filename$, offset, size
```

where

```
FILENAME$ is the string file name.
OFFSET    is the position on the screen to start.
SIZE      is the size in bytes.
```

For the CGA, you would write

```
DEF SEG = &HB800
BSAVE "screen.dmp", 0, 80*200
```

The analogous statement BLOAD can be used to read in these files:

```
BLOAD file$, offset
```

The EGA memory must be saved in four planes of 80 × 350 bytes each. This is done by selecting each plane using the read map mask and writing it to disk using BSAVE, as illustrated here:

```
'Program to demonstrate saving and loading of EGA planes
SCREEN 9                           'set to 350 x 640 graphics mode
LINE (20, 20)-(150, 150), 12, BF 'draw  red filled square
CIRCLE (400, 260), 70, 3           'draw open blue circle
DEF SEG = &HA000                   'select start of display memory
CALL saveplane("plane1", 0)        'save each of 4 planes
CALL saveplane("plane2", 1)
CALL saveplane("plane3", 2)
CALL saveplane("plane4", 3)
CLS                                'clear the screen
CALL loadplane("plane1", 1)        'and reload the display from
                                   'the files

CALL loadplane("plane2", 2)
CALL loadplane("plane3", 4)
CALL loadplane("plane4", 8)

END
'------------------------------------
```

```
SUB loadplane (file$, pl%)
   OUT &H3C4, 2                        'select map mask
   OUT &H3C5, pl%
   BLOAD file$, 0                      'load that plane from a file
END SUB
'-----------------------------------
SUB saveplane (file$, pl%)
   OUT &H3CE, 4                        'select read map
   OUT &H3CF, pl%                      'select plane
   BSAVE file$, 0, 350 * 80            'save that plane in a file
END SUB
```

WRITING TO THE EGA REGISTERS

The EGA display can be programmed to drive a monochrome monitor or a CGA monitor as well as the Enhanced Color Display (ECD) monitor. On the ECD display it can behave as either a CGA or an EGA display so that programs for the CGA will run on the EGA.

The EGA display in character mode has a character size of 9 × 14 instead of the 9 × 8 dot character used by the CGA. In graphics mode, you can draw in 320 × 200, 640 × 200 or 640 × 350 pixel resolutions. The EGA 640 × 350 resolution mode allows you to display 16 colors out of a palette of 64 as shown previously in the PALETTE command.

The actual setting of bits to draw dots or lines in the EGA is a lot more versatile, although the two most important graphics modes are write mode 0 and write mode 2.

In mode 0, you can write to any combination of the four planes using a bit mask to select the planes of interest and thus the color you wish to draw. The value you write to each screen byte represents the bits you wish to turn on.

```
'Drawing a line on the EGA Display in write mode 0

SCREEN 9                   'set to 640 x 350 graphics
DEF SEG = &HA200           'address of screen memory
OUT &H3CE, 5               'select mode
OUT &H3CF, 0               'write mode 0

OUT &H3C4, 2               'select write map
OUT &H3C5, 9               'color 9 is blue

FOR i = 1 TO 200           'write a color into 200 bytes, all 8 bits
   POKE i, &HFF
NEXT i
```

In mode 2, you select the bits you wish to write to with a bit mask, and the value you write to memory (0 <= N <= 15) is the color you turn on in each bit. In write mode 2, we can write a color by number to all the bits of any given byte which are selected with the bit mask. The following program shows how this can be done:

```
'Drawing a line on the EGA Display in write mode 2

SCREEN 9                'set to 640 x 350 graphics
def seg = &Ha200        'address of screen memory
out &h3ce,5             'select mode
out &h3cf,&h2           'write mode 2
out &h3ce,8             'select bit mask
out &h3cf,&hff          'set bit mask to select all 8 bits at once

for i = 1 to 200        'write a color into 200 bytes, all 8 bits
   poke i,&H9
next i
```

The mode 2 display is generally less frequently used, because characters are always written to the screen in mode 0.

12 Programming the Printer in QuickBASIC

In this chapter, we will discuss printing characters on dot matrix printers, particularly the IBM Graphics Printer (made by Epson) and the IBM Proprinters, made by IBM.

The IBM Graphics Printer can print 10 characters per inch (cpi) or 16 cpi in either draft or emphasized mode. It can also print graphics at 480 dots across the page.

The IBM Proprinter can print 10, 12, or 17 cpi in draft or near-letter-quality (NLQ) modes, and any of these charactern widths can also be emphasized to simulate boldface. The IBM Proprinter XL and Proprinter II have an additional higher quality character mode, called NLQ-II mode. The Proprinter can also print graphics at 480 or 960 dots across the page.

PRINTER CONTROL CODES

Nearly all of the printer functions can be changed by an *escape sequence* consisting of the ESC character (chr$(27)) followed by a character and some arguments. Some of the most common of these are:

```
esc$; "-"; chr$(1);      'start continuous underlining
esc$; "-"; chr$(0);      'stop  continuous underlining
esc$; "-"; chr$(1);      'start continuous overscore
```

```
esc$; "-"; chr$(0);       'stop  continuous overscore
esc$; "S" chr$(1);        'start superscript printing
esc$; "S" chr$(0);        'stop  superscript printing
esc$; "T" chr$(1);        'start subscript printing
esc$; "T" chr$(0);        'stop  subscript printing
esc$; ":";                'start 12 cpi
chr$(15);                 'start 17 cpi
chr$(18);                 '17 cpi off, return to 10 cpi
chr$(14);                 'double wide printing to end of line
esc$; "W"; chr$(1);       'start continuous double wide
                          'printing
esc$; "W"; chr$(0);       'stop  continuous double wide
                          'printing
esc$; "G";                'start NLQ printing
esc$; "H";                'stop NLQ printing
esc$; "I"; chr$(1)        'start NLQ-II printing
esc$; "I"; chr$(2)        'start NLQ printing
esc$; "I"; chr$(0)        'stop NLQ-II printing
esc$; "E";                'start emphasized printing
                          '(boldface)
esc$; "F";                'stop emphasized printing
```

Many of these functions can be combined, so that the following combinations are legal and useful:

Emphasized, NLQ, underlined

12 cpi, emphasized, NLQ

17 cpi, NLQ

Double wide, NLQ, underlined

The following combinations are not allowed, and give the results shown:

Combinations	Result
Condensed, emphasized	Emphasized
Condensed, 12 cpi	12 cpi
Condensed, NLQ, emphasized	NLQ, emphasized

THE WIDTH STATEMENT FOR THE PRINTER

QuickBASIC assumes that any printing device has a maximum width of 80 characters unless you tell it differently. If you have a Proprinter XL (14-inch wide carriage), or if you print in compressed mode, you can print more characters on the line than this. To prevent QuickBASIC from inserting a carriage return after 80 characters, you should give the WIDTH statement as follows:

```
WIDTH "lpt1:",132        'set printer width to 132
```

You can use a larger value for paper wider than 8 inches in compressed mode, but the width must be less than 256 characters.

PRINTING GRAPHIC IMAGES

Most printers also allow you to control each dot of the dot matrix to print graphic images. On the IBM Proprinter and Graphics Printer, you can send 8 bits at a time in graphics mode, each bit controlling one pin of the top eight pins of the nine-pin hammer. The bits are organized so the most significant bit controls the top pin and the least significant bit the bottom pin:

Pin	Value
7	128
6	64
5	32
4	16
3	8
2	4
1	2
0	1

There are several escape sequences you can use to print these graphic images on the printer:

Esc$; "K"; n1 n2 val1 . . . valn	480-bit graphics
Esc$; "L"; n1 n2 val1 . . . valn	960-bit graphics (half speed)
Esc$; "Y"; n1 n2 val1 . . . valn	960-bit graphics (full speed)
Esc$; "Z"; n1 n2 val1 . . . valn	1920-bit graphics

where

n1	is the number of dots in MOD 256
n2	is the number of dots divided by 256.
val1 . . . valn	are the 8-bit values to print.

These commands print N2 × 256 + N1 columns of dots on the same line where the following N2 × 256 + N1 bytes sent to the printer are the values of the bits to be struck to make up the graphic image. For example, you could print the image of the character π:

```
o o o o o o o o
  o     o
  o     o
  o     o
  o     o
  o     o
```

by using the following bit patterns:

00100000	&h20
00100000	&h20
00111111	&h3f
00100000	&h20
00100000	&h20
00111111	&h3f
00100000	&h20
00100000	&h20

This can be printed by the statements

```
'print PI in 480-bit graphics mode
    esc$ = CHR$(27)
    LPRINT esc$; "K"; CHR$(8); CHR$(0);                 'print 8
                                                        'graphics chars
    LPRINT CHR$(&h20); CHR$(&h20); CHR$(&h3f);          '1st 3
    LPRINT CHR$(&h20); CHR$(&h20); CHR$(&h3f);          '2nd 3
    LPRINT CHR$(&h20); CHR$(&h20);                      'last 2
```

The difference between the various graphics modes is the resolution and density of the dots. The 480-bit mode is rather like the draft character mode in quality, the 960-bit normal speed is like NLQ, and the 960-bit half speed is like emphasized print.

The 1920-bit mode is unusual in that it prints at the slow 960-bit rate but prints every other byte of the array sent to the printer. This is for compatibility with higher density printers and has no general applicability.

PRINTING A GRAPHICS SCREEN ON THE PRINTER

The example that follows draws a circle, square, and triangle on the screen and also draws them on the printer in graphics mode assuming the CGA display. This display is only 200 lines high by 640 lines wide in screen 2 mode, and thus would produce a long, thin picture if the vertical screen dimension were not filled in more densely. In the program, each horizontal byte is duplicated 4 times so that the final picture just fills a normal printer page. On an EGA display the lines would only have to be doubled from 350 to 700. The CGADUMP routine also includes a RES argument so you can print in either 480-dot mode, 960 full-speed or 960 half-speed mode.

The graphics printing mode requires that there be no distance between print lines and thus there is a command to set the vertical spacing in graphics mode:

```
esc$; "3"; chr$(n);
```

where N is the number of 216ths of an inch to advance the paper between lines. For normal eight-wire graphics, you should advance the paper by 24/216 of an inch between lines. Note that you must use the WIDTH statement to make sure that QuickBASIC does not insert a carriage return in the middle of your graphics character stream.

```
'Draw rectangle, triangle and circle
'and dump them to the IBM Proprinter in graphics mode
CONST LORES = 0, MEDRES = 1, HIRES = 2
SCREEN 2
LINE (20, 20)-(100, 50), 1, BF  'draw a filled rectangle

LINE (190, 90)-(260, 40)        'draw a hollow triangle
LINE STEP(0, 0)-STEP(50, 50)    'note use of STEP modifier
LINE STEP(0, 0)-(190, 90)

CIRCLE (500, 130), 60           'draw a hollow circle

LINE (0, 0)-(639, 0)            'outline the borders
LINE (639, 0)-(639, 199)        'of the screen
LINE (639, 199)-(0, 199)
LINE (0, 199)-(0, 0)

CALL cgadump(LORES)             'draw the screen on the printer
END
'*************************************************************
```

```
SUB cgadump (res)
'dumps contents of cga screen mode 2 to Proprinter or graphics
'printer in 960-bit mode, by quadrupling each column 200 cols
'becomes 800 columns
DIM buf(800) AS INTEGER, i AS INTEGER, j AS INTEGER
DIM col AS INTEGER
esc$ = CHR$(27)
WIDTH "lpt1:", 255                        'required for 960 mode
SELECT CASE res
   CASE LORES:
      ctrlchar$ = "K"
      incr = 4
      bytes = 400
   CASE MEDRES:
      ctrlchar$ = "Y"
      incr = 8
      bytes = 800
   CASE HIRES:
      ctrlchar$ = "L"
      incr = 8
      bytes = 800
END SELECT
LPRINT esc$; "3"; CHR$(24);               'set vertical advance to
                                          '24/216 in
FOR col = 0 TO 79                         'draw 80 columns of bytes
  DEF SEG = &HB800                        'even columns are at b8000
  i = bytes - 1                           'index in buffer array reverse
                                          'l to r
  FOR j = 0 TO 99                         '100 cols at b8000
     buf(i) = PEEK(j * 80 + col)          'read screen byte
     buf(i - 1) = buf(i)                  'double each one for better
                                          'plot
    IF (res <> LORES) THEN
       buf(i - 2) = buf(i)
       buf(i - 3) = buf(i)
    END IF
    i = i - incr                          'next even group of 4
 NEXT j
 DEF SEG = &HBA00                         'odd columns are at ba000
 i = bytes - 1 - incr / 2                 'reverse left to right
 FOR j = 0 TO 99                          '80 columns of odd rows
    buf(i) = PEEK(j * 80 + col)           'read screen byte
    buf(i - 1) = buf(i)
    IF (res <> LORES) THEN
       buf(i - 2) = buf(i)
       buf(i - 3) = buf(i)
    END IF
    i = i - incr                          'next even group of 4
  NEXT j
  hibyte = bytes \ 256
```

```
  lobyte = bytes - (hibyte * 256)
  LPRINT esc$; ctrlchar$;
  LPRINT CHR$(lobyte); CHR$(hibyte); 'set up 960-bit graphics
  FOR i = 0 TO bytes - 1             '800 bytes across
      LPRINT CHR$(buf(i));
  NEXT i
  LPRINT                             'advance paper by 24/216 in
NEXT col                             'on to next column
LPRINT CHR$(12);                     'eject page
END SUB
```

SCREEN DUMP OF AN EGA OR VGA DISPLAY

Reading bits from an EGA or VGA display involves setting the read map mask to each plane and reading in that byte. All four bytes are then ORed together to produce the monochrome image bits which the printer prints. The subprogram that follows allows you to select either full or half speed 960-bit mode and either an EGA or VGA display, with either 350 or 480 lines of resolution.

```
SUB egadump (resolution%, display%)
'dumps contents of EGA screen to Proprinter or graphics printer
'in 960 bit mode, by doubling each column.
' The RESOLUTION% argument determines the printer resolution:
'       0 = 960 bit full speed
'       1 = 960 bit half speed
' The DISPLAY% argument determines which display resolution:
'       350     EGA screen mode 9
'       480     VGA screen mode 12
' Thus, 350 becomes 700 columns, and 480 becomes 960
CONST GRADD = &H3CE, GRVAL = &H3CF
DIM buf%(960)
esc$ = CHR$(27)                     'define escape character
IF (resolution% > 0) THEN
   ctrlchar$ = "L"                  'high resolution, slower printing
ELSE
   ctrlchar$ = "Y"                  'low resolution, faster printing
END IF
WIDTH "lpt1:", 255                  'required for 960 mode
LPRINT esc$; "3"; CHR$(24);         'set vertical advance to 24/216 in
FOR col% = 0 TO 79                  'draw 80 columns of bytes
   DEF SEG = &HA000                 'display starts at &ha000
   i = (display% * 2) - 1           'reverse left to right
   FOR j = 0 TO display% - 1        'do all lines of display, 350 or 480
      OUT GRADD, 4                  'select read map register
      OUT GRVAL, 0                  'select map 0
      sbyte = PEEK(j * 80 + col%)
```

```
      OUT GRADD, 4                    'select read map register
      OUT GRVAL, 2                    'select map 2
       sbyte = sbyte OR PEEK(j * 80 + col%)
      OUT GRADD, 4                    'select read map register
      OUT GRVAL, 3                    'select map 3
       sbyte = sbyte OR PEEK(j * 80 + col%)
      buf%(i) = sbyte
      i = i - 1
      buf%(i) = sbyte                 'double each byte
      i = i - 1                       'next group
   NEXT j
   numbytes = display% * 2
   hibyte = numbytes \ 256
   lobyte = numbytes - (hibyte * 256)
   LPRINT esc$; ctrlchar$; CHR$(lobyte); CHR$(hibyte); 'set up
                                      '960-bit graphics
   FOR i = 0 TO (display% * 2) - 1         'up to 960 bytes across
      LPRINT CHR$(buf%(i));
   NEXT i
   LPRINT                                  'advance paper by 24/216 in
NEXT col%                                  'on to next column
LPRINT CHR$(12);                           'eject page
END SUB
```

PRINTING SPECIAL CHARACTERS

Some of the characters the printer normally interprets as control characters, with values between 128 and 159, can be printed as having character values by setting the printer to use character set number 2. To do this, you need to send the printer the code ESC$;"6"; once to change to this set:

```
LPRINT esc$;"6";          'change to character set 2
```

The characters available only in set 2 are those shown in the table in Chapter 9 between 128 and 159. Those in character set 1 at those values are:

128	NUL	145	DC1	Select printer
135	Bell	146	DC2	Set 10 cpi
136	Backspace	147	DC3	Deselect printer
137	Tab	148	DC4	Cancel double width
138	Linefeed	152	Can	Cancel printing

139	Vertical Tab	155	ESC	Escape
140	Formfeed			
141	Carriage Return			

Note that these characters have values that are exactly 128 higher than the original values shown in the lower part of the table. These are provided for compatibility with older software which sends some control characters with bit 7 set.

13 Introduction to DOS

The disk operating system available for your PC is referred to as DOS. So far there have been eight versions of DOS, of which only the last five handle hard disk drives well: 2.1, 3.0, 3.1, 3.2, and 3.3. These versions differ primarily in the hardware they handle: different types of floppy disks, hard disks, and computer models. The commands and file structure among these versions is more or less the same, and we will treat them all as "DOS" in this chapter.

STARTING YOUR COMPUTER

When you start a PC that has only floppy disk drives, you must put a diskette in drive A: containing a copy of DOS. The code in the read-only memory (ROM) of the PC looks for a diskette in drive A: and then for a hard disk when it starts up. A DOS diskette has a file on it called COMMAND.COM, which is the command interpreter for DOS and is the program which interprets and executes commands such as DIR, DEL, and COPY.

The diskette also has two hidden system files which contain links to the code stored in the ROM of the PC, called IBMBIO.COM and IBMDOS-.COM. It is these files and the links to the ROM code that differentiate the DOS which will run on IBM PCs from the DOS which will run on IBM clones.

If you have a hard disk on your computer, it too has the three files COMMAND.COM, IBMBIO.COM, and IBMDOS.COM in its main directory. If there is no disk in drive A: and there is a hard disk on your computer, the ROM startup code looks for these files on the hard disk and runs them to start the DOS program.

In both cases, the DOS program starts and eventually types the "C>" prompt indicating that DOS is ready to accept commands. DOS is so designed that if it does not recognize a command as one of its few resident commands, it looks for a file by that name having the extension .COM or .EXE and loads and runs it.

Finally, DOS looks for the batch file AUTOEXEC.BAT and executes all the commands it contains. This is a useful place to put programs you always wish to run such as desktop managers, keyboard editors, color-setting programs and the PATH commands we will discuss in this chapter.

BASIC DOS COMMANDS

All DOS commands can be typed in either upper or lower case. A few are resident, and the rest are actually programs that are loaded and executed. Some of the most common commands are:

`type file`	Lists any file on the screen.
`dir`	Lists the directory for the current drive.
`copy file1 file2`	Copies one file to another.
`del file`	Deletes a file.
`ren file1 file2`	Renames *file1* as *file2.*

All DOS commands and filenames are *case insensitive:* you can type them in upper or lowercase or a mixture and they will be treated identically. In fact, DOS translates all such commands into uppercase before interpreting them.

FILENAMES IN DOS

All files on your disk or diskette have names which are made up of a one- to eight-character *name* and a zero to three-character *extension.* When you get a listing of the files on your disk using the DIR command, they will be listed with a space separating the filename and the extension. However, if you want to type this filename, you type it with a *dot* between the name and the extension. This dot is not actually part of the name, but serves to make the separation clear between the name and the extension:

`A`	`EXE`	Referred to as A.EXE
`AUTOEXEC`	`BAT`	Referred to as AUTOEXEC.BAT
`QB`	`EXE`	Referred to as QB.EXE
`COMMAND`	`COM`	Referred to as COMMAND.COM

Filenames may consist of any combination of alphabetic or numeric characters, but most punctuation characters are illegal and cannot be used in filenames. The following characters can *not* be used in a filename:

```
. " / \ [ ] : | < > + = ; ,
```

Note that the hyphen (-) and underscore (_) can be used in filenames and often are. Unlike some other systems, filenames in DOS can start with numbers. Thus, the popular spreadsheet program can be called 123.EXE.

It is quite common for related files to have the same base name but different extensions. Thus a QuickBASIC program source will have the name TEMP.BAS, the compiled program TEMP.EXE, and the intermediate file generated for linking would be named TEMP.OBJ.

DOS WILDCARD CHARACTERS

Many DOS commands allow you to operate on a group of files by specifying filenames which include a *wildcard* character, which can represent any character. DOS allows you to use the question mark (?) to represent any single character and the asterisk (*) to represent a group of characters:

`dir *.exe`	Lists names of all files with the .EXE extension.
`dir ?team.tea`	Shows all files with the name *x*TEAM.TEA where *x* can be any character.
`del ?tea*.*`	Deletes files whose second through fourth characters are TEA.

THE DIR COMMAND

You can use the DIR command to list the names of all files in the current directory on the current device. If the prompt is "C>", the current device is hard disk C. If the prompt is "A>", the current device is diskette A:. The files listed are only those in the current subdirectory as described below. The DIR command can be modified with two "switches" as follows:

`dir/w`	Lists all filenames, five per line without details of size and date.
`dir/p`	Pauses at the end of each screen of files and waits for a key to be pressed.

THE COPY COMMAND

The COPY command is used primarily to copy files from one drive to another:

`copy a:*.* c:`	copies all files on drive A: to drive C:

You do not need to specify the filename over again if it is the same. You can also use the COPY command to make a copy of a file on the same drive using another name for backup purposes:

```
copy file.ext filenew.ext
```

FORMATTING DISKS AND DISKETTES

One of the first programs you learn to use when you start using DOS is the FORMAT command. The format program is started whenever you type FORMAT followed by a drive name. In most systems, diskette drives are called "a:" and "b:", and hard disks are called "c:" and "d:." If you give the command

```
format a:
```

the program will start and print the message

```
Insert diskette in drive a: and press Enter
```

When you do this, the program will begin writing format information on the diskette: each track and sector are numbered so they can be found by programs trying to write data on them.

If you want to create a diskette with the DOS system files on it, you instead give the command

```
format a:/s
```

which will format and copy the COMMAND.COM, IBMBIO.COM, and IBMDOS.COM files.

To format a hard disk, you must do two things. First run the program FDISK, which writes information on track zero of the disk describing how it is partitioned; then format the disk using the FORMAT program. You *always* format the C disk using the /S switch to transfer the system files:

```
format c:/s
```

DIRECTORIES AND SUBDIRECTORIES

If you are used to working with diskette-only systems, you may not be familiar with the concept of subdirectories. If you regard the directory of all the files on the disk as a file drawer, then the *subdirectories* can be conceptually regarded as large file folders containing smaller files.

It is important that you recognize the limitations of the DOS file system and use the subdirectory approach to organize your files more effectively. Even on a diskette a collection of 50–60 files can be somewhat confusing, especially if they are files with several purposes. It is more logical to group them by function and store them on the diskette with each group in its own subdirectory. The directory of a well-organized diskette might consist only of subdirectory entries, with each subdirectory containing 10–20 related files.

To create subdirectories, you use the MKDIR command. Let us suppose that we want to store files relating to spectra, spectrum-processing programs, reports, letters, and plotting. We might create subdirectories named SPECTRA, PROC, REPORTS, LETTERS, and PLOTS:

```
mkdir spectra
mkdir proc
mkdir reports
mkdir letters
mkdir plots
```

This command can also be abbreviated as MD, so we could type

```
md spectra
md proc
```

etc. Then to access files in these subdirectories, we must either make those subdirectories the current subdirectory using the CHDIR command, or we must tell DOS to always look in that subdirectory by entering that subdirectory in the PATH list. To change to a subdirectory, we type one of the following:

```
chdir \proc
cd \proc
```

Then, if we give the DIR command to look at the directory, we will see only the files in that subdirectory. This not only decreases clutter, but allows you to organize your thoughts and files more logically. The backslash character (\) is used to start a pathname at the root directory:

```
cd \proc            look for subdirectory at root level
```

If you omit the backslash, DOS looks for a subdirectory below the directory you are in currently:

```
cd proc             look for lower level subdirectory PROC
```

Thus, if you are in the subdirectory \DATA and type

```
cd proc
```

DOS will put you in the directory subsidiary to DATA named PROC, or \DATA\PROC. The command

```
cd\
```

will return you to the root directory, but the command

```
cd
```

will simply print out the name of the current subdirectory.

THE IMPORTANCE OF SUBDIRECTORIES

The main reason for adopting subdirectories is clearly for organization. On diskettes, however, there is a more compelling reason whenever you have a large number of small files: a main directory can only hold 112 files no matter how small the files are. It is perfectly possible for a diskette to have 280,000 bytes of free space but have no room in the directory to store another file.

To avoid this annoying and confusing occurrence, you should store all related files in subdirectories together. There is no limit to the number of files you can store in a subdirectory, since a subdirectory is in fact a special type of file.

On a hard disk, it is critical that you immediately organize your files into subdirectories by topic, since disks holding 20–40 megabytes are not uncommon, and even larger disks are frequently used. A well-organized disk will have only a few *files* in the main directory and a list of subdirectories. The subdirectories may themselves have further subdirectories to any level of nesting that you wish.

REMOVING DIRECTORIES

Once you are done using a subdirectory, you can erase it from your disk using the RMDIR or RD command.

```
rmdir proc        remove subdirectory "proc"
rd teams          remove subdirectory "teams"
```

This command will fail and an error message will be generated if these subdirectories are not empty.

QUICKBASIC COMMANDS FOR SUBDIRECTORIES

QuickBASIC allows you to create and remove subdirectories by using commands from within your program. These commands cannot be abbreviated as their DOS counterparts can:

```
CHDIR   "teams"     change to subdirectory "teams"
MKDIR   "proc"      make a new subdirectory "proc"
RMDIR   dirname$    remove the subdirectory in the string
                    DIRNAME$
```

THE PATH COMMAND

While you can apparently only access files in the current subdirectory on your disk directly, you can use the PATH command to tell DOS to look in other directories for files in the order listed in the command:

```
path c:\dos;c:\utils;c:\bin;\lib;c:\swim;c:\;
```

This command says that if the file is not found in the current directory, DOS should look in the subdirectories \DOS, \UTILS, \BIN, \LIB, \SWIM and the main or "root" directory C:\. However, you should note that DOS will only look for *executable* files having the .EXE or .COM extensions along the path, and not for other source files such as .BAS files or the text of documents.

When you start up DOS by turning on the computer or rebooting by pressing Ctrl+Alt+Del, DOS reads in the file AUTOEXEC.BAT and executes the commands in it. This file is the usual place to put the PATH command.

SUBDIRECTORIES AND THE DOT COMMANDS

If you create a new subdirectory and change to it, you will immediately find that there are two files in it named "." and "..". These files represent links to the parent directory and to any further "child" subdirectories. Note that these "dot" filenames are *not related* to the dot separating a filename and extension in a directory listing. For example, you might create a directory called \SWIM and then subdirectories called \TEAMS and \MEETS. The complete path to the directories containing the teams is

```
\swim\teams
```

and if you are in any subdirectory, you can change to the \TEAMS subdirectory by typing

```
cd \swim\teams
```

However, if you are in the \SWIM subdirectory, you can use the "." pointer to refer to the current subdirectory:

```
cd .\teams
```

Similarly, if you are two or more levels deep in subdirectories and wish to move up one level, you can do this with the ".." pointer by typing

```
cd ..
```

which will move you up to the \SWIM subdirectory from the \SWIM \TEAMS subdirectory.

SUBDIRECTORIES USED BY QuickBASIC

Usually, when you set up a hard disk, you put the executable files such as QB.EXE in the subdirectory \BIN and the library files BRUN40.EXE and BRUN40.OBJ in the library subdirectory \LIB. Then, if these subdirectories are in your path, DOS will have no trouble finding them. However, since DOS only finds executable files, library files have to be treated specially, and this is where DOS introduces the "environment" variable.

If you put a series of SET commands in the AUTOEXEC.BAT file, you can set variable names to be equal to any path you want. This is primarily used to allow you to put files wherever you want but still have certain programs know where to look for them. In the case of QuickBASIC as well as IBM programs such as IBM C, the library files are assumed to be kept in a subdirectory whose environment variable is named LIB. This is set up with the command

```
set lib = \lib
```

which sets the environment variable LIB equal to the pathname \lib. Note that you could keep your files in a subdirectory called RALPH, by issuing the command

```
set lib = \ralph
```

and QuickBASIC and other programs would find them correctly.

THE PROMPT COMMAND — KEEPING TRACK OF SUBDIRECTORIES

The usual prompt that DOS presents when you start up is simply the "C>" prompt. This is considered by many to be less than useful and even daunting by others. You can improve on what DOS prints out by using the PROMPT command. This command sets any of a number of possible values that DOS will print each time a prompt is generated. These are:

$	The "$" character
t	The time
d	The date
p	The current subdirectory
v	The DOS version number
n	The default drive letter
g	The ">" character
l	The "<" character
b	The "|" character
q	The "=" character
h	A backspace, erasing the previous character
e	The ESC character
-	A Return Linefeed combination to start a new line

The PROMPT command has the form

```
prompt $x$y$z
```

where X, Y, and Z are options from the above list. The most useful of these are the P and G options:

```
prompt $p$g
```

which print out the current subdirectory name, including the drive letter and a greater-than sign (>).

A TYPICAL AUTOEXEC.BAT FILE

Usually, you will include in this file the following commands:

```
path c:\utils;c:\dos;c:\bin;c:\lib;c\;
set lib=c:\lib
getclock
prompt $p$g
```

where the GETCLOCK program may read the clock calendar of an on-board clock calendar. This last is not necessary in PC/AT or PS/2 systems which automatically set the system clock from the battery-backed-up clock.

REDIRECTING INPUT AND OUTPUT

DOS allows you to change the input and output devices used by a program using input/output redirection and piping. The following characters can be included in a DOS command to indicate this redirection:

`< file`	Takes input from FILE.
`> file`	Puts output in FILE.
`p1 | p2`	Pipes output from program *P1* to program *P2*.

For example, you can get all commands to a given program to come from a file by creating a file such as SWIN.ASC and using it as the input to the file MEET.EXE:

```
meet < swin.asc
```

Conversely, if the program MEET puts all its output on the screen, you can redirect it to the file SWOUT.ASC and take its input from SWIN.ASC by typing:

```
meet < swin.asc > swout.asc
```

Note that the name of the executing program comes first, and the names of the input and output files follow in either order.

PIPING DATA TO THE SORT PROGRAM

One example of the uses of the piping feature (|) is the SORT program provided with DOS. SORT normally takes its input from the keyboard and puts its output on the screen. This is not very useful as it stands, but can be improved by using pipes from commands such as the DIR command:

```
dir | sort
```

will take the directory of the current subdirectory and pipe it through the SORT program and out to the screen in alphabetical order. You can also sort by date by starting your sort with column 24, where the data normally starts:

```
dir | sort /+24
```

More important, you can sort the directory and put in a new file called SORTDIR.ASC by typing:

```
dir | sort/+24 > sortdir.asc
```

14 Advanced Use of Files and DOS Functions

RECORD FILES

Thus far we have only discussed files as an extension of the screen and keyboard: those made up of characters that can be read and printed just as they were on the screen. QuickBASIC also allows you to keep files organized as *records,* where each record can be made up of *fields* of information, and each record field can be a string, a single precision or double precision number, or an integer.

There are two advantages to creating record files: random access and compactness of storage. A file which is organized in fixed-length records can be accessed at random simply by telling QuickBASIC the number of the record you want to access. If a substantial amount of the data in your records is numeric, there can also be a great saving of file space in using this format, since each number can be stored in binary form rather than as the characters that you type in or print out.

Integers are stored in record files in 2 bytes and single precision numbers in 4 bytes. In order to store them in this format QuickBASIC provides you with the TYPE declaration and the ability to define records as a collection of data types. The advantage of representing a number like 1.07465E23 in binary can be substantial: the written form takes 10 bytes, while the binary form takes only 4. This can be an important saving in space if you want to store thousands of data values efficiently in disk files.

DEFINING A RANDOM ACCESS RECORD FILE

There are two statements that tell QuickBASIC you want a file to be treated as a record file, the OPEN statement and the TYPE statement. The TYPE statement defines the positions and lengths of the variables in the record, and the LEN modifier to the OPEN statement tells QuickBASIC how long the record actually is. Suppose we wanted to make up address records for a group of people. These records might contain their first names, last name, address, town, state, zip code, and some account information such as an integer billing code and an account total stored as a single precision number. We first decide how much space to allocate for each member of the record:

First name	15	characters
Last name	15	characters
Address	15	characters
City	15	characters
State	2	characters
Zip code	10	characters (to accommodate foreign codes)
Account balance	4	bytes as a single precision number
Billing code	2	bytes as an integer
TOTAL	78	bytes

We next define a record consisting of these fields:

```
TYPE AccountRec                          'account record
  frname  AS STRING * 15                 'first name
  lname   AS STRING * 15                 'last name
  addr    AS STRING * 15                 'address
  city    AS STRING * 15                 'city name
  state   AS STRING * 2                  'state name
  zip     AS STRING * 10                 'zip code
  balance AS SINGLE                      'account balance
  billnum AS INTEGER                     'billing code
END TYPE
```

Then we define one record variable to hold the contents of a record read in from disk or to be written to disk:

```
DIM acc AS AccountRec                    'define record variable
```

We then open the file as a random access record file by writing

```
OPEN "account.rec" FOR RANDOM AS #addfile LEN = LEN(acc)
```

Note that we do not have to say "for input" or "for output" since we can read and write to any existing file record and add new records to the end of an existing file. In fact, QuickBASIC will insert the phrase "FOR RANDOM" automatically if you specify the record length with the LEN = modifier. Note that this way of defining records completely eliminates the complex and wordy FIELD statements.

DATA IN RECORD FILES

You can then access the data in record files using the GET and PUT statements. These statements read and write an entire record from the file to the file buffer area in memory, which is one record length long:

```
GET #1,, acc        'get the next record from file 1
PUT #2,, acc        'put the current record on disk in the next
                    'available space in the record file
GET #1,rnum,acc     'read in record number RNUM to the record
PUT #4,12,acc       'put the current record information in record 12
```

You can get data out of the record you just read in by referring to the record name followed by a period and by the name of the variable within the record:

```
GET #1, recnum,acc                  'read in record number RECNUM
PRINT acc.frnm ;" ";acc.lname       'print out that person's name
```

Putting data into a record is done in an analogous fashion:

```
acc.lname = "Smith"
```

You can read data into a variable using an INPUT statement in the same way:

```
PRINT "Enter name: ";          'ask for new name
INPUT acc.frnm                 'put it into the record field
```

READING A RECORD FILE

The following program illustrates all of the steps for reading a record file and printing out the account balances and total balance:

```
'Read in records from a record file and print out the total
'account balance
'--------------------------------------------------------------
TYPE AccountRec                      'account record
  frname  AS STRING * 15             'first name
  lname   AS STRING * 15             'last name
  addr    AS STRING * 15             'address
  city    AS STRING * 15             'city name
  state   AS STRING * 2              'state name
  zip     AS STRING * 10             'zip code
  balance AS SINGLE                  'account balance
  billnum AS INTEGER                 'billing code
END TYPE
'---------------------------------------------------------------
DIM acc AS AccountRec                'define record variable
'open the record file
addfile = FREEFILE
OPEN "account.rec" FOR RANDOM AS #addfile LEN = LEN(acc)

'read in the records until the file is exhausted, adding into
balance
sum = 0                            'sum of balances in file

WHILE NOT EOF(addfile)
   GET #addfile, , acc             'read in each record
   PRINT acc.billnum;              'convert and print billing code
   PRINT acc.frname; " ";
   PRINT acc.lname;                'print out names
   sum = sum + acc.balance         'add together balances
   PRINT TAB(40);                  'print out balance
   PRINT USING "$###.##"; acc.balance ' in $-format
WEND
PRINT USING "Total balance = $####.$$"; sum  'print out sum

END
```

CONVERTING VALUES WRITTEN BY OLDER VERSIONS OF BASIC

Older versions of BASIC, such as Microsoft BASIC, BASICA, and QB versions 1.0, 2.0, and 3.0 write single and double precision real numbers in Microsoft Binary Format (MBF). If you have data written with these programs and are now running QB 4.0, which reads and writes values in IEEE floating point format, you must convert these old values to the new binary format. This only applies to record files written with the old program and has no effect on calculations done internally to either program version. However, if you are reading such a file, you must use the following functions to convert the data:

```
real = CVSMBF(r$)           'convert MBF single precision data
double# = CVDMBF(d$)        'convert MBF double precision data
```

These functions only apply to the FIELD method of describing records as a series of strings. They are not applicable to the TYPE record format described previously, since this feature only exists in QuickBASIC 4.0. Conversely, if you are writing data back to files which you wish to keep in the old format, reconvert the data in the program to the old format in the record files:

```
lset r$ = MKSMBF$(real)     'convert single precision to MBF
lset d$ = MKDMBF$(double#) 'convert double precision to MBF
```

BINARY FILES

QuickBASIC also allows you to access files as *binary* strings of bytes, regardless of the meaning of the bytes in that file. This is particularly useful for reading files written by other programs which set up unusual formats. The syntax for reading such a file is

```
OPEN "foo.bin" FOR BINARY AS #n
```

In binary mode, you can read a string of bytes into a record:

```
GET #n, recnum, acc
```

where RECNUM is the byte number (position in the file) and ACC is the record variable. However, the size of these variables is not fixed, and you can read in any variable size you wish. It is important to note that in BINARY mode there is no record length value associated with the file as in RANDOM mode, and that it is possible to construct a file with a mixture of different record lengths.

You can directly access any byte in a BINARY mode file or any record in a RANDOM mode file using the SEEK statement:

```
SEEK #file, position
```

where POSITION is the byte or record number depending on the file type.

THE INPUT$ FUNCTION

You can also read any specified number of bytes from a binary or a record file using the INPUT$ function:

```
x$ = INPUT$(k, #n)   'read K bytes from file #N into string X$
```

The value of K, the number of bytes, can vary from one call to the next in binary mode. Note the unusual syntax of this expression—the file number is the *second* argument.

CALLING DOS FROM WITHIN QUICKBASIC

QuickBASIC provides a convenient way for you to call DOS commands from within your QuickBASIC program using the SHELL statement. It has the form:

```
shell command$   'execute command in string command$
                 '          and
shell            'start DOS command intepreter
```

For the SHELL command to work, a copy of the DOS command interpreter program COMMAND.COM must be available in the current directory or in your directory path. You can execute specific commands by putting them in the string following the command:

```
shell "dir *.bas/w"     'list short directory of .bas files
```

or you can start the command intepreter by giving the SHELL statement by itself:

```
shell
```

causes DOS to be loaded, to print out

```
The IBM Personal Computer DOS
Version 3.x
                Copyright 1987 (c) ... etc.
```

and then to print out the current prompt, for example:

```
C\BASIC>
```

You can enter commands and run other programs from this prompt. To return to your QuickBASIC program, type EXIT on the command line, and DOS will unload and return to your program.

ERROR HANDLING IN QUICKBASIC

Whenever you execute an input or output operation which involves any mechanical device, there is the possibility that an error will occur. Some of the most common of these errors are:

Error Number	Cause
58	Destination file already exists in rename
24	Device timed out
71	Disk(ette) drive not ready
55	File already open
53	File not found
5	Illegal value for function
62	Input past end-of-file
27	No paper in printer
7	Not enough memory for file buffer
63	Record number = 0 for PUT or GET

If one of these errors occurs, and you have taken no special action, and have compiled with DEBUG on QuickBASIC, will exit from the program after printing one of these error messages. However, if you want to intercept these errors and tell the user to try again, QuickBASIC provides the ON ERROR statement, which causes the program to jump to a specified location when any error condition occurs:

```
ON ERROR GOTO error.handler
```

where ERROR.HANDLER is a label of a routine to be entered when an error occurs. This is known as *error trapping* because the actual QuickBASIC program traps the error instead of letting the system handle it.

When one of these errors occurs, the program will automatically jump to the error handler routine, which must then decide which error occurred and what action to take. You can then return from the error routine using the RESUME statement, which has the following forms:

```
RESUME          'resume where you left off
RESUME NEXT     'resume at the next line
RESUME label    'where LABEL: names a location to continue from
```

The first two forms are the most useful, and are used depending on the nature of the error:

- If you can correct the error, you should resume where you left off. Use this form for printer errors, and when disk drive doors are open.
- If you cannot correct the error, you should set some flag and resume on the next line, so that the program doesn't keep trying to execute the same error over and over. Use this form for errors such as "file not found."

DETECTING THE KIND OF ERROR

The variable ERR in QuickBASIC always contains the number of the most recent error. It will usually be one of the numbers listed in the previous section, and you can easily check which one occurred and handle it accordingly. Since it is possible that other errors could occur while you are checking, it is best to copy the value of ERR into some other variable while checking.

The variable ERL always contains the *line number* of the last line which was numbered before the error. This is only useful if you number the lines in your program, and has little value in a modern structured, numberless program.

HANDLING "FILE NOT FOUND"

The error of a file not found by a BASIC program deserves special consideration, since it happens so often and since the error is easily corrected. For example, if the user of the program mistypes the file name he wants to use, the program should not "bomb," but should print an error message and allowing the user to correct his error. In the following routines, we create the COMMON variable FILE.ERR which is zero unless a file is not found in an OPEN statement. It is then set to 1 by the error handler and the program continues at the next line. Thus, if a program tests FILE.ERR after any OPEN, it can decide whether any action has to be taken. For example:

```
DO
OPEN filename$ FOR INPUT AS #1
    IF (file.err = 1) THEN                    'if there is an error
        PRINT "File "; filename$; " does not exist"
        PRINT "Enter new filename: ";  'get a new filename
        INPUT filename$
        file.err = 0                          'reset error flag
        CLOSE #1
    END IF
LOOP UNTIL (file.err = 0)
```

The complete program follows, illustrating how a number of these errors can be handled:

```
'Error handler program
'This statement must occur near the beginning of any program
'which handles errors internally

              ON ERROR GOTO error.handler

'now try to execute some statements that will cause errors:

'open a file that doesn't exist:
file.err = 0                         'set error flag initially to 0
filename$ = "glotch.foo"
      DO
      OPEN filename$ FOR INPUT AS #1
          IF (file.err = 1) THEN                    'if there is an error
              PRINT "File "; filename$; " does not exist"
              PRINT "Enter new filename: ";   'get a new filename
              INPUT filename$
              file.err = 0                          'reset error flag
              CLOSE #1
          END IF
      LOOP UNTIL (file.err = 0)

'Try to print on the printer
      CALL mesg.key("Be sure the printer is turned off")
      LPRINT "This will fail if the printer is off"
```

```
'Try to write to empty floppy drive
        OPEN "a:foo.asc" FOR OUTPUT AS #2

'Try a function with an illegal argument
        y = SQR(-18)

END
'------------------------------------------------------------
'Error handler routine
CONST FILE.EXISTS = 58, TIME.OUT = 24, NOT.READY = 71
CONST FILE.NOT.FOUND = 53, ILLEGAL.VALUE = 5, NO.PAPER = 27,
CONST ILLEGAL.RECORD = 63, DEVICE.FAULT = 25

error.handler:
        errnum = ERR    'variable set by  QuickBASIC

        SELECT CASE (errnum)

        CASE FILE.EXISTS
                CALL mesg.key("File already exists")
                RESUME NEXT
        CASE TIME.OUT
                CALL mesg.key("Device timed out")
                RESUME
        CASE NOT.READY
                CALL mesg.key("Printer or floppy not ready")
                RESUME
        CASE DEVICE.FAULT
                CALL mesg.key("Printer not on")
                RESUME
        CASE NO.PAPER
                CALL mesg.key("No paper in printer")
                RESUME
        CASE ILLEGAL.VALUE
                CALL mesg.key("Illegal value for function")
                RESUME NEXT
        CASE FILE.NOT.FOUND
                file.err = 1 'This is trapped by the main program
                RESUME NEXT
        CASE ELSE
                err$ = STR$(errnum)  'convert error number to string
                CALL mesg.key("Found error #" + err$)
                RESUME NEXT
        END SELECT

SUB mesg.key (mesg$) STATIC
   PRINT mesg$;
   PRINT ". Press any key to continue"
   k$ = ""
```

```
   WHILE (LEN(k$) = 0)
      k$ = INKEY$
   WEND
END SUB
```

ERROR HANDLING IN MULTIPLE MODULE PROGRAMS

QuickBASIC 4.0 requires that the line number or label in the ON ERROR statement be in the same program module. Upon entry to a routine in a module, you must enable error trapping with an ON ERROR statement which will be active for that module. This means that errors may be localized by module and each module can have its own error routines.

QuickBASIC also provides the ability to trap for specific *events* such as key presses, light pen and joy stick button presses.

```
ON event GO TO label
```

where EVENT can be

COM	characters received at a COM port
KEY(n)	pressing of a function key
PEN	light pen activated
PLAY	when background music queue is emptied
STRIG(n)	when joystick trigger is pressed
TIMER(n)	when N seconds have passed.

This event trapping is *not* localized by module, and a single ON statement will cause a jump to the event handling subroutine regardless of what module is executing when the event occurs.

15 Software Interrupts and Use of the Mouse

The 8086, 80286, and 80386 microprocessors used in the IBM PC, PC/AT and PS/2 families have a series of machine instructions called *software interrupts.* These instructions enable a program to jump to predetermined locations in memory where special code for handling these interrupts has been loaded. DOS allows you to set up such programs as handlers for interrupts and leave them resident in memory while you run other programs. It is through these interrupts that you can call DOS functions and functions for handling added devices such as the mouse. QuickBASIC does not have built-in calls to these software interrupts, but it allows you to make up a user library containing a call to the INTERRUPT function. This function is provided with QuickBASIC in the file QB.QLB, which you can load when you start QuickBASIC. The form of the calls is:

```
CALL INTERRUPT(intnum%, inreg, outreg)
        and
CALL INTERRUPTX(intnum%, inreg, outreg)
```

where

INTERRUPT	is the subprogram to use—*unless* the function you are calling *requires* the use of the segment registers DS and ES.

INTERRUPTX	is the subprogram to use—*when* the function you are calling *requires* the use of the segment registers DS and ES.
inreg, outreg	are records of the type RegType.

THE RegType RECORD STRUCTURE

The RegType record structures is a group of 16-bit integer values which are the names of the 8088 internal registers. All of the INT calls require that some of these registers be set to values and some return values in these registers. The INTERRUPT subprogram copies the values in this record into the actual hardware registers, and executes the desired INT call, and then copies the resulting register values back into the output structure. These records consist of the following fields:

```
'Define the type needed for INTERRUPT
TYPE RegType
     ax    AS INTEGER
     bx    AS INTEGER
     cx    AS INTEGER
     dx    AS INTEGER
     bp    AS INTEGER
     si    AS INTEGER
     di    AS INTEGER
     flags AS INTEGER
END TYPE
'
'Define the type needed for INTERUPTX
TYPE RegTypeX
     ax    AS INTEGER
     bx    AS INTEGER
     cx    AS INTEGER
     dx    AS INTEGER
     bp    AS INTEGER
     si    AS INTEGER
     di    AS INTEGER
     flags AS INTEGER
     ds    AS INTEGER
     es    AS INTEGER
END TYPE
```

Note that the two structures differ only in that the registers DS and ES are included in INTERRUPTX. You should only use INTERRUPTX where the DS and ES registers are specifically required. Otherwise, you should use RegType and the INTERRUPT call.

SOFTWARE INTERRUPTS

A number of software interrupts are used by the code in the read-only memory on the system board of your PC to control hardware functions on your system. The most important of these are as folows:

`int &h10`	Video mode control
`int &h11`	Equipment determination
`int &h12`	Memory size of system
`int &h13`	Diskette and disk control
`int &h14`	Asynchronous communcations control
`int &h15`	System services (modem, joystick)
`int &h16`	Keyboard
`int &h17`	Printer
`int &h1a`	System and real-time clock
`int &h20`	Terminate program
`int &h21`	DOS function calls, argument in AX
`int &h25`	Absolute disk read
`int &h26`	Absolute disk write
`int &h27`	Terminate program and stay resident
`int &h2f`	PRINT.COM interface
`int &h33`	Mouse driver

All of these functions are designed to be called from assembly language with the function numbers and arguments in the various hardware registers of the 8088 microprocessor. QuickBASIC provides a way for you to put these arguments into an integer array in a particular order and make a call to the INTERRUPT function, with the results to be returned in another integer array. The names of these registers are as follows:

AX	Accumulators A-D
BX	
CX	
DX	

BP	Base pointer
SI	Source index
DI	Destination index
FLAGS	Flag register
DS	Data segment register
ES	Extra segment register

Most of the functions listed above have analogs as statements in QuickBASIC. However, the INTERRUPT calls are particularly useful when you need to access new hardware devices which are not yet supported by QuickBASIC. In particular, while QuickBASIC uses the mouse for selecting arguments and functions from the compiler and editor, you can not use it from within your program in any simple way.

USING THE MOUSE IN QUICKBASIC

There are a number of manufacturers who make mouse products for the PC and PS/2, which have different hardware characteristics such as sensing methods and number of buttons. However, a standard for making calls to these mice has evolved so that all manufacturers now provide a *driver program* which allows you to call the mouse functions in the same way no matter which mouse you are using.

In the case of the Microsoft mouse, a program called MOUSE.COM is provided which you run when you start your computer. This installs the driver as a resident program which responds to interrupt &h33. Similarly, Mouse Systems provides a program called MSMOUSE.COM which operates in the same way.

The most useful functions which these drivers support include the following:

INT &h33	Function
AX = 0	Resets the mouse driver: on return, BX = status (−1 installed) CX = number of buttons
AX = 1	Shows cursor.
AX = 2	Hides cursor.

AX = 3	Gets button status: on return, BX = 1 for left down 2 for right down 4 for midddle down CX = current X position DX = current Y position
AX = 4 CX = x-position DX = y-position	Sets cursor position:
AX = 5	Gets button press information: BX = button(0,1,2) on return, AX = button status BX = count of button presses CX = X position when pressed DX = Y position when pressed

RANGE OF ARGUMENT VALUES FOR MOUSE FUNCTIONS

The mouse driver should be reset using function AX = 0 in the table above after you have put the screen into the mode you wish to use. If you are going to use the mouse in text mode, you do not need to do anything but call the initializing function. The rows and columns are returned as follows:

Screen	Column	Row
0	0 - 79	0 - 24
1	0 - 319	0 - 199
2	0 - 639	0 - 199
9	0 - 639	0 - 349
12	0 - 639	0 - 479

For two-button mice, the button number for function AX = 5 is 0 for the left button and 1 for the right button. If you have a three-button mouse, button number 2 indicates the middle button.

The button status function (AX = 3) returns the current state of all mouse buttons in a single integer. If the left button 1 is pressed, a 1 is returned; if the right button is pressed a 2 is returned; and if the middle button is pressed, a 4 is returned. If two or more buttons are pressed, the value returned is the sum of these values.

THE MOUSE CURSOR

In text mode, when you initialize the mouse driver, a square block will appear on the screen which you can manipulate with the mouse without any programming on your part. Drawing the cursor and saving and restoring the screen under it are handled automatically by the driver. Thus, you have a pointing device under your control which you need not program, but only read its position.

In graphics mode, the driver displays a diagonal arrow pointing towards the upper left, with the cursor's "hot spot" one pixel above and to the left of this arrow. It is important that you change to the graphics mode in which you intend to use the mouse in before initializing the mouse driver, so it knows which kind of cursor to display.

DESIGNING MOUSE FUNCTIONS

Since the mouse functions all require up to four arguments, we will set up a general subprogram named MOUSE which passes and returns these arguments:

```
SUB MOUSE (func%, arg1%, arg2%, arg3%)
'-------------------------------------------------------------------
' subprogram to call all mouse functions
' on entry FUNC% holds the mouse function number and ARG1% the
argument
' on return, all 4 may hold values from that function
'-------------------------------------------------------------------
DIM inreg AS RegType     'input register record

inreg.ax = func%         'pass function number in AX
inreg.bx = arg1%         'and argument in BX
inreg.cx = arg2%         'other arguments in CX and DX
inreg.dx = arg3%

' call INT 33 to pass arguments to mouse driver
CALL INTERRUPT(&H33, inreg, inreg)

' return arguments to calling routine
func% = inreg.ax
arg1% = inreg.bx
arg2% = inreg.cx
arg3% = inreg.dx

END SUB
```

Then we can set up some simple subprograms to call the MOUSE subprogram and perform the functions listed above. First, we will define some constant names for the numbers of the functions:

```
CONST MOUSE.INIT =      0   'reset mouse driver
CONST SHOW.CURSOR =     1   'turn cursor on
CONST HIDE.CURSOR =     2   'turn cursor off
CONST BUTTON.STAT =     3   'get mouse position and button status
CONST SET.CURSOR  =     4   'set position of cursor
CONST BUTTON.PRESSES = 5    'get button press count
CONST LEFT.BUTTON =     0   'arg to button presses to get left
                            button
CONST RIGHT.BUTTON =    1   'arg to button presses to get right
                            button
CONST MID.BUTTON =      2   'for 3-button meese
```

Then, it is easy to write a series of simple-to-use functions for handling the mouse from our QuickBASIC programs:

```
'****************************************************************
SUB buttonstatus (BUTTON%, row%, column%)

CALL MOUSE(BUTTON.STAT, BUTTON%, column%, row%)

END SUB
'****************************************************************
SUB getpresses (BUTTON%, count%, column%, row%)
'----------------------------------------------------------------
' Returns the number of times button number BUTTON% has
' been pressed since this function was last called
' COLUMN% and ROW% contain the column and row in the
' current text or graphics coordinate system.
'----------------------------------------------------------------
func% = BUTTON.PRESSES  'call with this one
arg1% = BUTTON%         'button number in this argument
CALL MOUSE(func%, arg1%, column%, row%)
count% = arg1%          'return count since last called

END SUB
'****************************************************************
SUB hidecursor

CALL MOUSE(HIDE.CURSOR, arg1%, arg2%, arg3%)

END SUB
'****************************************************************
SUB initmouse (instld%, mtype%)
'----------------------------------------------------------------
' Initializes mouse and returns type=2 for 2-button, 3 for
3-button.
' If driver is not installed, instd% is 0 and error is printed.
```

```
' Reset the driver after you are in the desired graphics mode.
'-----------------------------------------------------------------
CALL MOUSE(MOUSE.INIT, instld%, mtype%, arg3%)
END SUB
'*****************************************************************
SUB setcursor (column%, row%)

CALL MOUSE(SET.CURSOR, column%, row%, arg3%)

END SUB
'*****************************************************************
SUB showcursor

CALL MOUSE(SHOW.CURSOR, agr1%, arg2%, arg3%)

END SUB
```

Now, with these functions all defined, we can write a simple program to draw lines on the screen in graphics mode. This program simply initializes the mouse, waits for a button to be pressed and draws a dot at the point where the button was pressed. Then it waits for a second button press and draws a line from the original position to the new one.

```
' main program to display cursor and draw lines
 SCREEN 2                           '320 x 200 graphics mode
CALL initmouse(instld%, mtype%)     'initialize mouse driver

' If mouse  driver is not installed, print error message and
' quit.
IF instld% = 0 THEN
    PRINT "Mouse driver not installed"
ELSE                                'otherwise start reading
                                    'buttons
    CALL showcursor                 'turn on cursor
    RIGHT% = 0                      'count of right button
                                    'presses
    WHILE RIGHT% = 0                'loop until right button
                                    'pressed
        count% = 0                  'button press count
        WHILE count% = 0
           CALL getpresses(LEFT.BUTTON, count%, column%, row%)
        WEND
        PSET (column%, row%)        'mark that point on the
                                    'screen

        count% = 0                  'look for 2nd press
        WHILE count% = 0
           CALL getpresses(LEFT.BUTTON, count%, col1%, row1%)
        WEND
```

```
        'draw line between 2 points
        CALL hidecursor              'turn off cursor when drawing
        LINE (column%, row%)-(col1%, row1%)
        CALL showcursor              'turn back on when done

        ' exit if right button was pressed
        CALL getpresses(RIGHT.BUTTON, RIGHT%, column%, row%)

    WEND                             'while right button not
                                     'pressed
END IF                               'if mouse installed
END
```

ON KEY INTERRUPTS IN QuickBASIC

The ON KEY statement allows you to tell your program to jump to a particular routine when a specific key is pressed, usually one of the function keys. In order for the ON KEY trap to work, you must first have turned on key trapping with the KEY(*n*) ON statement. The value *n* is the code for that key and can be any of the following:

1 - 10	F1 - F10
11	Cursor Up
12	Cursor Left
13	Cursor Right
14	Cursor Down
15 - 25	User defined keys
30 - 31	F11, F12

While this method is not recommended for handling regular key presses within a program, it is particularly useful for handling abort-restart interrupts:

```
'Illustrates key trap
KEY(9) ON                        'turn on key trapping
ON KEY(9) GOSUB keytrap          'direct trap

WHILE (1)                        'endless loop
        i = i
WEND

keytrap:                         'key trap message printed
        PRINT "Key F9 pressed"
        RETURN                   'and continue program
```

You can define any key as one of the cases from 15–25 using the statement:

```
key n, chr$(scancode) + chr$(keyboardflag)
```

where the keyboard flag has the values

```
Shift   1, 2, or 3                'Shift keys are depressed
Ctrl    4                         'Control key depressed
Alt     8                         'Alt key depressed
```

and the scan codes are given in Table 15.1 below.

TABLE 15.1 Scan Codes for the PC Keyboard

<table>
<tr><th>Key</th><th>Code</th><th>Key</th><th>Code</th><th>Key</th><th>Code</th></tr>
<tr><td>Esc</td><td>1</td><td>Ctrl</td><td>29</td><td>Space</td><td>57</td></tr>
<tr><td>1</td><td>2</td><td>A</td><td>30</td><td>CapsLock</td><td>58</td></tr>
<tr><td>2</td><td>3</td><td>S</td><td>31</td><td>F1</td><td>59</td></tr>
<tr><td>3</td><td>4</td><td>D</td><td>32</td><td>F2</td><td>60</td></tr>
<tr><td>4</td><td>5</td><td>F</td><td>33</td><td>F3</td><td>61</td></tr>
<tr><td>5</td><td>6</td><td>G</td><td>34</td><td>F4</td><td>62</td></tr>
<tr><td>6</td><td>7</td><td>H</td><td>35</td><td>F5</td><td>63</td></tr>
<tr><td>7</td><td>8</td><td>J</td><td>36</td><td>F6</td><td>64</td></tr>
<tr><td>8</td><td>9</td><td>K</td><td>37</td><td>F7</td><td>65</td></tr>
<tr><td>9</td><td>10</td><td>L</td><td>38</td><td>F8</td><td>66</td></tr>
<tr><td>0</td><td>11</td><td>: ;</td><td>39</td><td>F9</td><td>67</td></tr>
<tr><td>- -</td><td>12</td><td>' "</td><td>40</td><td>F10</td><td>68</td></tr>
<tr><td>+ =</td><td>13</td><td>‘ ˜</td><td>41</td><td>NumLock</td><td>69</td></tr>
<tr><td>Backsp</td><td>14</td><td>L Shft</td><td>42</td><td>ScrollLock</td><td>70</td></tr>
<tr><td>Tab</td><td>15</td><td>\ |</td><td>43</td><td>Home 7</td><td>71</td></tr>
<tr><td>Q</td><td>16</td><td>Z</td><td>44</td><td>Up 8</td><td>72</td></tr>
<tr><td>W</td><td>17</td><td>X</td><td>45</td><td>PgUp 9</td><td>73</td></tr>
<tr><td>E</td><td>18</td><td>C</td><td>46</td><td>—</td><td>74</td></tr>
<tr><td>R</td><td>19</td><td>V</td><td>47</td><td>Left 4</td><td>75</td></tr>
<tr><td>T</td><td>20</td><td>B</td><td>48</td><td>5</td><td>76</td></tr>
<tr><td>Y</td><td>21</td><td>N</td><td>49</td><td>Right 6</td><td>77</td></tr>
<tr><td>U</td><td>22</td><td>M</td><td>50</td><td>+</td><td>78</td></tr>
<tr><td>I</td><td>23</td><td>, <</td><td>51</td><td>End 1</td><td>79</td></tr>
<tr><td>O</td><td>24</td><td>. ></td><td>52</td><td>Down 2</td><td>80</td></tr>
<tr><td>P</td><td>25</td><td>/ ?</td><td>53</td><td>PgDn 3</td><td>81</td></tr>
<tr><td>[</td><td>26</td><td>R Shft</td><td>54</td><td>Ins 0</td><td>82</td></tr>
<tr><td>]</td><td>27</td><td>* PrtSc</td><td>55</td><td>Del .</td><td>83</td></tr>
<tr><td>Enter</td><td>28</td><td>Alt</td><td>56</td><td></td><td></td></tr>
</table>

OTHER ON STATEMENTS

In a similar way, you can tell QuickBASIC to respond to interrupts on the light pen, COM port, joystick, and music PLAY command:

```
ON COM(m) GOSUB n          'when characters are received
                           ' at a COM port
ON PEN GOSUB n             'when lightpen is pressed
ON PLAY GOSUB n            'when music queue has less than 4 notes
ON STRIG GOSUB n           'when joystick is pressed
ON TIMER(M) GOSUB n        'causes interrupt every M seconds
```

where N is the name of a subroutine (not a subprogram).

These devices are activated using the commands:

```
        COM(n) ON          COM(n) OFF          COM(n) STOP
        PEN ON             PEN OFF             PEN STOP
        PLAY ON            PLAY OFF            PLAY STOP
        STRIG ON           STRIG OFF           STRIG STOP
        TIMER ON           TIMER OFF           TIMER STOP
```

16 Sorting in QuickBASIC

One of the most common tasks you have to perform in programming is the sorting of lists of data. These data can be either numbers or alphabetical lists, such as names. In his chapter we will look at several simple ways of sorting data, each a little more efficient than the last.

INTERCHANGING PAIRS OF DATA

All sorting routines have in common the need to interchange pairs of data points as they work through the data arrays. In BASIC this is done most efficiently using the SWAP command, which can operate on integer, floating point, or string data:

```
swap x, y         'interchange values of X and I
swap i%, j%       'interchange integer values I% and J%
swap a$, b$       'interchange strings A$ and B$
```

GENERATING DATA TO SORT USING THE RND FUNCTION

In order to test these sorting routines, we will use the RND function to generate 100 pseudorandom numbers. So that the results will be comparable, we will set the random number to the same starting seed using the RANDOM-

IZE statement before calling the function. For all of the sorting subprograms that follow, the main program has the following structure:

```
'Copy sort from one array to another
CONST MAX = 100
DIM x(MAX), todata(MAX)

RANDOMIZE (1.23)      'set the seed for the random number generator
FOR i = 1 TO MAX
  x(i) = RND          'fill X with random numbers
NEXT i
start = TIMER         'begin timing the sort

CALL copysort(x(), todata(), MAX)
finish = TIMER        'stop timing the sort
PRINT "total time = "; finish - start
END
```

In each case, the TIMER function is called before and after the sort so we can compare the times each method takes.

THE COPY SORT ROUTINE

The most straightforward way of sorting data is to search one by one for the smallest remaining value in the array, copy it into the next position in a new array and delete that value from the old array. This can be very simple to program and use, as long as you can select a suitable number to use to "cross out" the numbers you've already found and copied. For example, if the set of numbers is all positive, you can cross them out by negating, or if the range is known, you can use a very large or very small number to cross out with. In the following example, the value 1×10^{37} is used as a cross-out number.

```
SUB copysort (x(), todata(), N%) S
'sorts the array X into the array TODATA
'the array X is destroyed.

FOR j = 1 TO N%                   'scan list MAX times
   small = 1.0E37                 'set to be large compared to data
   FOR i = 1 TO N%                'look for smallest remaining value
       IF x(i) < small THEN
          isave = i               'save location
          small = x(i)            'and value
       END IF
   NEXT i
```

```
todata(j) = small                'copy next smallest found into to
                                 'array
x(isave) = 1E+37                 'blot out this value
NEXT j
END SUB
```

The obvious disadvantage of sorting in this way is that you require another array to sort into. This can lead to problems when the arrays are very large or when memory space is otherwise limited.

THE BUBBLE SORT

By far the most commonly used sorting routine is the *bubble sort.* The bubble sort can be done in place in the same array without any additional storage space. The routine works by comparing the adjacent values in the array and swapping them if the later one is smaller than the earlier one. This scanning process is repeated N times, where N is the size of the array, resulting in a sorted array from smallest to largest values:

```
SUB bubble (fdata(), N%)

FOR i = 1 TO N%                  'scan list N% times
   FOR j = i TO N%               'look for 1st value > 2nd value
   IF fdata(i) > fdata(j) THEN
      SWAP fdata(i), fdata(j)    'swap values if first > second
   END IF
   NEXT j
NEXT i
END SUB
```

THE SHELL SORT

For very large sorting problems, programmers often use the Shell sort. While the copy sort requires scanning the data N^2 times, and the bubble sort *N!* times, the Shell sort typically requires only $(N/2)^2$ passes through the data and is somewhat more time-efficient for large arrays.

The method works by scanning the array and comparing the size of values a fixed distance apart, such as half the length of the array. In any cases where the first one is larger, the values are swapped as before. The array is again scanned at this separation until no swaps occur. Then the separation distance is decreased and the process repeated:

```
SUB shellsort (x(), N%)
'Shell sort the array X of N% points
sep% = N%                           'start separation at N but
                                    'divide by 2 at once

DO
sep% = sep% / 2                     'halve separation
   DO
   swapflag = 0                     'set to 1 if a pair was swapped
   FOR i = 1 TO MAX - sep%
      IF x(i) > x(i + sep%) THEN
         SWAP x(i), x(i + sep%) 'swap if first > second number
         swapflag = 1               'set a flag showing a swap occurred
      END IF
   NEXT i
   LOOP UNTIL swapflag = 0          'repeat until there are no swaps
LOOP UNTIL sep% <= 1                'repeat until the separation is <=1
END SUB
```

COMPARISON OF EFFICIENCY OF SORTING PROCEDURES

Running the three sort programs on 100 random numbers will produce some interesting differences:

Time* to Sort 100 Random Numbers

	Without 8087	With 8087
Copy sort	13.01 sec	6.09 sec
Bubble sort	12.51 sec	5.55 sec
Shell sort	6.08 sec	2.64 sec

*Data obtained on an IBM PC/XT (R) running at 4.77 MHz.

The copy sort and bubble sort take about the same amount of time, but the bubble sort requires half as much array space to execute. The Shell sort requires less than half the time of either of the other sorting routines.

THE QUICK SORT

The Quick Sort routine is an extremely rapid recursive method for sorting data. It involves picking a random point in the list and sorting the points on each side by the same procedure. The sort exits when the a division results in only one member. A complete example of this method is included with the QuickBASIC 4.0 diskette set and will not be presented here. While it is quite rapid, it has the usual disadvantage of recursive programs that it may use up a substantial amount of memory in continually calling itself.

17 Matrix Algebra in QuickBASIC

A *matrix* is a square or rectangular array of numbers which has certain useful mathematical properties. Matrices can be added, subtracted, multiplied, inverted, and diagonalized using standard rules of matrix algebra. The matrix inversion and diagonalization methods are particularly useful for solving simultaneous equations and finding eigenvalues. While these matrix manipulation routines were part of the original definition of timesharing BASIC for large computers they are seldom part of BASICs included with microcomputers. Therefore we present the QuickBASIC code for these operations in this chapter. We will start by defining a few fundamental properties of matrices.

PROPERTIES OF MATRICES

If we consider the general matrix

$$\begin{bmatrix} a_{11} & a_{12} & a_{13} \\ a_{21} & a_{22} & a_{23} \\ a_{31} & a_{32} & a_{33} \end{bmatrix}$$

we see that we have written a square array of numbers having subscripts referring to their rows and columns, in that order. Matrices are often represented by a single capital letter, such as A. If A and B are two 2×2 matrices,

$$A = \begin{bmatrix} a_{11} & a_{12} \\ a_{21} & a_{22} \end{bmatrix}, \quad B = \begin{bmatrix} b_{11} & b_{12} \\ b_{21} & b_{22} \end{bmatrix}$$

then the matrix sum $A + B$ is obtained by adding together the corresponding elements of the two matrices. Matrix addition and subtraction is only defined for matrices having the same number of rows and columns.

$$A + B = \begin{bmatrix} a_{11} + b_{11} & a_{12} + b_{12} \\ a_{21} + b_{21} & a_{22} + b_{22} \end{bmatrix}$$

You can only multiply matrices together when the number of columns in the first matrix is equal to the number of rows in the second matrix. Then the product $A \times B$ is obtained by multiplying each element in each row of the first matrix by each element in the corresponding column of the second matrix and summing these products for a given row and column. If A is a matrix of m rows and p columns and B is a matrix of p rows and m columns, then

$$A \times B = c_{ij} = \sum_{k=1}^{p} a_{ik}\, b_{kj}$$

Multiplication is always row by column—with the rows of the first matrix multiplied by the columns of the second to produce the new matrix element. The order that you specify the matrices in is important: matrix multiplication is not commutative.

The following subprogram can be used for multiplying two matrices of arbitrary size:

```
SUB matmul (a(), b(), c(), M%, p%)
'Performs the matrix multiplication
'
'       C = A x B
'
'where A is a matrix of M% rows and P% columns and
'      B is a matrix of P% rows and M% columns


FOR i = 1 TO M%
  FOR j = 1 TO p%
     sum = 0
```

```
        FOR k = 1 TO p%
            sum = sum + a(i, k) * b(k, j)
        NEXT k
        c(i, j) = sum
    NEXT j
NEXT i

END SUB
```

MATRIX INVERSION

Matrices cannot be divided as such, but they can be *inverted*. If we define the *unit matrix I* as a matrix having ones in the diagonal and zeroes in the off-diagonal elements,

$$I = \begin{bmatrix} 1 & 0 & 0 & 0 \\ 0 & 1 & 0 & 0 \\ 0 & 0 & 1 & 0 \\ 0 & 0 & 0 & 1 \end{bmatrix}$$

we can define the inverse A^{-1} of a matrix A as one which when multiplied by the original will produce the unit matrix:

$$A \times A^{-1} = I$$

The most important use for matrix inversion is in solving a set of simultaneous equations, as we see in the next section.

SOLVING SIMULTANEOUS EQUATIONS BY MATRIX INVERSION

Let us consider a series of simultaneous equations such as:

$$\begin{aligned} a_1x_1 + b_1x_2 + c_1x_3 &= k_1 \\ a_2x_1 + b_2x_2 + c_2x_3 &= k_2 \\ a_3x_1 + b_3x_2 + c_3x_3 &= k_3 \end{aligned}$$

This can be written in matrix form as

$$\begin{bmatrix} a_1 & b_1 & c_1 \\ a_2 & b_2 & c_2 \\ a_3 & b_3 & c_3 \end{bmatrix} \begin{bmatrix} x_1 \\ x_2 \\ x_3 \end{bmatrix} = \begin{bmatrix} k_1 \\ k_2 \\ k_3 \end{bmatrix}$$

or just as

$$MX = K$$

where M represents the matrix of coefficients and X and K the column matrices (vectors) of variables and constants. If we rearrange this above equation, we can write

$$(M^{-1})K = X$$

which implies that the inverse matrix M^{-1} multiplied by the constant matrix K will give us the solution for the variables X.

Let us consider the equations

$$\begin{aligned} x_1 + x_2 - x_3 &= 4 \\ 3x_1 + x_2 - 2x_3 &= 1 \\ -x_1 + x_2 - x_3 &= 34 \end{aligned}$$

These can be written in matrix form as

$$\begin{bmatrix} 1 & 1 & -1 \\ 3 & 1 & -2 \\ -1 & 1 & 1 \end{bmatrix} \begin{bmatrix} x_1 \\ x_2 \\ x_3 \end{bmatrix} = \begin{bmatrix} 4 \\ 1 \\ 34 \end{bmatrix}$$

The inversion of matrix X will give us X^{-1}, which we can multiply by the constant matrix to give us the solutions for X. This is illustrated in the following program. It is important in inverting matrices that none of the diagonal elements become zero, or division by zero will occur. This can be avoided by simply rearranging the rows of the input matrix.

In this program, we read in these values from the keyboard, and have the main program print out the result.

```
'Matrix inversion routine main program:
CONST MAX = 20
DIM x(MAX, MAX), constants(MAX), solns(MAX)

'get the data from the keyboard
```

```
INPUT "Size of matrix: "; size    'get size of matrix
PRINT "Enter values of coefficients by row: "
FOR i = 1 TO size
    PRINT "row"; i; ":"
    FOR j = 1 TO size
       PRINT "  "; j; ":";
       INPUT x(i, j)                'get matrix row
    NEXT j
    PRINT "Constant for row"; i; ":";
    INPUT constants(i)              'get constants
NEXT i

CALL matinv(x(), size, determ)    'invert the matrix

IF determ = 0 THEN
   PRINT "Matrix is singular"     'check for singularity
ELSE

'calculate the  solutions to the matrix
   FOR i = 1 TO size
      solns(i) = 0
      FOR j = 1 TO size
         solns(i) = solns(i) + x(i, j) * constants(j)
      NEXT j
   NEXT i

PRINT "Solutions of equations:"
FOR i = 1 TO size
   PRINT i, solns(i)
NEXT i
END IF
END
'*****************************************************************
'Matrix inversion procedure:
SUB matinv (a(), n, determ)

'This subprogram inverts a real symmetric matrix of size N x N.
'following the procedure given by Johnson.
'The routine assumes nonzero diagonal elements. If the matrix
'is singular, the variable DETERM is set to zero.

CONST tol = 1E-34                 'very close to zero

DIM ipv%(n, 3)
determ = 1!                       'start with nonzero determinant

FOR j = 1 TO n
       ipv%(j, 3) = 0             'initialize pivot numbers
NEXT j
```

```
i = 1
DO                                          'until I > N or determ is zero
   'search for pivot element
   amax = 0!
   FOR j = 1 TO n
      IF ipv%(j, 3) <> 1 THEN
         FOR k = 1 TO n
            IF ipv%(k, 3) <> 1 THEN
               IF amax < ABS(a(j, k)) THEN
                  irow = j                  'save row and column
                  icolumn = k               ' of pivot element
                  amax = ABS(a(j, k))
               END IF
            END IF
         NEXT k
      END IF
   NEXT j

'if pivot element is near 0 the determinant will be 0
IF amax <= tol THEN
   determ = 0   'you could use a GOTO statement here to get out
ELSE
   ipv%(icolumn, 3) = ipv%(icolumn, 3) + 1
   ipv%(i, 1) = irow
   ipv%(i, 2) = icolumn

   'interchange rows to put pivot element on diagonal
   IF irow <> icolumn THEN
      FOR k = 1 TO n
         SWAP a(irow, k), a(icolumn, k)
      NEXT k
   END IF

   'divide pivot row by pivot element
   pivot = a(icolumn, icolumn)
   determ = determ * pivot
   a(icolumn, icolumn) = 1!

   FOR k = 1 TO n
      a(icolumn, k) = a(icolumn, k) / pivot
   NEXT k

   'reduce the nonpivot rows by subtraction
   FOR k = 1 TO n
      IF k <> icolumn THEN
         t = a(k, icolumn)
         a(k, icolumn) = 0!
         FOR m = 1 TO n
            a(k, m) = a(k, m) - a(icolumn, m) * t
         NEXT m
```

```
      END IF
   NEXT k
   i = i + 1                  'go on to next i
   END IF                     'end of else clause
LOOP UNTIL (i > n) OR (determ = 0!)

'interchange the columns and modify the determinant
nswap = 0                                'this is the sign flag
IF determ <> 0 THEN
   FOR i = 1 TO n
      l = n - i + 1
      IF ipv%(l, 1) <> ipv%(l, 2) THEN
         jrow = ipv%(l, 1)
         jcolumn = ipv%(l, 2)
         nswap = nswap + 1           'count swaps
         FOR k = 1 TO n
            SWAP a(k, jrow), a(k, jcolumn)
         NEXT k
      END IF
   NEXT i

   IF (nswap \ 2) * 2 <> nswap THEN       'if # of swaps is odd
      determ = -determ                    'negate determinant

   END IF
END IF
END SUB
```

In this case the solution of these equations is

$$x_1 = 12$$
$$x_2 = 19$$
$$x_3 = 27$$

SINGULARITY

A *singular* matrix has a zero determinant. Singular matrices usually occur when the simultaneous equations are not independent, such as

$$x + y + z = 5$$
$$2x + 2y + 2z = 10$$

In such a case, the subprogram MATINV exits with DETERM = 0, and the calling program prints out this fact as an error message.

MATRIX DIAGONALIZATION

In scientific problems, a system of linear equations often occurs which can be solved by matrix diagonalization. Such a series of equations has the form

$$Ax = \lambda x$$

where λ is a constant, A is a matrix of coefficients, and X is a column vector of unknowns. Constant values which satisfy this equation are termed *eigenvalues*, and the corresponding X's are called *eigenvectors*.

We find that one way computer programs can be used to solve such systems of linear equations is by *diagonalizing* the matrix, or subtracting values from rows and columns in an orderly fashion, so that the result is a matrix whose only nonzero values lie on the diagonal. These values are the eigenvalues solving the equations. A second array which starts out as a unit matrix, if transformed in the same way, will contain the eigenvectors.

MATRIX DIAGONALIZATION AND MOLECULAR ORBITAL THEORY

In chemistry, the relative energies of planar cyclic conjugated molecules can be calculated using matrix diagonalization to determine the eigenvalues, which in this case are the energies of the various molecular energy levels. This theory, called Simple Hückel Molecular Orbital theory, says that we can determine the relative energies of conjugated molecules, having alternating single and double bonds, by considering only the overlap of the π-orbitals and writing down a matrix related to the connectivity of the molecule. For the simple molecule benzene, C_6H_6, we write down a matrix where all the diagonal elements are $\alpha - E$ and all the off-diagonal elements which relate to where bonds connect are β.

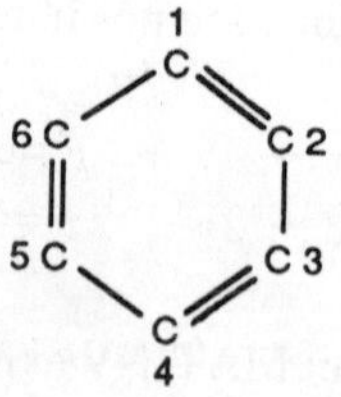

$$\begin{bmatrix} \alpha-E & \beta & 0 & 0 & 0 & \beta \\ \beta & \alpha-E & \beta & 0 & 0 & 0 \\ 0 & \beta & \alpha-E & \beta & 0 & 0 \\ 0 & 0 & \beta & \alpha-E & \beta & 0 \\ 0 & 0 & 0 & \beta & \alpha-E & \beta \\ \beta & 0 & 0 & 0 & \beta & \alpha-E \end{bmatrix}$$

By letting

$$x = \frac{\alpha - E}{\beta}$$

we can convert the above determinant to a matrix equation of the form

$$\begin{bmatrix} 0 & 1 & 0 & 0 & 0 & 1 \\ 1 & 0 & 1 & 0 & 0 & 0 \\ 0 & 1 & 0 & 1 & 0 & 0 \\ 0 & 0 & 1 & 0 & 1 & 0 \\ 0 & 0 & 0 & 1 & 0 & 1 \\ 1 & 0 & 0 & 0 & 0 & 1 \end{bmatrix} \begin{bmatrix} x_1 \\ x_2 \\ x_3 \\ x_4 \\ x_5 \\ x_6 \end{bmatrix} = \begin{bmatrix} \lambda & 0 & 0 & 0 & 0 & 0 \\ 0 & \lambda & 0 & 0 & 0 & 0 \\ 0 & 0 & \lambda & 0 & 0 & 0 \\ 0 & 0 & 0 & \lambda & 0 & 0 \\ 0 & 0 & 0 & 0 & \lambda & 0 \\ 0 & 0 & 0 & 0 & 0 & \lambda \end{bmatrix} \begin{bmatrix} x_1 \\ x_2 \\ x_3 \\ x_4 \\ x_5 \\ x_6 \end{bmatrix}$$

Then by diagonalizing the left-hand matrix above, we can find the energy levels of benzene. The eigenvalues and eigenvectors are given below. The energy levels are expressed in terms of α and β, which are generally not evaluated. The eigenvalues are

$$2, \quad 1, \quad 1, \quad -1, \quad -1, \quad -2,$$

leading to the following energy levels

$\alpha + 2\beta$ -----

$\alpha + \beta$ ----- -----

$\alpha - \beta$ ----- -----

$\alpha - 2\beta$ -----

and the eigenvectors to the coefficients of the individual wave functions:

−0.4082	0.5724	−0.0757	−0.5429	0.1963	−0.4082
−0.4082	0.2206	−0.5335	0.1014	−0.5684	0.4082
−0.4082	−0.3517	−0.4578	0.4415	0.3720	−0.4082
−0.4082	−0.5724	0.0757	−0.5429	0.1963	0.4082
−0.4082	−0.2206	0.5335	0.1014	−0.5684	−0.4082
−0.4082	0.3517	0.4578	0.4415	0.3720	0.4082

The matrix diagonalization subprogram used in these calculations is shown here:

```
'matrix diagonalization routine

SUB matdiag (a(), s(), n) STATIC

'This procedure diagonalizes a real symmetric matrix of size N x N
'using the method of Jacobi as described by Ralston and Wilf.

rho = .0000001              'small value to represent off-diagonal

'generate an identity matrix having off-diagonal elements = 0
'and diagonal elements = 1.0

FOR i = 1 TO n
   FOR j = 1 TO n
      IF i <> j THEN
         s(i, j) = 0!
      ELSE
         s(i, j) = 1!
      END IF
   NEXT j
NEXT i

'compute initial norm of matrix
nu = 0!
FOR i = 1 TO n
   FOR j = 1 TO n
      IF i <> j THEN nu = nu + a(i, j) * a(i, j)
   NEXT j
NEXT i

nu = SQR(nu)                'square root of nu

nufinal = nu * rho / n

DO                          'until n <= nufinal and no off-diagonals
                            found
```

```
  nu = nu / n
  FOR q = 2 TO n
     p = 1
     DO                    'until p> q-1
        off.diag.found = 0      'not found
        IF ABS(a(p, q)) > nu THEN
           off.diag.found = 1
           'save elements of pivotal set
           app = a(p, p)
           aqq = a(q, q)
           apq = a(p, q)
           lambda = -apq
           mu = (app - aqq) / 2!
           IF (mu = 0) OR (mu < rho) THEN
                omega = 1
           ELSE
                omega = lambda / SQR(lambda * lambda + mu * mu)
                omega = omega * SGN(mu)
           END IF
           sine = omega / SQR(2 * (1 + SQR(1 - omega < 2)))
           cosine = SQR(1 - sine < 2)
           FOR i = 1 TO n
              temp = a(i, p) * cosine - a(i, q) * sine
              a(i, q) = a(i, p) * sine + a(i, q) * cosine
              a(i, p) = temp
              temp = s(i, p) * cosine - s(i, q) * sine
              s(i, q) = s(i, p) * sine + s(i, q) * cosine
              s(i, p) = temp
           NEXT i

           'now do the diagonal elements
           co2 = cosine < 2
           si2 = sine < 2
           sico = sine * cosine
           sico2 = 2 * sico * apq
           a(p, p) = app * co2 + aqq * si2 - sico2
           a(q, q) = app * si2 + aqq * co2 + sico2
           a(p, q) = (app - aqq) * sico + (co2 - si2) * apq
           a(q, p) = a(p, q)
           FOR i = 1 TO n
              a(p, i) = a(i, p)
              a(q, i) = a(i, q)
           NEXT i
        END IF
        p = p + 1
        LOOP UNTIL p > (q - 1)
    NEXT q
LOOP UNTIL (nu <= nufinal) AND (NOT off.diag.found)
END SUB
```

18 Using the Fast Fourier Transform

In many scientific applications, data are acquired from some sort of instrument as a series of varying sine waves. Such waves may be sound harmonics as in speech analysis, data from infrared interferograms (1), data from nuclear magnetic resonance (NMR) free-induction decays (2,3) or even periodic chartings of stock behavior. In every case, these groups of added sine waves can be difficult to interpret, even if displayed or plotted for inspection. For example, consider the single decaying sine wave and peak in Fig. 18.1.

These plots illustrate the same data in two different ways. The upper trace is a plot of intensity versus *time*, and the lower trace is a plot of intensity versus *frequency*. In other words, time varies from left to right in the upper trace, and frequency varies from left to right in the lower trace. We refer to these representations as *time domain* and *frequency domain* respectively.

While you can determine the frequency by inspection in either trace in Fig. 18.1, consider the two waves coadded in Fig 18.2. These are again fairly easily distinguished, but the actual frequencies are obtained only with difficulty since counting the waves is somewhat harder.

Finally, in Fig. 18.3, we see a plot of a free-induction decay from the ^{13}C NMR spectrum of Pro-Leu-Gly amide, and its corresponding frequency domain spectrum (Fig. 18.4). In this case the frequencies are far too tightly mingled to discern in the time domain spectrum (Fig 18.3). The frequency domain spectrum (Fig 18.4) was obtained by the use of a *Fourier transform* on

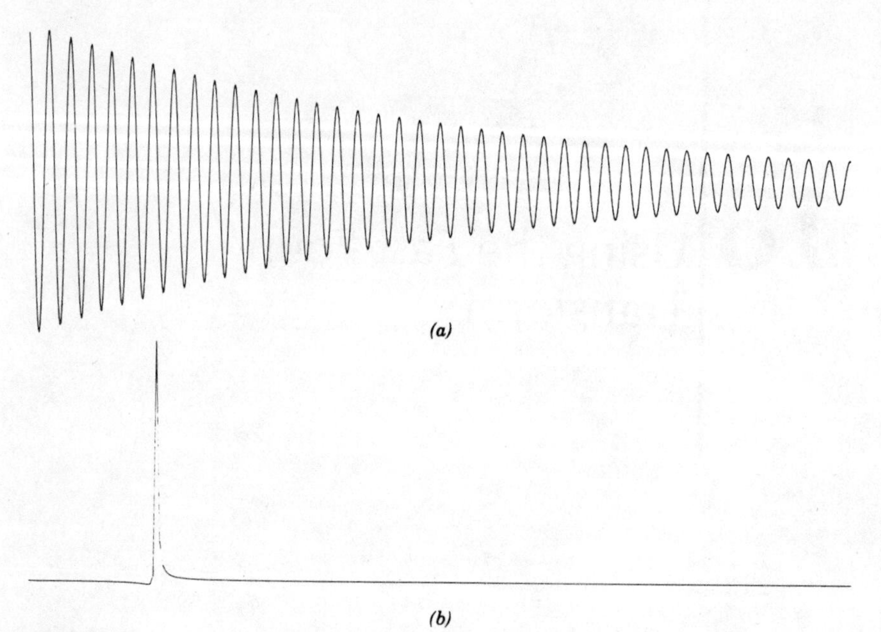

Figure 18.1(*a*) A single decaying sine wave. (*b*) The Fourier transform of the single decaying sine wave.

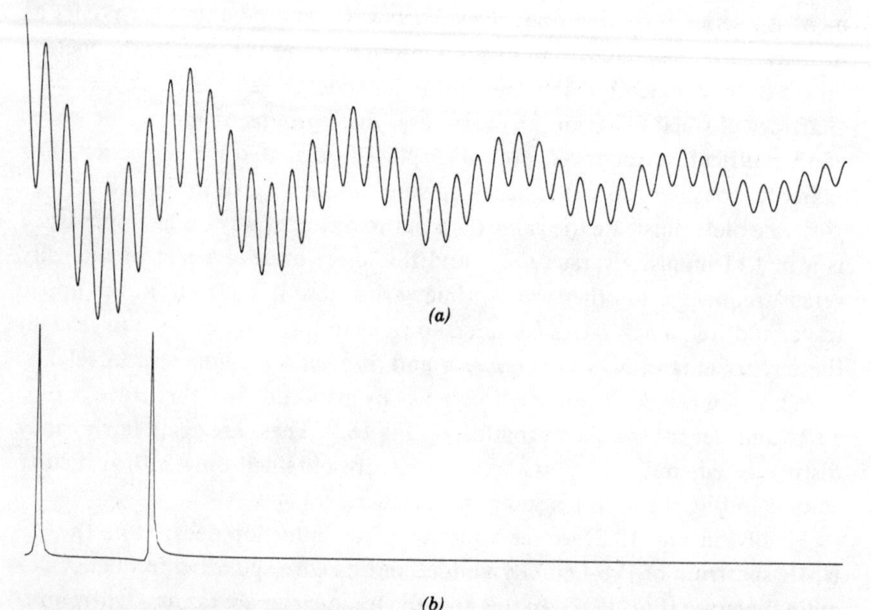

Figure 18.2(*a*) Two coadded decaying sine waves. (*b*) The Fourier transform of two coadded decaying sine waves.

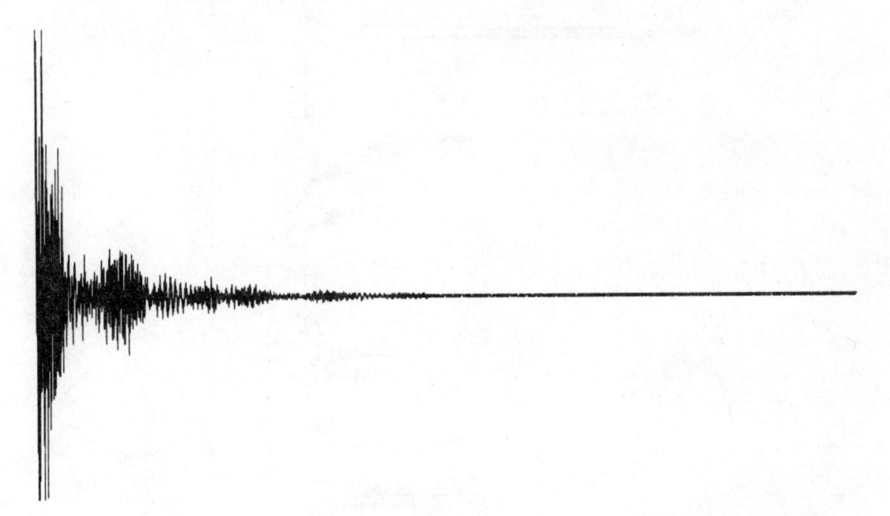

Figure 18.3 The free-induction decay from the ^{13}C NMR spectrum of Pro-Leu-Gly amide.

the original data. The conversion from time to frequency domain is commonly referred to as a *forward transform,* and the conversion back to time domain as an *inverse transform.*

THE EQUATIONS FOR THE FOURIER TRANSFORM

The actual transform of an array of time domain points X_k is given by

$$A_r = \sum_{k=0}^{N-1} X_k W^{-k}, \qquad r = 0, \ldots, N-1$$

where

$$W = \exp(-2\pi i/N)$$

In this equation, X_k is the kth time domain point and A_r is the rth frequency domain point. It is assumed that both arrays are complex numbers, having real and imaginary parts. We will see in the following sections how data arrays of purely real numbers can be handled.

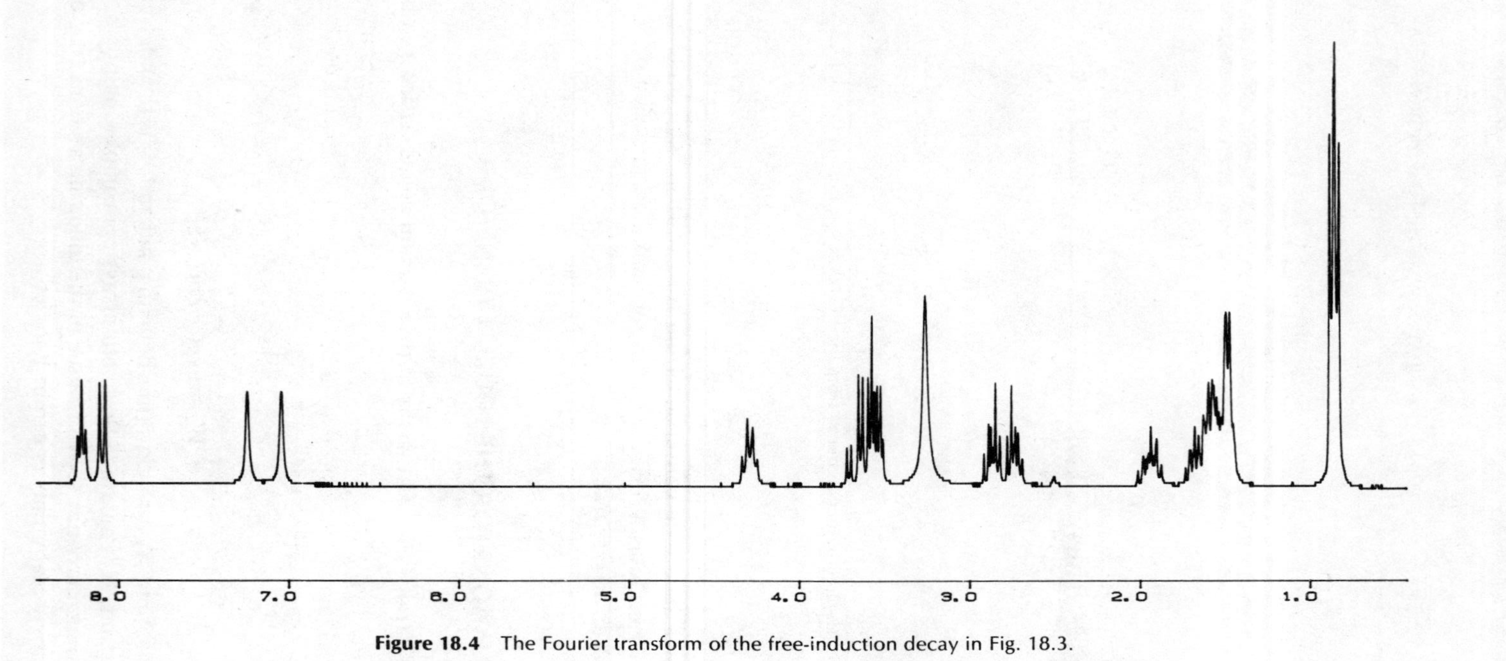

Figure 18.4 The Fourier transform of the free-induction decay in Fig. 18.3.

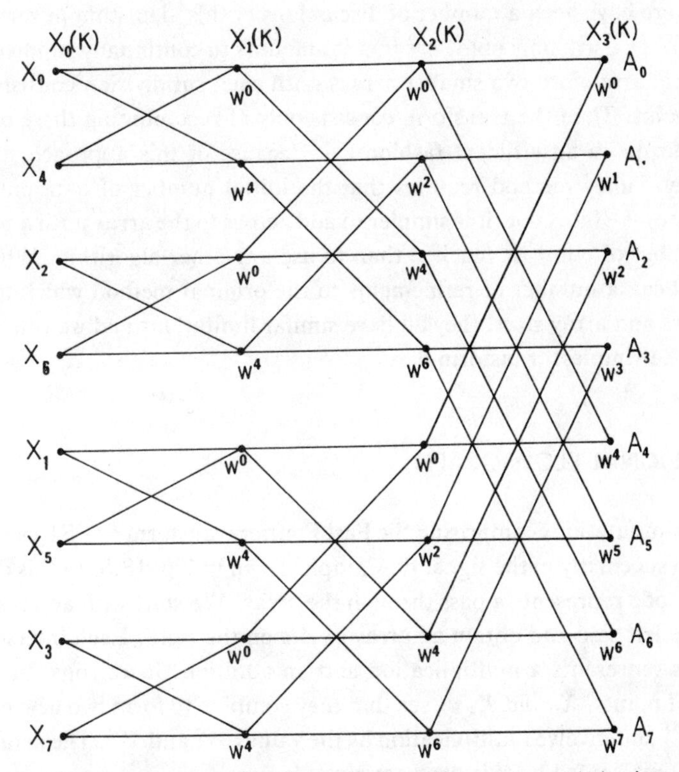

Figure 18.5 The signal flow graph for a fast Fourier transform, starting with the data points in bit-inverted order.

THE COOLEY-TUKEY ALGORITHM

Clearly such a series of operations contains N^2 multiplications of X's times W's. Since multiplications are the slowest of the common computer operations, the Fourier transform would appear to be quite time consuming.

However, in 1965, Cooley and Tukey (4) proposed an algorithm or method for calculating the Fourier transform which was termed the *fast Fourier transform* (FFT) because it only required $N \log_2(N)$ multiplications. This can be an enormous savings in computation time. For example, suppose that we wanted to transform an array of 1024 data points. Using the conventional transform, this would require 1024 × 1024 or 1,048,576 multiplications. By contrast, the Cooley–Tukey method requires only 1024 × 10 or 10,240 multiplications, a savings of a factor of 102 in time.

There have been a number of discussions of this algorithm in various articles, and we will only note here that it amounts to continually subdividing the original array into two smaller arrays until each subdivision consists of only one point. Then the transform consists only of recombining these one-point transforms in an efficient fashion (5). Because of this approach, the basic Cooley–Tukey method requires that the initial number of data points be a *power of 2.* If it is not, it is simpler to add zeroes to the array until a power-of-2 number of points is reached than to use any other algorithm. While there have been a number of refinements to the original method which use other powers and array sizes, they all have similar limitations and we will illustrate only the simplest transform here.

THE SIGNAL FLOW GRAPH

The computations comprising the Fast Fourier transform or FFT can be illustrated succinctly in the signal flow graph shown in Fig. 18.5. In this diagram, each node represents a pass through the array. We start with an array of X's on the left side and obtain an array of A's on the right. Each intersection of points represents a multiplication and an addition. If we consider the first pair of points, X_0 and X_4 we see that they combine to form two new points X_0^1 and X_4^1 and involve multiplication by the values W^0 and W^4. The actual equations represented by this diagram are

$$X_0^1 = X_0 + W^0 X_4$$

and

$$X_4^1 = X_0 + W^4 X_4$$

where

$$W = \exp(-2\pi i/N)$$

SIMPLIFYING W

We see that if we are to carry out this computation, we must evaluation W efficiently. This can be done using Euler's formula:

$$e^{iy} = \cos(y) + i\sin(y)$$

This allows us to write W as

$$W^y = \exp(-2\pi iy/N) = \cos(-2\pi y/N) + i\sin(-2\pi y/N)$$

Since all of the X's are themselves complex numbers, we have the multiplication of X's by the complex numbers derived from W. It can be shown that if we write

$$X_1 = X_1 + X_2 W^y$$

$$X_2 = X_1 - X_2 W^y$$

and if

$$X_1 = R_1 + iI_1$$

$$X_2 = R_2 + iI_2$$

then we can collect terms and write

$$R_1 = R_1 + R_2 \cos(y) - I_2 \sin(y)$$

$$R_2 = R_1 - R_2 \cos(y) + I_2 \sin(y)$$

$$I_1 = I_1 + R_2 \sin(y) + I_2 \cos(y)$$

$$I_2 = I_1 - R_2 \sin(y) - I_2 \cos(y)$$

It is these equations that we will use in the FFT routine shown later.

BIT-INVERTED ORDER

If you examine Fig. 18.5, you will notice that the order of X's on the left side of the graph is not the usual linear order, but an apparently scrambled order:

Decimal	Binary
0	000
4	100
2	010
6	110
1	001
5	101
3	011
7	111

If we examine these numbers in binary as shown in the right-hand column, we see that if we read these terms backwards, we have the usual 0,1,2,3,4,5,6,7 order. In fact, the order that we start in is called the *bit-inverted* order, and this order can easily be calculated by reversing the binary digits of the indices and interchanging the respective X's.

THE COMPLEX FFT

The routine shown here will operate on an array *X* of N complex pairs.

```
        SUB fft (x(), N)
'       X is an array of real and N is the number of complex pairs
          CONST PI = 3.141592654#

'calculate NU = log2(N)
          nu = 0
          n1 = N / 2
          n2 = n1

          WHILE n1 >= 1                  'calculates power of 2 of
                                         complex size
            nu = nu + 1
            n1 = n1 \ 2
          WEND
          FOR i = 0 TO N - 1             'shuffle into bit-inverted order
              k = ibitr%((i), nu)
              IF (k > i) THEN
                 ri = i * 2 + 1
                 rk = k * 2 + 1
                  SWAP x(ri), x(rk)
                  SWAP x(ri + 1), x(rk + 1)
              END IF
          NEXT i

'The first pass is all addition and subtraction
x1 = 1
x2 = 3
          FOR i = 0 TO n2 - 1
            xtemp = x(x1)
            x(x1) = xtemp + x(x2)
            x(x2) = xtemp - x(x2)
            x1 = x1 + 1
            x2 = x2 + 1
            xtemp = x(x1)
            x(x1) = xtemp + x(x2)
            x(x2) = xtemp - x(x2)
            x1 = x1 + 3
            x2 = x2 + 3
          NEXT i

          deltay = PI / 2                'set up delta Y for 2nd pass
          celnum = N / 4
          parnum = 2
          celdis = 4
```

```
'       Each pass after the first starts here
WHILE celnum > 0
       celloff = 1
       y = 0

       FOR p = 1 TO parnum                       'do the number of pairs
                                                 'in each cell
           IF (y <> 0) THEN
               cosy = COS(y)                     'calculate sine and cos
                                                 'once each
               siny = SIN(y)                     'and use in all cells
           END IF
               i = celloff                       'start with top cell
               j = i + celdis                    'j is offset to 2nd pair
           FOR celcnt = 1 TO celnum              'do the same pair in
                                                 'each cell
               oldr1 = x(i)                      'save original values
               oldi1 = x(i + 1)
               IF (y = 0) THEN
                   x(i) = oldr1 + x(j)  'only add/subtract at
                   x(j) = oldr1 - x(j)  'first point of cell
                   x(i + 1) = oldi1 + x(j + 1)
                   x(j + 1) = oldi1 - x(j + 1)
               ELSE
                   r2cosy = x(j) * cosy 'otherwise use sines
                                        'and cosines
                   r2siny = x(j) * siny
                   i2cosy = x(j + 1) * cosy
                   i2siny = x(j + 1) * siny
                   x(i) = oldr1 + r2cosy + i2siny
                   x(i + 1) = oldi1 - r2siny + i2cosy
                   x(j) = oldr1 - r2cosy - i2siny
                   x(j + 1) = oldi1 + r2siny - i2cosy
               END IF
           i = i + celdis + celdis               'go on to same pt in
                                                 'next cell
           j = i + celdis
           NEXT celcnt
        celloff = celloff + 2                     'next position in each
                                                  'cell
        y = y + deltay                            'next angle
        NEXT p                                    'count total pairs per
                                                  'cell
        pass done, change cell dist and number of cells
        celnum = celnum \ 2                       'next pass has half as
                                                  'many cells
        celdis = celdis * 2                       'twice as far apart
        parnum = parnum * 2                       'twice as many pairs
                                                  'per cell
        deltay = deltay / 2                       'half as big an
                                                  'increment to the angle
```

```
'go back for additional passes until number of cells becomes
'zero
WEND                                        'while celnum > 0

END SUB
'****************************************************************
FUNCTION ibitr% (i, nu)

'bit invert J through NU bits
        k = 0
        FOR j = 1 TO nu
            k = k * 2
            IF (i AND 1) THEN k = k + 1
            i = i \ 2
        NEXT j

        ibitr% = k          'return bit-inverted value

END FUNCTION
```

FOURIER TRANSFORMS OF REAL ARRAYS

So far our discussion has been of Fourier transforms of complex numbers, where it was assumed that the array X alternated between real and imaginary coefficients. Such scientific data could come from the measurement of frequencies when two detectors are used, one set in quadrature to the other. This is common in NMR data processing but uncommon nearly everywhere else. Consequently, we need to know how to process arrays of purely real numbers which have no imaginary parts.

One of the simplest ways to process real arrays is to convert them into complex arrays with all of the imaginary coefficients set to zero. An FFT of such an array will give you the correct answer as long as you have room for storage of the expanded array.

A more sophisticated method for processing real data has been given by Brigham (5).

1. Using the original real data, arbitarily call every even point real and every odd point imaginary.
2. Perform a complex transform as usual.
3. Perform postprocessing on the complex result by applying a simple one-pass algorithm.

If B_r is the transformed array, we can obtain the desired real transformed array A_r by the following method:

$$A_r(n) = R_r + \cos(\pi n/N)\, I_p - \sin(\pi n/N)\, R_m$$

$$A_i(n) = I_m + \sin(\pi n/N)\, I_p - \cos(\pi n/N)\, R_m$$

$$N = 0, 1, \ldots, N-1$$

where

$$R_p = R_n + R_{M-n}$$

$$R_m = R_n - R_{M-n}$$

$$I_p = I_n + I_{M-n}$$

$$I_m = I_n - I_{M-n}$$

and

$$M = N/2$$

While the evaluation of the equations generate $N/2$ complex points, it requires $N/2 + 1$ input points. The symmetry of the transform allows us to calculate the first and last points separately:

$$R_p = R_0$$

$$R_m = 0$$

$$I_p = 0$$

$$I_m = -R_0$$

The postprocessing routine is given below:

```
  SUB post (x(), N)
' Postprocessing of complex data for real FT's
' converts output of complex FFT to alternating real/imaginary
' points
' from real FFT
' Input X is an array of N pairs of points, N is the complex
' size of the array
       CONST PI = 3.141592654#
       count = N / 2           'number of pairs of points
' start at ends of array and work towards middle
       first = 3               'start with 2nd point pair,
                               'pair 1 is unchanged
```

```
        last = 2 * N - 1            'pointer to last pair
        index = PI / (N)            'angle increment
        arg = index

        FOR c = 1 TO count
           sine = SIN(arg)           'calculate the sine and cosine
           cosn = COS(arg)
           rp = x(first) + x(last)
           rm = x(first) - x(last)
           ip = x(first + 1) + x(last + 1)
           im = x(first + 1) - x(last + 1)
           x(first) = rp + ip * cosn - rm * sine
           x(first + 1) = im - ip * sine - rm * cosn
           x(last) = rp - ip * cosn + rm * sine
           x(last + 1) = -im - ip * sine - rm * cosn
           last = last - 2
           first = first + 2
           arg = arg + index          'increment the angle for next
                                      'point pair
        NEXT c
        END SUB                       'end of postprocessing routine
```

DEMONSTRATION OF THE FFT

The FFT is best illustrated by example. The calling program below generates five sine waves at frequencies of 100, 200, 300, 400, and 500 Hz into an array of 1024 points, and then displays the coadded result shown in Fig. 18.6*a*. The FFT and postprocesssing routines are called, and the resulting transform is shown in Fig. 18.6*b*. Note that the coadded sine waves are multiplied by a decaying exponential function. This widens the peaks and makes them more visible in the plots. Furthermore, it simulates a number of physical processes, such as the free-induction decays of nuclear magnetic resonance. The transformed lines then have a Lorentzian shape, since the Fourier transform of an exponential is a Lorentzian curve.

```
'Fast Fourier transform test routine
CONST XMAX = 1024
CONST PIE = 3.141592654#

DIM x(XMAX)

FOR i = 0 TO XMAX - 1                 'set array to zero to start
   x(i) = 0
NEXT i
FOR j = 100 TO 500 STEP 100           'calculate array of cosine waves
cycles = j * PIE                      'number of cycles in wave
```

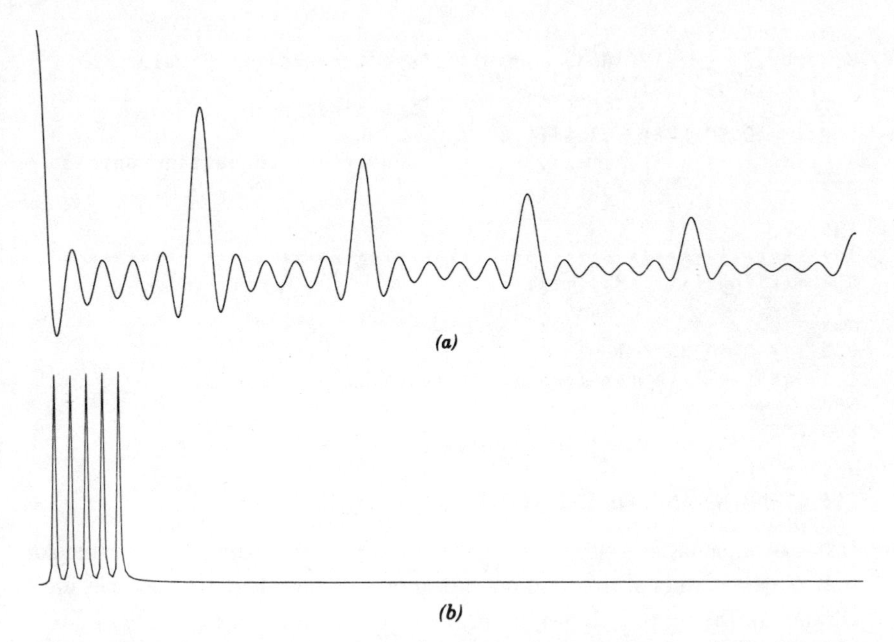

Figure 18.6(*a*) The coadded sine waves generated by the FFT test routine. (*b*) The FFT of the sine waves generated in *a*.

```
    FOR i = 0 TO XMAX - 1              'calculate test data
        x(i) = x(i) + 10 * COS((i) * cycles / XMAX)
    NEXT i
NEXT j                                 'apply exponential decay widow
                                       'function
FOR i = 0 TO XMAX - 1 STEP 2
    x(i) = x(i) * EXP(-10 * i / XMAX)
    x(i + 1) = x(i + 1) * EXP(-10 * i / XMAX)
NEXT i
CALL maxfind(x(), XMAX, max)           'find the maximum in the array
ymax = max * 4                         'set y scale to 4 x this maximum

SCREEN 1                               'set to graphics mode
WINDOW (0, ymax)-(XMAX, -ymax)         'define window for display

PSET (0, max), 1                       'draw first point
FOR i = 0 TO XMAX - 1 STEP 2           'display calculated data
    LINE -(i, x(i) - max), 1           'offset by max
NEXT i

CALL fft(x(), XMAX / 2)                'call the comple. transform
CALL post(x(), XMAX / 2)               'post processing converts to
                                       'real FFT

CALL maxfind(x(), XMAX, max)
```

```
ymax = max * 4
WINDOW (0, ymax)-(XMAX, -ymax)     'set scale of FT'd data

PSET (0, 0), 2                     'set first point
FOR i = 0 TO XMAX - 1 STEP 2
   LINE -(i, x(i) + max), 2        'draw lines connecting points
NEXT i

END
'*****************************************************************
SUB maxfind (x(), N%, max)

max = 0
FOR i = 0 TO N% - 1
  IF ABS(x(i)) > max THEN max = ABS(x(i))
NEXT i
END SUB
```

EFFICIENCIES IN THE FFT ROUTINE

It has been usual in writing FFT routines to provide a sine lookup table so that large amounts of time are not consumed in the calculation of sines and cosines. In the routine shown above, however, we see that each sine and cosine is calculated only once and used in all of the cells that require them. Unless the FFT is of an exceptionally large array, probably larger than the memory of a PC, the sine table is an unnecessary luxury, because calculating it once will occupy more time than calculating the sines used in the FFT will. Further, with the advent of math coprocessor chips such as the 8087, 80287, and 80387, the computational requirements are significantly reduced, as the floating point computations are now extremely fast.

In the case of the 1024-point FFT above, removing the computation of the sine and cosine from the FFT reduces the time for the FFT by 2.5%.

REFERENCES

1. P. R. Griffiths, *Chemical Infrared Fourier Transform Spectroscopy,* Wiley-Interscience, New York, 1975.
2. T. C. Farrar, *Pulse and Fourier Transform NMR,* Farragut Press, Madison, WI, 1987.
3. J. W. Cooper, *Spectroscopic Techniques for Organic Chemists,* Wiley-Interscience, New York, 1980.
4. J. W. Cooley and J. W. Tukey, *Math. Comput.,* 19, 297 (1965).
5. E. O. Brigham, *The Fast Fourier Transform,* Prentice-Hall, Englewood Cliffs, NJ, 1974.

19 Structured Programming and the GOTO Statement

If you have previously written programs in BASIC, you may have already noticed that we have never made any use of the GOTO statement. This is because the structured looping commands of QuickBASIC make the GOTO statement completely unnecessary. For example, the traditional way to read in lines of text from a file was

```
100 OPEN "TEXT.ASC" FOR INPUT AS #1
110 IF EOF(1) GOTO 200
120 LINE INPUT#1, S$
130 PRINT S$
130 GOTO 110
200 '......
```

Today, we can write the same code without these confusing GOTOs by writing

```
OPEN "text.asc" FOR INPUT AS #1
WHILE NOT EOF(1)                'open the file
 LINE INPUT #1,s$               'read in a line
 PRINT s$                       'print out the line
WEND                            'until end of file found
```

The use of these looping commands and the avoidance of GOTO statements is part of a programming discipline called *structured programming*.

Structured programming forces you to write programs in a more organized fashion, so that they are more readable and less likely to contain errors. Some of the main rules of structured programming are

1. Every loop and subprogram must have only one entry point and one exit point.
2. Programs should be designed from the top down, with the most general routines outlined first, and the calls to the specific routines written before the specific routines are written.
3. Programs should be well commented, describing their purpose and the method they use to accomplish this purpose.
4. Loops should be indented so that their nesting is immediately apparent to the eye.
5. Programs should not be *gullible,* as explained later in this chapter.

AVOIDING THE USE OF GOTO STATEMENTS

It is principle 1 in the previous list that leads to the avoidance of the GOTO statement. If any loop or subprogram can have only one entry and exit point, then it is not permissible to jump out of or into the middle of a loop using a GOTO. This is not as difficult as it sounds, since we have not yet used a GOTO statement in this text. Let's consider the case of avoiding division by zero, a common error condition that GOTOs are used to avoid. The traditional approach is illustrated by the following:

```
100 'Program to print out the reciprocal of the entered number
110 PRINT "Enter value: ";
120 INPUT NUM
130 IF NUM = 0 GOTO 110              'go back if zero
140 PRINT "Reciprocal = "; 1/NUM
150 IF NUM <> 0 GOTO 110             'get new value if num <> 0
```

A more structured approach would be

```
    'Program to print out the reciproal of the entered number
    num = 1                              'initalize value
    WHILE (num <> 0)                     'loop indefinitely
      PRINT "Enter value: ";
      INPUT num
```

```
   IF (num <> 0) THEN
        PRINT "Reciprocal = "; 1/num
   ELSE
        PRINT "Illegal value: exiting"
   END IF
 END                                    'exit when num = 0
```

When your program discovers an unrecoverable error deep inside a number of nested loops, some programmers make the argument that a GOTO is the only elegant way out of the programming dilemma. Such a case, and the non-GOTO solution is illustrated in the matrix inversion routine in Chapter 17. In this case, if a pivot element AMAX has become very small, the determinant will be zero and the matrix will be singular. Thus, there is no point in continuing the calculation. This is best handled by

```
IF amax <= tol THEN
        determ = 0      'set the determinant to 0
ELSE
  'do rest of subprogram
  '  :
END IF
```

The important thing about this approach is that the subprogram must have only one entry and one exit point. Then if you have to modify the subprogram later, or try to debug it, you can count on the fact that, whenever a call to the subprogram occurs, the beginning of the subprogram will be executed and the last statement in the subprogram will be executed. Any code that is not executed will be skipped because of an IF–THEN–ELSE statement or a SELECT CASE statement. Note that this stricture specifically prohibits such constructs as

```
IF max < 0 THEN EXIT SUB            'exit if < 0
IF ans$ = "N" THEN END              'end if "N"
```

Instead you should write

```
IF max >= 0 THEN                    'execute only if >= 0
  'program code
END IF
END SUB
```

and

```
IF ans$ = "Y" THEN                  'execute if Y
  'program code
END IF
END
```

PROGRAM GULLIBILITY

A gullible program believes that all the values it will receive are legal. It does not check for cases out of range, of the wrong sign, zero values, or unexpected answers. The most common example is asking for an answer of "Y" or "N" but not having the program check for any other answers. Some of the most common programming errors of this type include:

1. Not checking for answers other than those expected
2. Checking for only upper case text answers.
3. Assuming that the file you wish to open always exists.
4. Assuming that all variables are initialized to a desired value, say 0, or 1.
5. Assuming that there is a diskette in the drive or that the user is in the correct subdirectory.
6. Not checking for a zero or negative value describing the number of loops the program is to perform.
7. Not checking for "end effects." The first or last time through a loop may require special processing.
8. Assuming that the printer is turned on and has paper in it.
9. Assuming that the user of the program has exactly the same hardware you do. Ask questions, print reminders, or check the hardware status bits.
10. Errors in transcendental functions: square root of a negative number, logarithm of zero or a negative number, or a number too large to use as exponent.

It is important that you check before any critical operations to be sure that no errors can occur that will make the program fail. We have already illustrated how to check for hardware errors. Testing for the range of numbers allowed by functions is trivial but prevents awkward run-time error messages when a person unfamiliar with your program or with programming is using your program.

20 Plotting Techniques

In addition to plotting data on a graphics printer, you can also plot data on *x*–*y* plotters. Most of today's modern plotters are attached to the COM port of the PC and are driven using simple commands which are easily programmed in BASIC. The most common of these plotters use Hewlett–Packard's HP–GL or IBM's IBM–GL graphics language, a simple series of character commands followed by integer parameters.

THE PLOTTER COMMAND LANGUAGE

There are a number of commands in the HP-GL language; here we will illustrate only the most common of these which are available in all plotters. Some of the more esoteric commands are only available in the more expensive plotters.

The syntax of the HP-GL language is a two-letter command followed by a parameter, followed by a terminator. If there are several parameters they must be separated by a comma or space. If there are several commands on the same line, they must be separated by a semicolon. All commands except the label instruction (LB) must be terminated with a semicolon. The LB instruction must be terminated with an ETX character, ASCII 3. Table 20.1 gives the common HP-GL commands.

TABLE 20.1 HP-GL Commands

`CI r,a`	Plot circle of radius *r*, thru angle *a*
`LBstring etx$`	Plot label "string"
`PA x,y;`	Plot absolute to position *(x,y)*
`PD;`	Pen down
`PU;`	Pen up
`PR x,y;`	Plot relative to position *(x,y)*
`SI w,h;`	Set character size to *(w,h)*
`SP n;`	Select pen #n

The usual US 8½ × 11 plotter page or metric A4 plotter page is divided into 10,000 *x* units and 7200 *y* units, with a resolution of .025mm. While many plotters have some ability to plot in a user-coordinate space in floating point, for greatest generality it is better to convert your pen movements to plotter steps directly. This means that you determine the total number of plotter units in each direction and divide into the total number of steps to determine the number of plotter steps per coordinate unit.

Note that there is no "plot" instruction. The PA (plot absolute) instruction is used for both movement and plotting depending on whether the pen is currently up or down.

Different plotters have different numbers of pens in pen holders. The SP (select pen) instruction determines which pen is to be selected next. This instruction causes the plotter to return the current pen to the carousel and pick up the one specified.

SETTING UP THE COM PORT

The PC's COM port can be set to operate at speeds from 300 to 9600 *baud*, or bits per second. All commercial plotters will also operate at all of these speeds. There is no reason, however, for not operating at the highest possible baud rate, since more data can be transferred with less computer overhead. To set the COM port to 9600 baud, we use the OPEN COM instruction, which has the form

```
OPEN "COMn: baud, p,d,s " FOR OUTPUT AS #f
```

where

n = port 1 or 2
$baud$ = 110, 300, 1200, 2400, 4800 or 9600
p = parity N (none), S (Space), E (even) or O (odd)
d = number of data bits, 5–8
s = number of stop bits (1, 1.5, or 2)

Any parameters which are not to be changed from the default may be omitted. A typical setting statement is

```
OPEN "COM1:9600,S" FOR OUTPUT AS #1
```

PLOTTING X–*T* DATA

The routine that follows plots NUM% data points from a real array *X*, advancing ALT% points between plots (where alt% is 1 or 2).

```
SUB plot (x(), num AS INTEGER, alt AS INTEGER)
'plots a continuous series of equidistant x points across the page
xstep = 10000 / (num / alt)                'number of plot steps
max = 1E-30
min = 1E+30

FOR i = 1 TO num

  IF x(i) > max THEN max = x(i)
  IF x(i) < min THEN min = x(i)
NEXT i
range = (max - min) * 2                    'make the scale 1/2 of
                                           'full vertical

ystep = 7200 / range
OPEN "COM2:9600,S" FOR RANDOM AS #1
etx$ = CHR$(3)
PRINT #1, "SP1"                            'select pen #1  xpos = 0
ypos = 5000
PRINT #1, "PU;PA"; xpos; ypos; etx$        'move to first point
PRINT #1, "PD;"                            'put pen down
FOR i = 1 TO num STEP alt
  xpos = i * xstep                         'calculate the x position
  ypos = (x(i) - min) * ystep              'and the y-position
  PRINT #1, "PA"; xpos; ypos; etx$         'plot to that point
NEXT i
CLOSE #1
END SUB
```

21 Advanced Display Techniques

Thus far, we have only used QuickBASIC's built-in methods for displaying data on the screen. While these routines are quite efficient, we sometimes need to improve on them for special cases where large amounts of data are to be displayed. The important factor here is the response time your program will have in *changing* the display. The time it takes to draw it the first time is not so noticeable as the time it takes to redraw the screen once the first data has been displayed.

LARGE DATA ARRYAS

Let us consider the case of a large number of data points, such as might occur in an array which has been calculated and Fourier transformed. For example, suppose that we need to display a plot of 4096 data points on the screen, repesenting some sort of spectrum. Since there are only 640 pixels across the x-axis of any of the display screens, we would be drawing line segments between 4096/640 or 6.4 data points which will end up on top of each other. In other words, if we simply write

```
PSET(1,x(1))
FOR i = 2 TO 4096
  LINE -(i,x(i))
NEXT i
```

we will be drawing the lines between $x(1)$, $x(2)$, . . ., $x(6)$ all in pixel 1 on the screen. Clearly, even for this relatively small array, there is nearly sixfold wasted effort in using the LINE function provided by QuickBASIC.

DISPLAY BUFFERS

A more efficient method is to calculate a short integer array of the maximum and minimum points that will be placed in each column and use this *display buffer* to actually draw the spectrum. It is important that we use an integer array, because integer calculations are much faster than floating point calculations. To pack this buffer, we search points 1–6 for the largest and smallest values and put these into the first two points in the buffer array, then search 7–12 for the next maximum and minimum, and search 13–19 ($3 \times 6.4 = 19.2$) for the next maximum and minimum. When we have completed our search through the array, we will have a 1280-point integer display buffer representing the maximum and minimum values that will occur in each pixel column on the screen, and our display task is reduced to drawing a series of vertical lines in successive columns on the screen.

```
ix = 1
FOR ib = 1 TO 1280 STEP 2
  LINE (ix, ibuf(ib)) - (ix, ibuf(ib + 1))
  ix = ix + 1
NEXT ib
```

Here we are drawing 640 vertical lines instead of 4095 lines, and the display will be refreshed that much faster.

BUFFER DISCONTINUITIES

In creating this display buffer, it can happen that the maximum and minimum for one column do not overlap with the maximum and minimum for the next column, so that unconnected vertical stripes occur:

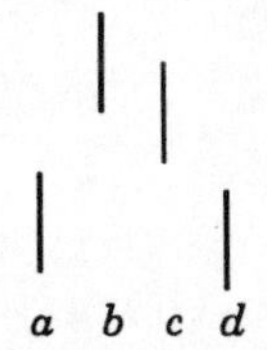

Column *a* has a maximum which is less than the minimum of column *b*, and column *c* has a minimum which is greater than the maximum of column *d*. Before displaying this buffer, you must scan it looking for these two types of discontinuities, and correcting them by extending the max of column *a* to meet the min of *b* and the min of *c* to meet the max of *d*:

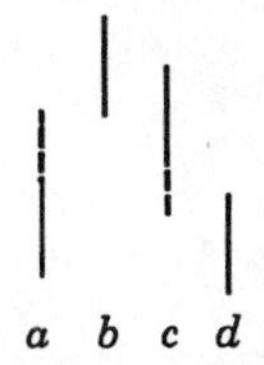

In the example that follows, we read in the file FT.DAT, create a max-min buffer as we have just described, correct for discontinuities, and then display it. We also look for keyboard commands "+", "−", and "Q" and use them to shift the display up and down and to exit from the program.

```
'Buffered display routine
CONST REALDIM = 4096, BUFDIM = 1280, FOREVER = 1
DEFINT I-N                    'NOTE all variables i-n are integers
'
---------------------------------------------------------------------
' x is a large array of real numbers
' ibuf is a small 1280 point array of integers representing the
' maximum and minimum excursion within each screen pixel column
'
---------------------------------------------------------------------


TYPE realdat                  'define single precision binary record
x AS SINGLE
END TYPE

DIM x(REALDIM), ibuf(BUFDIM), xdat AS realdat

'read in data file from disk
OPEN "ft.dat" FOR RANDOM AS #1 LEN = LEN(realdat)
```

```
dmax = -1E+30                                'and find the overall
                                             'maximum
FOR i = 1 TO REALDIM
   GET #1, , xdat
   x(i) = xdat.x
   ax = ABS(x(i))
   IF ax > dmax THEN dmax = ax
NEXT i
CLOSE #1

scale = 75 / dmax                            'convert x(j) to +/- 75
                                             'range

pts.per.column = REALDIM * 2 / BUFDIM 'number of points to be
                                             'compressed

ib = 1                                       'buffer pointer
j = 1                                        'array pointer
pend = j + pts.per.column                    'end of region for this
                                             'buffer
' -------------------------------------------------------------------
' For each packet of points, find the maximum and minimum values
' and scale them to be pixel values between 25 and 125
' -------------------------------------------------------------------
WHILE (pend <= REALDIM)
   xmax = -1E+30                             'initialize max and mins
   xmin = 1E+30
   WHILE j <= pend                           'find max and min in each
                                             'packet
      xj = x(j)
      IF xj > xmax THEN xmax = xj
      IF xj < xmin THEN xmin = xj
      j = j + 1
   WEND
   ibuf(ib) = 100 - xmin * scale     'save min and max in display
                                             'buffer
   ibuf(ib + 1) = 100 - xmax * scale
   ib = ib + 2
   pend = pend + pts.per.column      'on to next group WEND
'
--------------------------------------------------------------------
' correct any discontinuities in the buffer
' if a max is less than the next min make the max larger
' if a min is greater than the next max, make it smaller
' note that the signs are reversed since UP is a smaller pixel
' number
' -------------------------------------
FOR ib = 3 TO BUFDIM - 2 STEP 2
   IF ibuf(ib - 1) > ibuf(ib) THEN ibuf(ib - 1) = ibuf(ib)
   IF ibuf(ib) < ibuf(ib + 2) THEN ibuf(ib) = ibuf(ib + 2)
NEXT ib
```

```
'now display the resulting integer buffer
SCREEN 2
joff = 0
WHILE (quit = 0)
   CLS
   ix = 1
   FOR ib = 1 TO BUFDIM STEP 2
     LINE (ix, ibuf(ib) + joff)-(ix, ibuf(ib + 1) + joff)
     ix = ix + 1
   NEXT ib
   CALL getkey(s$)
   IF s$ = "+" THEN joff = joff - 10
   IF s$ = "-" THEN joff = joff + 10
   IF s$ = "Q" THEN quit = 1
WEND
END
```

CREATING A DRAWUP ROUTINE

Rather than using the general LINE function to draw these vertical lines, we can create a special DRAWUP procedure which is specialized for vertical line drawing and contains no routines for calculating how to draw the best diagonal line, since all the lines will indeed be vertical.

For the CGA display, this will require that the address of the relevant byte be calculated and the segment offset of &Hb800 or &Hba00 be used to determine the correct display memory address. Such a routine would be of the type

```
FOR ib = 1 TO BUFDIM STEP 2
  CALL drawup(ibuf(ib) + joff, ix, ibuf(ib) - ibuf(ib + 1))
  ix = ix + 1
NEXT ib
```

where

`ibuf(ib)`	is the value of the lower pixel
`ibuf(ib + 1)`	is the value of the upper pixel
`joff`	is the vertical offset
`ix`	is the x pixel address

Such a routine would be of the following form in QuickBASIC:

```
SUB drawup (irow, icol, icount)
' draws a line from row,col up count rows
iadd = (irow \ 2) * 80 + (icol \ 8)
```

```
ibit = jbit(icol MOD 8)           'get actual bit to turn on
IF (icount = 0) THEN icount = 1

WHILE (icount > 0)
    IF (irow AND 1) THEN          'calculate the segment address
        DEF SEG = &Hb800          'for odd rows
    ELSE
        DEF SEG = &Hba00          'or even rows
    END IF
    iword = PEEK(iadd)            'get current contents of this
                                  'byte
    iword = iword OR ibit         'OR in this bit
    POKE iadd, iword              'put it back
    IF (irow AND 1) = 0 THEN
        iadd = iadd - 80          'decrement address on even rows
                                  'only
    END IF
    irow = irow - 1               'next row
    icount = icount - 1           'continue till all done
WEND

END SUB
```

While such a routine is marginally faster than the original LINE call, the rate of display refresh is still quite slow, primarily because of the slow rate at which the PEEK and POKE instructions calculate the correct addresses from floating point arguments.

ASSEMBLY LANGUAGE INTERFACING

In order to improve the speed of this routine substantially it is necessary to rewrite a portion of DRAWUP in assembly language. While we will not attempt to describe the complete 8086/80286/80386 assembly language in Chapter 22, we will illustrate two such routines, and how to interface them with the calling program. For simplicity, we will assume that you can use the Microsoft MASM assembler, version 5.0, which has directives which are greatly simplified over earlier versions.

22 Elements of Assembly Language Programming

The fundamental reason for writing a routine in assembly language is to handle bit and address manipulation when it dominates over numeric calculation, as is usually the case in display routines. Such manipulations are always faster in assembly language because you can select the minimum number of integer instructions to get the job done without having the overhead which the compiler may impose on such calculations. For example, you can keep all the important values in registers and never store them back into memory unless they are actually needed later.

THE 80XXX MICROPROCESSOR FAMILY

The original IBM PC was built around the 8088 microprocessor, which has the instruction set we will be discussing here and an 8-bit data path to and from the chip. The 8086 microprocessor is a somewhat more efficient implementation of the same instruction set and has a 16-bit data path to and from the chip.

The 80286 microprocessor is the chip used in the Personal Computer AT (PC/AT) and and the PS/2 models 50 and 60. It has the same instruction set as the 8088 in *real* address mode, but with a few enhancements, considerably faster operating speeds, a 16-bit data path, and in *protected* address mode the ability to address up to 16 megabytes of memory.

The 80386 microprocessor is the chip used in the PS/2 model 80 as well as in a number of machines with the "386" designation in their names. It runs even faster than the previous generation and has much more sophisticated additional processor modes. It has a 32-bit data path and can address up to 2^{48} bytes or four *gigabytes* of memory. It also will operate as a very fast 8088 processor in real address mode.

INSTRUCTIONS AND DATA

Memory in the 8088 is organized into 8-bit *bytes.* Two bytes make up a 16-bit word, and most integer operations take place on 16-bit words. In digital computers, an instruction pointer (IP) register is set to contain the address of some memory location where numbers called *instructions* are stored. Locations which contain instructions are no different than locations that contain other numbers except that the programmer tells the computer to begin executing the numbers at some address and continue executing from that point. Obviously, if a computer begins executing locations containing data values, it will probably behave strangely, usually resulting in a "crash."

ORGANIZATION OF THE 8088 INSTRUCTIONS

The 8088 microprocessor is fundamentally an *accumulator machine* in which the four registers AX, BX, CX, and DX can be used as places to put values and carry out calculations. Each of these registers is 16 bits wide and can be broken into two 8-bit registers:

16-bit	8-bit
AX	AH, AL
BX	BH, BL
CX	CH, CL
DX	DH, DL

These "general" registers also have special purposes inherent in their names:

AX	Accumulator register
BX	Base register
CX	Counter register
DX	Data register

You can carry out 8- or 16-bit operations depending on whether the instruction refers to the 8- or 16-bit register name.

As noted earlier, the 8088 has a segmented address scheme in which a 16-bit address can refer to 65,536 bytes of memory relative to a *segment register.* These registers are assumed to point to the code, the data, the stack, and to another "extra" data set:

CS	Code segment register
DS	Data segment register
ES	Extra segment register
SS	Stack segment register

Thus, while the basic 8088 instruction set can only address 65,536 bytes directly, you can change a segment register so that you can address 1 megabyte of memory or 1,048,586 bytes. This 1-megabyte limit is enforced by a 20-bit internal address bus: the newer 80286 and 80386 have much larger potential address spaces, but not when running the instruction set and addressing modes of the 8088 chip. It is this 20-bit limit which leads to the 640K limit on a PC's memory, where the upper 384K of the 1 megabyte are reserved for the addresses of the video screens and the read-only memory which makes up the basic input/output system (BIOS) code of the PC.

The actual address of any memory location is made up of a segment register value and an offset. A *segment address* is simply the absolute 20-bit address with the lowest 4 bits dropped. Thus the address of the EGA screen memory is $a0000_{16}$ and the segment address is just &ha000. Thus, only every 16th address can be described directly by a segment register value, and these addresses are called *paragraph* addresses.

If we want to refer to a given location relative to a segment address, we usually write a 32-bit number with a colon between the upper and lower 16 bits: a000:0123 means address a0123.

The other registers in the basic 8088 are two index registers and two pointer registers:

SP	Stack pointer
BP	Base pointer
SI	Source index
DI	Destination index

Each of these has special purposes, as we will see in the examples that follow.

FUNDAMENTAL MACHINE INSTRUCTIONS

There are a number of instructions for carrying out arithmetic and logical operations in the 8088 microprocessor, but we will only mention a few common ones here. Most are *dual operand instructions:* they have two parts, a *source operand* and a *destination operand.* The source operand is never changed and the destination operand is almost always changed. The syntax of these two operand instructions is

```
opr dest, source        ;perform operation on source
                        ; and put in destination
```

Note that unlike some other instruction syntaxes, the destination operand is written *first* followed by the source operand. Note that *comments* in assembly language always start with *semicolons,* unlike QuickBASIC where apostrophes were used.

CAPITALIZATION IN ASSEMBLY LANGUAGE

MASM recognizes instructions in either upper or lower case as being equivalent. We will follow Microsoft's recommended convention and write all of our instructions in lowercase and all of the *directives* that tell the assembler how to carry out the assembly in uppercase.

DUAL OPERAND INSTRUCTIONS

Some of the most common dual operand instructions include the following:

```
mov b, a                ;move A to B
add b, a                ;add A to B
sub b, a                ;subtract A from B
xchg b, a               ;swap A and B
and b, a                ;AND A with B
```

```
or   b, a                ;OR A with B
xor b, a                 ;exclusive OR A with B
cmp b, a                 ;subtract A from B and set
                         ; the condition flags
test b, a                ;AND A with B and set
                         ; the condition flags
```

In each case the source A and the destination B may be registers or memory addresses, but both cannot be memory addresses. To move a value from one address to another, you must first move it to a register and then move the register to another memory address. There are also multiplication and division instructions, but they are seldom necessary since such operations are usually better written in QuickBASIC.

SINGLE OPERAND INSTRUCTIONS

Some of the most common *single operand instructions* include

```
inc a                    ;add 1 to A
dec a                    ;subract 1 from A
neg a                    ;negate A
not a                    ;take ones complement of A
jmp x                    ;jump to location named "x"
```

SHIFT INSTRUCTIONS

Shift instructions move the bits in a register to the right and left. The bits on the end fall off and are lost in the chronosynclastic infundibulum.[1] A *logical shift* causes the bits on the source end to be filled with zeroes. A right *arithmetic shift* causes the sign bit (bit 15) to be copied into each of the vacated left-most bits.

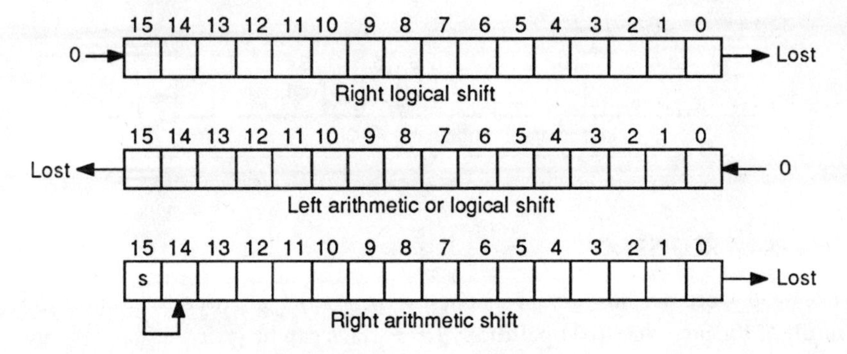

The shift instructions have the syntax:

```
sal a, 1        ;shift A 1 place left
sal a, cl       ;shift A left the number of places
                ;contained in register CL
shr a, 1        ;logical shift A right 1 place
shr a, cl       ;logical shift A right by CL
sar a, 1        ;arithmetic shift A right 1 place
sar a, cl       ;arithmetic shift A right by CL
```

ROTATE INSTRUCTIONS

There are also four *rotate instructions* in which the data are rotated out of one end of the register and into the other. Two of them also include the carry flag register in the rotation.

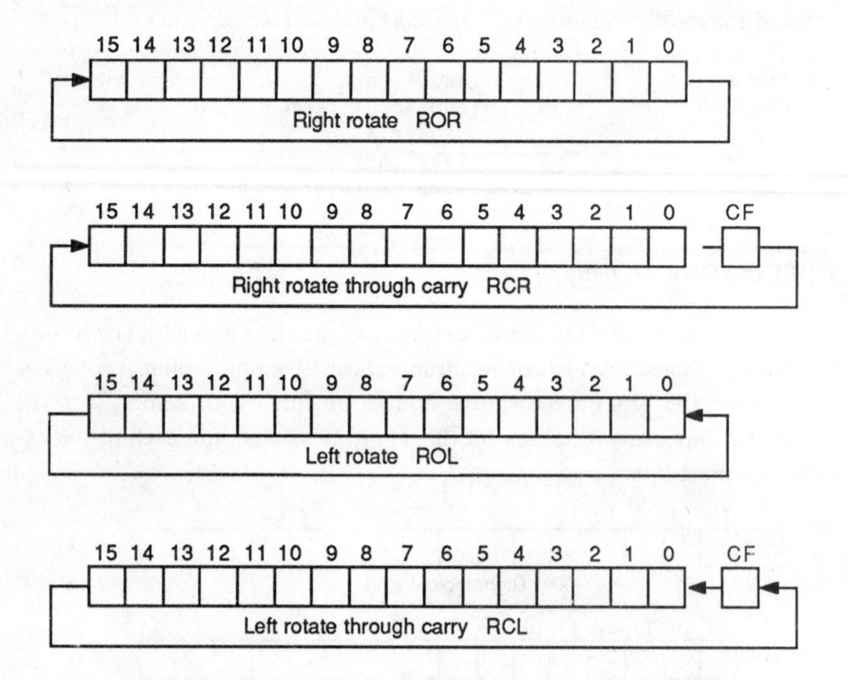

THE FLAG REGISTERS

The 8088 processor has a set of six one-bit flags which are used to monitor the result of the last executed operation. These flags can be tested as part of conditional jump instructions to make decisions which control the flow of the program:

CF	Carry flag	Set if there is a carry out or borrow in.
ZF	Zero flag	Set if the result is zero.
SF	Sign flag	Set if the result is negative.
OF	Overflow flag	Set if the signed result is out of range.
PF	Parity flag	Set if the result has an even number of bits set to 1.
AF	Aux carry flag	Set if there is a carryout from the low 4 bits to the high 4 bits of the lowest byte of the operand.

DECISION-MAKING INSTRUCTIONS

The conditional jump instructions test one or more of the flag register bits and jump if and only if the condition tested for is true. These flag bits are set by arithmetic operations and by CMP and TEST instructions, but *not* by MOV instructions:

```
jmp     ;jump always
jc      ;jump if carry
jnc     ;jump if not carry
je      ;jump if equal zero
jcxz    ;jump if cx is zero
```

Signed comparisons:

```
jne     ;jump if not equal to zero
jg      ;jump if greater than
jge     ;jump if greater than or equal to zero
jle     ;jump if less than or equal to zero
jl      ;jump if less than
```

Unsigned comparisons:

```
ja      ;jump if above
jae     ;jump if above or equal
jbe     ;jump if below or equal
jb      ;jump if below
```

THE LOOP INSTRUCTION

The LOOP instruction is used to loop through a small section of code extremely quickly. Each time the loop instruction is encountered, it decrements

CX by 1 and loops back to the specified address if CX is nonzero. When CX becomes zero, the loop is completed and the next instruction is executed:

```
        mov cx, 5       ;set counter
c10:    mov dx, ax      ;copy AX into DX, for instance
        ; :             ;other instructions
        loop c10        ;go back until CX is 0
```

There also two special forms of the LOOP instruction which are useful for searching a table for the first zero or nonzero element:

```
    LOOPE   addr    ;loop until ZF is set or CX is zero
    LOOPNE  addr    ;loop until ZF is clear or CX is zero
```

ADDRESSING MODES IN THE 8088

Thus far we have discussed the various 8088 registers and the condition flags, but have not discussed how we can address memory locations using the previous instructions. The 8088 has seven basic addressing modes:

```
    mov ax, bx          ;register addressing
    mov ax, 5           ;immediate addressing
    mov ax, fred        ;direct addressing
    mov ax, ds:010h
    mov ax, [di]        ;indexed indirect addressing
    mov ax, [si]
    mov ax, [bx]        ;based indirect addressing
    mov ax, [bp]
    mov ax, [bp+6]      ;base relative (6 off BP)
    mov ax, 6[bp]       ;base relative also 6 off BP
    mov ax, [bx-12]     ;base relative
    mov ax, [di+20]     ;direct indexed
    mov ax, [si+33]     ;direct indexed
    mov ax, [bx][di]    ;based indexed
    mov ax, [bp][di]
    mov ax, [bx][si]
    mov ax, [bp][si]
    mov ax, 12[bx][di]  ;based index with displacement
    mov ax, 25[bp][di]
    mov ax, 42[bp][si]
```

In all of these addressing modes, the segment register is assumed to be the DS register unless the BP register is used in the instruction. Using the BP register always implies that the SS register is used. In most cases, these registers are loaded for you by the calling program and you seldom have to load them or be aware of their contents when writing subroutines to be called from QuickBASIC.

Register Addressing

In this mode, the data are in one of the registers. In the first example above, the BX register is the source and in all of the examples, the AX register the destination.

Immediate Addressing

In this mode, a 16-bit constant is moved into a register. The constant is actually stored in a second location just after the instruction. Obviously, these constants can only be used as source operands.

Direct Addressing

Direct addressing is almost always used when a program wishes to move data to or from a memory location nearby. This could occur for local constants which are accessed from a number of places or when a routine uses local data storage for temporary results. In MASM syntax, a named or labeled location must start with an alphabetic character or with an underscore (_), a question mark (?), a dollar sign ($), or an "at" sign (@), and the label may be up to 31 characters long. You define a location as having a name by placing the name on a line followed by a colon. You use a name by simply referring to it as an address:

```
mov bx, tem32              ;get contents of location TEM32
                           ;and put in the BX register
        :
tem32:  03456h             ;address containing a constant
```

Usually, such labelled addresses are nearby in the code and are referred to as NEAR, meaning that they are addressed as part of the code segment pointed to be the CS register. This will always be true in the simple examples in this chapter, but it is possible to refer to FAR labels where another segment register is implied or used specifically.

Based and Indexed Indirect Addressing

In both of these addressing modes, a register contains the *address* of the memory location of interest. Unless a segment register is specified, the assembler assumes that the segment is pointed to by DS and the register contains an offset relative to this segment address for addresses pointed to by BX, SI, or DI. If BP is used, the stack segment register SS is assumed. The purpose of these modes is to calculate a pointer address which can be used to refer to a data location. Often these addresses are incremented or decremented in a loop so that a table of addresses can be referred to sequentially. This provides a way of stepping sequentially through an array.

Base Relative and Direct Indexed Addressing

In both of these modes, a register contains a fixed address and an offset is specified which is added to this register to calculate the final address. Several slightly different syntaxes have evolved over the history of the 8088 processors, and all are accepted by the current MASM assembler as identical:

```
mov cx, 6 [bp]            ;all refer to the same operation
mov cx, [bp + 6]
mov cx, [bp] + 6
```

In each of these examples, 6 is added to the contents of the BP register to form a new address. This address is the one used to retrieve the data. Since BP is used, the stack segment (SS) register is implied. The purpose of these modes is usually to fetch a value from a table of values passed to a subroutine, where the start of this table is pointed to by the base register.

Based Indexed Addressing

In this mode, the contents of a base register BX or BP is added to the contents of an index register SI or DI and a specified constant offset is added to this to form the effective address of the data. If BX is used, DS is implied, and if BP is used, SS is implied. As above, there are a number of equivalent syntaxes:

```
mov dx, [bp] [si] + 12    ;equivalent syntaxes
mov dx, 12 [bp] [si]      ; for based index addressing
mov dx, [bp + si +12]
mov dx, [bp][si + 12]
```

The main purpose of this mode is really to access elements in a table of fixed-length record. If BP contains the address of an array of records and SI contains the offset to a given record in the table, then the displacement (12) is the number of bytes to the address of a given element in that record.

THE STACK

The stack is an array of numbers pointed to by the stack pointer register. It is used for temporary storage of data passed to subroutines and for the return addresses from subroutine. The stack pointer always starts at a high memory location and grows towards low memory (address 0). The SP register always contains the address of the last value pushed onto the stack. For each value pushed onto the stack, the stack pointer is *decremented* by 2, and a value is put in the location whose address is represented by SS:SP. For each value popped off the stack, a value is moved from the address SS:SP and put into a destination register; then the stack pointer is *incremented* by 2.

```
push ax           ;put the contents of AX onto the stack
push bp           ;put the contents of BP onto the stack
  :
pop bp            ;retrieve old value of BP from the stack
pop ax            ;get old AX value from the stack
```

The address in SS and SP is usually controlled by the calling program and does not need to be calculated in your subroutines. However, if you push values onto the stack, you must retrieve them before exiting so that the stack pointer has the same value when you leave a subroutine as it did when you enter it.

CALLING SUBROUTINES IN ASSEMBLY LANGUAGE

The CALL instruction is used to call subroutines in assembly language. This instruction saves the address following the call on the stack and then jumps to the address named in the instruction:

```
call ztest        ;call ZTEST subroutine
```

This has the effect of:

```
push IP           ;save the instruction pointer
jmp ztest         ;jump to address "ztest"
```

The reason this instruction is so powerful is that this gives us a way to call a routine from many places and return to those locations after executing the subroutine, since the address we came from is saved on the stack.

Of course, there must be a complementary instruction to return to the address following the call:

```
ret                     ;return to the address on the stack
```

The RET instruction pops the address of the stack and puts it into the IP, so that the next instruction fetched is that at the new address in the IP, thus causing a return from the subroutine to the address after the original CALL statement.

NEAR AND FAR PROCEDURES

Since the 8088 addresses are always made up of a segment value and an offset value, the "true" address of any procedure is also 32 bits long, made up of a segment and offset. Therefore, if you call a procedure, it may be in the current segment or in a different 64K segment of memory. We call a procedure in the same segment a NEAR procedure and one in another segment a FAR procedure. In order to call a FAR procedure, we need to save both the code segment register CS and the current address offset in IP on the stack, and load a new values into the CS and IP. Likewise, to return from a FAR procedure, we need to pop both of these values off the stack.

The MASM assembler has NEAR and FAR directives to be used with each subroutine so that it can decide whether to generate a near or a far call and return for each procedure:

```
ztest: PROC NEAR        ;the subroutine starts here and is near
       :
       ret              ;return from a near procedure
       ENDP             ;tell MASM this is the end of ZTEST
ftest: PROC FAR         ;start of far procedure
       :
       ret              ;this will be a far return
       ENDP             ;tell MASM this is the end of FTEST
```

We will see the uses of the stack and PROC directives in the following chapter.

THE STRING INSTRUCTIONS

The 8088 series also has a set of instructions for transferring blocks of data from one location to another. These instructions are very efficient ways of moving, comparing, and scanning strings of up to 64K bytes in length. Actually we refer to "strings" for this instructions, although the compilers often use these instructions for moving many types of numbers from one place to another. We will not use them in our programming but merely list them here for completeness:

```
movsb   ;move string of bytes
movsw   ;move string of words
cmpsb   ;compare string of bytes
cmpsw   ;compare string of words
scasb   ;scan string of bytes
scasw   ;scan string of words
```

Each time one of these instructions is executed, one element of the string is moved, compared, or scanned, and SI and DI are changed by 1 or 2. The entire operation can be carried out in a single pair of instructions by adding the REP prefix to the instructions:

```
rep movsw        ;move entire word string
repne cmpsb      ;repeat while not equal (zf=0)
repe cmpsb       ;repeat while equal (zf=1)
```

In each of these instructions, the length of the strings is contained in CX, the address of the source string in DS:SI, and the address of the destination string in ES:DI. The strings can be scanned from low memory to high memory or vice versa, depending on the state of a special flag called the *direction flag*. If the direction flag is 0, the SI and DI registers increment after each use, and if DF is 1, they decrement.

```
CLD              ;clear direction flag
STD              ;set direction flag
```

This concludes our brief summary of the 8088 assembly language. In Chapter 23, we will show how you can call subroutines from QuickBASIC.

REFERENCES

1. K. Vonnegut, Jr., *The Sirens of Titan,* Dell, New York, 1959.

2. L. J. Scanlan, *IBM PC and XT Assembly Language,* Brady, New York, 1985.
3. A. Singh and W. Trebel, *IBM PC 18088 Assembly Language Programming,* Prentice Hall, Englewood Cliffs, NJ, 1985.
4. D. Bradley, *Assembly Language Programming for the IBM PC,* Prentice-Hall, Englewood Cliffs, NJ, 1984.

23 Calling Assembly Language Procedures from QuickBASIC

The QuickBASIC environment allows you to declare procedure names and their arguments even if the procedures aren't in the current source module. While the main purpose of this is to allow you to link together a number of different QuickBASIC modules, you can also link in assembly language routines that perform some function more efficiently than QuickBASIC can.

GENERAL STRATEGY FOR ASSEMBLY LANGUAGE PROCEDURES

The whole reason for writing an assembly language procedure is to make some critical routine run faster. Thus, we want to put in the assembly code only those operations which we can code significantly more efficiently than the compiler can. Thus, we will not include any multiplication, division, floating point arithmetic, or manipulations that are not part of a loop that must be passed through several times.

In addition, we should strive to keep all of the important variables in registers in assembly language, because operations on registers take place within the microprocessor chip, while operations on memory require interaction with the bus and fetching of memory contents. This is always significantly slower than register-based operations.

CALLS IN ASSEMBLY LANGUAGE

When you write a call to a procedure with arguments, QuickBASIC pushes the arguments onto the stack in the order they are listed, and then does a far call to the procedure address specified in the call:

```
CALL fred(ab%, cd%)
```

generates code equivalent to push the *address of* AB% and CD% onto the stack. When you enter your procedure, then, you will find that the stack pointer points to the stack with the following values on it:

```
sp---> oldip     ;calling return address
       oldcs     ;calling value of CS
       acd       ;address of CD%
       aab       ;address of AB%
```

What you must do is to save the value of any registers you change from the group of BP, SI, DI, SS, and DS. You do not have to save the accumulators AX–DX or the extra segment register ES. Saving the registers means simply pushing them onto the stack and retrieving their values before you exit. In the examples in this chapter, we will need to save BP and DI. In addition, since we need to address the arguments we passed to the procedure, we will need to copy the final value of SP into the base pointer register BP, so we can use it in based indexed addressing moves. Thus, the first three instructions in any routine we write in assembly language will be:

```
push bp          ;save the old value of SP
push di          ;save the value of DI
mov bp, sp       ;copy SP into the base pointer
```

Our stack now looks like this:

```
0     sp---> olddi     ;saved value from DI
2            oldbp     ;saved value from BP
4            oldip     ;calling return address
6            oldcs     ;calling value of CS
8            acd       ;address of CD%
10           aab       ;address of AB%
```

Thus, if we want to access the 16-bit address of CD%, we will need to refer to the address offset 8 from the value in BP:

```
mov bx, [bp + 8]     ;get address of CD%
```

Then, if we want to get the actual *value* of CD%, we simply use the BX register as a pointer to that value, in indirect addressing mode:

```
mov ax, [bx]        ;get value of CD, address in BX
```

In this manner, we can access any of the values passed to the procedure.

THE STRUC STATEMENT IN MASM

Rather than calculating the offsets of all the arguments relative to BP, and recalculating them each time you change the number of arguments or save registers, the STRUC statement in the MASM assembler allows the assembler to assign values to constants that are automatically correct. As we are using this statement, it generates no code and it does not refer to a real record or structure. Rather, it provides a convenient way for the assembler to calculate these offsets for us. It has the form:

```
stack STRUC      ;beginning of a structure named "stack"
olddi   DW ?     ;saved DI
oldbp   DW ?     ;saved BP
retadr  DD ?     ;return address to calling program

;parameters pushed onto stack in this order:
cd      DW ?     ;address of CD
ab      DW ?     ;address of AB

stack  ENDS
```

The constants OLDDI, OLDBP, RETADR, CD, and AB are now assigned the values 0, 2, 4, 8, and 10. Note the directives DW and DD for "define word" and "define doubleword" which keep us from having to keep our 2s and 4s straight.

Now we can refer to these offsets symbolically, without ever having to know what they actually are:

```
mov bx, [bp + cd]        ;get address of CD
mov ax, [bx]             ;get value of CD
mov bx, [bp + ab]        ;get address of AB
mov dx, [bx]             ;get value of AB
```

It is this method that we will use in the actual programs that follow.

RETURNING FROM PROCEDURES

Before we exit from a procedure we have called from QuickBASIC, we have to be careful to put back the registers we used and remove the arguments from the stack. The RET instruction can take an optional argument telling how many bytes to remove from the stack after the calling address and CS are popped off. This is done as follows:

```
pop bp          ;restore BP
pop di          ;restore DI
ret 4           ;return and add 4 to SP
```

CODING OUR DRAWUP ROUTINE FOR THE CGA

Now, let us consider the DRAWUP routine we wrote in Chapter 21, and see how we might make it more efficient in assembly language. The call is

```
call cgadrawup(iadd, ibit, irow, icount)
```

where

iadd	is the number or rows to draw up.
ibit	is the address offset of the byte to change.
irow	is the bit in the word to set.
icount	is the odd or even row.

Recall that the even rows start at a segment offset of &Hb800 and the odd rows at a segment offset of &Hba00. We need to check whether each row is even or odd and load the ES segment register correctly to access the correct byte of screen memory:

```
du10:  mov ax, 0b800h        ;segment address of even rows
       and dx, 1             ;test odd-even row number
       je du20               ;leave if even
       mov ax, 0ba00h        ;segment address of odd rows
du20:  mov es, ax            ;load extra segment register with
                             ;correct value
```

We also need to subtract 80 from the row number only if the current row is *even* because the next lower odd row will have a different offset, but the next lower even row will have the *same* offset in the other segment:

```
        test dx,1           ;is this an even or an odd row?
        jne du30            ;if odd, lower even has same offset
        sub di,80           ;number of bytes in a row
du30:   inc dx              ;flip odd-even row counter
```

We also need to check to be sure that the value of ICOUNT is not zero, since we might only be setting the bit in one row, and this could result in a calculated count of zero. While this could be done in the calling program, this is an example of a task we can probably write more efficiently in assembly language:

```
    cmp cx,0                ;if count is 0 make it 1
    jne du10
    mov cx,1                ;set to 1
```

Finally, we actually set the bit in memory using an OR instruction so that we will not disturb other bits that are already set. In addition, we don't actually have to fetch the byte we are changing since we can address it in memory and perform the OR to memory in a single instruction:

```
    or es:[di], bx          ;OR this bit into display word
```

ASSEMBLER DIRECTIVES

Earlier versions of the MASM assembler required some fairly elaborate declarations regarding the code and data segments and the type of memory model to be used. These have been simplified in MASM 5.0, so we need only declare that the memory model to be used is the Medium Model, where all the code is in one segment and the data is in another segment. This tells the assembler what segments to use in generating the instructions. The directive:

```
    .MODEL MEDIUM
```

tells MASM that the medium model is to be used, and the directive

```
    .CODE
```

tell MASM that code follows.

We also need to tell MASM that other routines will wish to refer to the label defining the entry to the procedure CGADRAW. We do this by declaring this symbol to be public:

```
    PUBLIC cgadraw
```

This tells MASM to put this symbol in the .OBJ file so that the LINK program will find it and resolve the reference to this symbol from the calling program DISP. The complete routine follows:

```
;SUB cgadrawup(iadd, icol, irow, icount)

.MODEL MEDIUM
.CODE
        PUBLIC cgadrawup
;define stack offsets of variables used in setpnt
;------------------------------------------------------------
stack   STRUC
olddi   DW ?  ;saved DI
oldbp   DW ?  ;saved BP
retadr  DD ?  ;return address to calling program
;parameters pushed onto stack in this order:
count   DW ?  ;number of rows to draw up
row     DW ?  ;odd or evenness of first row
bitmask DW ?  ;bit to be set
addr    DW ?  ;address to be altered
stack   ENDS
;------------------------------------------------------------
cgadrawup PROC
        push bp                    ;save the base pointer
        push di                    ;and the destn index
        mov bp,sp                  ;set BP to pt to current SP
        mov bx,[bp+row]            ;get initial row address
        mov dx, [bx]               ;get its value
        mov bx,[bp+addr]           ;get address offset and load it
                                   ;into DI
        mov di, [bx]               ;get its value
        mov bx,[bp+count]          ;number of pixels to draw up
        mov cx, [bx]               ;get count value
        mov bx,[bp+bitmask]        ;get the bitmask address
        mov bx, [bx]               ;and its value
        cmp cx, 0                  ;if count is 0 make it 1
        jne du10
        mov cx,1                   ;set to 1
du10:   mov ax, 0b800h             ;segment address of even rows
        and dx, 1                  ;test odd-even row number
        je du20                    ;leave if even
        mov ax, 0ba00h             ;segment address of odd rows
du20:   mov es, ax                 ;load extra segment reg with
                                   ;correct value
        or es:[di], bx             ;OR this bit into display work
        test dx, 1                 ;is this an even or an odd row?
        jne du30                   ;if odd, lower even has same
                                   ;offset
```

```
        sub di,80                ;number of bytes in a row
du30:   inc dx                   ;flip odd-even row counter
        loop du10                ;go back COUNT times
        pop di                   ;restore old values
        pop bp
        ret 8                    ;and exit restoring 8 bytes off
                                 ;stack

        cgadrawup  ENDP
END
```

THE CALL FROM QUICKBASIC

Our original loop for drawing lines from the display buffer was

```
FOR ib = 1 TO BUFDIM STEP 2
  LINE (ix, ibuf(ib) + joff)-(ix, ibuf(ib + 1) + joff)
  ix = ix + 1
NEXT ib
```

We will modify this by replacing the LINE statement with a call to a drawup routine:

```
FOR ib = 1 TO BUFDIM STEP 2
  CALL drawup(ibuf(ib) + joff, ix, ibuf(ib) - ibuf(ib + 1))
  ix = ix + 1
NEXT ib
```

Then we will write a QuickBASIC DRAWUP routine which calculates the one-time values of the address and row and then calls CGADRAW:

```
SUB drawup (irow, icol, icount)
' draws a line from irow, icol up icount rows

iadd = (irow \ 2) * 80 + (icol \ 8)
ibit = icol MOD 8
ibit = jbit(ibit)                    'get actual bit to turn on
CALL cgadrawup(iadd, ibit, irow, icount)
END SUB
```

Finally, we need to declare this procedure at the beginning of the program so that it will be checked for the correct number and type of arguments:

```
DECLARE SUB cgadrawup (addr%, ibit%, irow%, icount%)
```

DRAWING VERTICAL LINES USING THE EGA OR VGA DISPLAY

Both the EGA and VGA displays treat display memory as four planes located at the same address. The actual planes which we access are controlled by a write map mask register. The combination of planes we write to determines which of the 16 colors we actually display. In addition, we need to OR the data into these planes. We don't do this directly, since there are actually up to four planes we are setting a single bit in. Instead, we set bits 3 and 4 of the mode register to one of the following:

00	put
01	AND
10	OR
11	XOR

All of the EGA registers are addressed in two steps: one in which a register selector address is specified and one in which the actual register is loaded. These addresses are part of the input-output address space rather than actual physical memory address, and they are addessed using the OUT instructions either in QuickBASIC or in assembly language. The relevant addresses are as follows:

3c4	Sequencer register select
3c5	Selector value
	0, reset
	1, clocking mode
	2, write map mask
	3, character map select
	4, memory mode select
3ce	Graphics controller register select
3cf	Selector value:
	0, set/reset
	1, enable set/reset
	2, color compare
	3, data rotate and write mode
	4, read map select
	5, mode register
	8, bit mask

You access the rotate and write mode register by setting output port 3ce to 3 and then setting 3cf to the correct mode:

&H00	put
&H08	AND
&H10	OR
&H18	XOR

using the instructions

```
out &h3ce, 3     'select write mode register
out &h3cf, &h10 'select OR
```

Similarly, you select the color you wish to display by selecting the write map register and setting it to the number of the color (0–15).

```
out &h3c4, 2
out &h3c5, color
```

In our EGADRAW program, which follows, the former is performed in QuickBASIC and the latter within the assembly language routine. While the EGA and VGA are extremely complex devices with a large number of registers, these are the only registers you probably ever need to change yourself.

```
;SUB egadrawup(addr,bitmask,color,pixcnt);
.MODEL MEDIUM
.CODE
       PUBLIC egadrawup
;------------------------------------------------------
;define stack offsets of variables used in setpnt
stack   STRUC

olddi   DW ?  ;saved DI
oldbp   DW ?  ;saved BP
retadr  DD ?  ;return address to calling program
pixcnt  DW ?  ;number of rows to draw up
color   DW ?  ;color to draw in (0-15)
bitmask DW ?  ;bit to set
addr    DW ?  ;number of pixels to draw up and draw down
stack   ENDS
;------------------------------------------------------

egadrawup  PROC                    ;beginning of procedure
        push bp                    ;save the base pointer
        push di                    ;and the destn index
```

```
        mov bp,sp                   ;copy current SP into BP
        mov ax, 0a000H              ;address of display
        mov es,ax                   ;set extra segment to point to it
        mov bx,[bp+addr]            ;get address of address offset
        mov di,[bx]                 ;load it into DI
        mov dx,03c4H                ;controller address register
        mov al, 02                  ;select write map
        out dx,al                   ;#2 is the write map register
        inc dx                      ;3c5 now addresses the writemap
                                    ;mask
        mov bx,[bp+ color]          ;get the address of the color
        mov ax,[bx]                 ;get the color value
        out dx,al                   ;and set the mask to pick the
                                    ;color
        dec dx                      ;back to address register
        mov bx,[bp+bitmask]         ;get address of bit mask
        mov ax, [bx]                ;put bits to set in AX
        mov bx,[bp+pixcnt]          ;get address of count
        mov cx, [bx]                ;put count into CX
        cmp cx, 0                   ;if count is 0 make it 1
        jne pixup10
        mov cx,1                    ;set it to 1
pixup10:   mov ah,es:[di]           ;read that byte into the latches
                                    ;(and AH)
        mov es:[di],al              ;OR new bit with that in the
                                    ;latches
        sub di,80                   ;go up one row (80 bytes)
        loop pixup10                ;loop back until all rows done
        pop di                      ;restore old values of DI
        pop bp                      ;and BP
        ret 8                       ;and exit removing 8 bytes from
                                    ;stack

egadrawup  ENDP END
```

CONCLUSIONS

We have seen throughout this book that it is possible to write logical, readable, structured code in QuickBASIC. This language provides the student, the scientist, and the professional programmer with extremely powerful tools for program development. It completely replaces the original BASICA interpreter and is many times faster and more versatile. QuickBASIC gives us a way to utilize our PC or PS/2 as never before for structured program development.

Index